Cast the First Stone

By

A. Keith Mack, M.D.

Printed by
Remnant Publications
Coldwater, MI

Cast the First Stone

This edition published 2005

Cover Photo by Corbis

ISBN 0-9742881-0-1

Acknowledgment

Many of the words which were written in the "Phonetic spelling of Mack" have been revised from those of the original document. Through the laborious efforts of my wife, the individual letters in many of these inscriptions have been rearranged to produce words more compatible, in spelling, with those commonly found in modern unabridged dictionaries.

I wish to thank my wife Sherrie for her love, help and patience in the writing of this book.

Thanks also to:

My daughter Cindi who painstakingly retyped page after page of manuscript for me after I pushed "Yes" to the question, would you like to replace the document? Thank you.

My son Kevin and daughter-in-law Amber who patiently tried to persuade me that the computer was really doing the very best it could with the information I was feeding it.

My daughter Teri who read portions of the manuscript and encouraged me to continue.

My buddy Carol who persuaded me to write a book in the first place.

In loving memory of our son, brother and friend, Steve. And to the mother that never had the privilege of knowing and loving him as we did. She will always be in our prayers.

Contents

Introduction

For many years I have wanted to write a book. It was to be an epic comedy about my children. The title that seemed most appropriate was, "Two ways to go through life, first class or with children." However, the book I have chosen to write is neither an epic nor a comedy. It's difficult to find humor in the life of a son who is diligently seeking God, and frantically searching for a way to find salvation, then surrenders his life at a party with the assistance of a heroin needle.

In the beginning God gave each of us the power to choose. The choices we make in life determine our destiny. Most choices are based on either right or wrong. Occasionally they are by chance. This book is not intended to be entertaining, but is written to the multitudes of parents who have watched their children's lives go completely askew through some ill twist of fate.

Usually we blame ourselves for our children's mistakes. At times we are to blame, sometimes we are not. Often their choices reflect innocent errors in judgment.

I sincerely hope that some father or mother out there will benefit from my ability to have completely mismanaged the frustrations in my own son's life. I did the best I knew to do. At times best is not good enough.

Too often the expectations that we as parents hold for our children are unrealistic and impossible for the child to obtain. Many times we choose to live our own lives vicariously through their lives. We expect them to have the same ambition, drives and goals that we ourselves have. This is often not the case.

In reading the story of David in the Old Testament, we find that David not only committed adultery, but also caused a man to be murdered. In spite of his poor choices, when he asked God for forgiveness, God not only forgave him, but said it was as if he had never sinned. This promise is extended to us, just as it was to David.

When Christ gave the parable of the prodigal son, the father waited and watched (and I am sure, prayed diligently) and when he saw his son returning he ran to meet him. He didn't immediately say how dirty he looked, or how unacceptable his behavior had been, or even mention the disgrace he had brought to the family. He chose to simply kiss him, drape his robe about him and welcome him home.

My son Steve wanted to live his life exempt from all authority, yet he sought desperately to find God. He was one of those people that plummeted into the trap of believing that he must of himself be perfect or be eternally lost to God's kingdom.

Although this book is written by a Seventh-day Adventist, and may be best understood by a Seventh-day Adventist audience, there are many in other faiths who have had to go through similar situations, and hopefully will find comfort in some of my personal experiences. I am a Seventh-day Adventist, but have not always been. If I were to speak truthfully, it would have to be said that even when claiming to be a member in good standing, I didn't always maintain strict adherence to the standards of my faith.

For those of you who do not understand about Seventh-day Adventist teachings I would like to give you a brief explanation of what the church teaches:

Jesus Christ is the central teaching of the church. It is through Christ, and only through Christ that we are able to achieve salvation. We believe that the Bible is God's inspired word, and the ultimate authority that leads us to Christ. Scripture teaches that Jesus is coming again to take the faithful to be with Him, and Seventh-day Adventists believe the time is soon.

Principles include, healthful living, which incorporates abstinence from alcohol, drugs, and tobacco. Vegetarianism is stressed as a part of a healthful diet. Worldly entertainment is discouraged as are high fashion and excessive adornment. Exercise, adequate rest and relaxation are also essential for healthful living. This is all felt to be in keeping with Christ's teachings.

We also observe the seventh day Sabbath in adherence to the ten commandments of the Old Testament. We believe that if we love the Lord, we will keep His commands. We are not saved because we keep the commandments, but we keep the commandments because we are saved.

This is a very elementary sketch on Adventist teachings. Unfortunately there are always those who take a more radical approach to the subject, as the Pharisees did in Christ's time. This way of thinking sometimes includes being saved by keeping the Sabbath, or not eating meat, not going to dances, or not drinking or smoking. The list goes on and on. The do's and do not's replace the love of Jesus, and salvation is thought to be achieved by our own efforts, rather than through the loving grace of our savior Jesus Christ. There are those in the church, as well as others who are nonmembers who hold these views.

This is the story of a father and son. The story of our battles against alcohol and drugs as we both tenaciously searched to find God. One of us lived to tell the story, the other did not.

Among the conclusions I would like to create from this writing are the following: Life goes on after tragedy. Through God's wonderful mercy there is forgiveness no matter how severe the indiscretion. We can find happiness without guilt regardless of the mistakes we have made. Faithfulness to God is not a prerequisite for His love. Last but not least, only those who are without faults should be considered worthy to "Cast The First Stone."

"If there is one among you who is without sin, let him cast the first stone."

John 8:7

Prologue

The service was over, the final notes of Amazing Grace had faded into oblivion. I was standing with friends and relatives yet feeling all alone. The entire scene was without emotion. I stared blindly at the little box at the grave site that contained the ashes of my son. There was the representation of twenty-eight wasted years of life. It all seemed like a dream. People came and went about me. Nothing made any sense.

My three remaining children seemed paralyzed with grief, one put his arm around me to console me, I felt nothing.

My wife Sherrie seemed insensitive to anything around her, wandering aimlessly throughout the crowd. This couldn't be happening. It had to be a bad dream. Faces appeared in front of me, then quickly disappeared. I knew people were speaking, but couldn't make myself hear. Embraces had no feeling.

My mind was racing through the twenty-eight years of Steve's misdirected life. Where had I gone wrong? What had I done? Did I kill my own son? The thought was too painful to consider. I am a physician. I know how to handle grief. I work with life and death every day. Nothing new, just another day, tomorrow everything will be back to normal. Everything will be fine.

More people offered their hands of comfort. "When will it stop hurting?" I cried out. "It has to stop hurting." I began to sob uncontrollably. My son Kevin put his arm around me. I knew he didn't know what to do, but it was helping. "God," I sobbed. "Why are you doing this to me? What have I done so wrong that I should have to endure such suffering?"

I took one last look at the box of ashes and whispered, "Goodbye, Steve. I'm so sorry it all had to end this way. Goodbye, my son. Your dad really has always loved you. Maybe I haven't always been able to express it in the right way."

"You know we both have pretty strong personalities and definite opinions. I wish I could tell you how much I really love you. That obnoxious laugh of yours always made me angry, but if only I could hear it one more time. If only we could have one more of our famous discussions. Maybe this time we wouldn't end up in a screaming match. If only we could start all over again.

"Well, son, the crowd is leaving. Your mother needs me. Kevin, Teri and Cindi need me. I guess you don't need me anymore. I only hope I was there at least part of the time when you did need me. So long."

There is a poem that goes something like this: "God pity them both! And pity us all, who vainly the dreams of youth recall; For of all sad words of tongue or pen the saddest of these: It might have been."

It didn't stop hurting the next day or the next, but over the years the pain has become bearable. The question still haunts me. Am I responsible for Steve's death, and as a result of my action will we not be able to spend eternity together.

I am so thankful for a merciful Heavenly Father who died for each and every one of us. God looks at the heart. I choose to believe that Steve will be counted with the redeemed when Christ returns. My prayer is, Thy will be done.

1

A Gift From Heaven

Christmas Eve 1966, was an exciting and unexpectedly eventful night. My parents had come to spend Christmas Eve with Sherrie and myself and our seven-month old son, Kevin.

Later in the evening we were to take Kevin to Sherrie's parent's home for their annual Christmas Eve party. This was to be a time to introduce their new grandson to their friends and have some Christmas cheer. The Togstad party was always a real bash that was looked forward to by a large number of friends and relatives. My mother-in-law spent hours of preparation in the kitchen. The eggnog and rum would flow freely with the blessings of their guests.

My parents were invited, but not knowing any of the other guests, they had declined the invitation. We had a light dinner at our home then began to open our gifts. In the process of the festivities we received a very exciting phone call. A nurse from the hospital called to inform me that the unwed young lady whose baby we had agreed to adopt was in the hospital in very active labor. This came as a complete surprise, as she was not due until late January or early February.

I walked into the living room and made the announcement. I looked at our seven-month-old son, who was already more than a handful and thought, what have we done? I didn't know whether to shout for joy or to cry.

Before we could get our thoughts together, the phone rang again, and I heard the voice on the other end of the line say, "You are the proud parents of a six-pound boy." This time I knew exactly what to do. I cried!

We abandoned the package opening, and headed for the hospital to see our new son. The nurse led the way to the nursery window chattering up a storm all the way. She informed us the ladies in the nursery had already dubbed our son "the love baby" because he was the product of an unwanted pregnancy, and had been chosen as special by our family. We were also informed that "love babies" always had a wonderful temperament.

We all peered through the window. Wow, I thought, he's cute and funny looking all at the same time. He was red as a beet, and had blond hair that stood straight up all over his head.

The chatty nurse, who hadn't stopped talking the entire time, said, "Isn't he beautiful?" I wanted to gag, but I nodded my head in agreement. Everyone stood around doing all the silly things that grownups do around newborns. I wasn't in a "goo-goo gaa-gaa" mood at the moment. All I could think was, why are we doing this and how are we going to take care of another baby? Nine months between babies is bad enough, but seven months is completely ridiculous.

Finally after an extended stay, we tore ourselves away from the window and headed for home. In spite of the fact that we were now working on a litter, this had been a fantastic Christmas Eve. What a great gift God had given us. My mother was especially happy as Christmas day was her birthday. (By the way, we always celebrated Steve's birthday on the 24th of June. He was the only one of our children who was one and one-half, two and one-half, etc.)

On the way home we decided to name the new baby Steven Ray. Ray was for my father (my father-in-law's name was Erling, not a good choice for a six-pounder) and to this day, I don't have a clue where the name Steve came from, but I have always liked it.

As we pulled into the driveway, I remembered the Togstad party. It was already well on its way, I was sure, but knew how excited my in-laws would be about a new grandson. Sherrie jumped out of the car and ran into the house to phone her folks with the exciting news.

Moments later she came into the living room crying hysterically. "They didn't even ask if it was a boy or girl" she sobbed. "They just said for us not to bother coming to the party tonight and they wouldn't be coming for Christmas dinner tomorrow either."

I jumped to my feet and headed for the phone. I was intercepted by my father who said "Keith," in a tone I haven't heard since I was ten years old. "Not now. Sit down and cool off. It's going to be all right. They need time to get used to having a new grandchild this soon."

Well everything wasn't all right. Sherrie spent most of the night awake crying and I spent the night fighting back the anger. How could they put their idiotic party above a new grandchild? I had no idea that in their minds an adopted child wouldn't really be their grandchild.

In the morning I called early and got my father-in-law. He told me Rosie wouldn't talk about it, and she wouldn't come to dinner. He didn't know what to do about it, so thought it would be best to do nothing.

Christmas day was a complete disaster at our house. We visited Steve at the hospital and decided not to have a real Christmas dinner. My parents left for home early. Sherrie spent the day in tears and Rosie refused to answer the phone.

The day after Christmas, we brought Steve home from the hospital. We were totally unprepared for a new baby but were able to make do with Kevin's old clothes and a borrowed crib. The boys shared bottles and cried constantly from the time we left the hospital until late into the night. So much for the "love baby" temperament concept.

The following day, Sherrie's dad came to the house. He thought Rosie would feel like coming over the following evening if it would be all right. We said it would be fine, and he left. He didn't mention anything about the new baby.

The grandparents did arrive the following evening with an armload of baby gifts. It was great to see them and know that our little misunderstanding was behind us. Sherrie said she was sorry and she and her mother hugged and exchanged tears appropriately.

The grandparents disappeared down the hall to see their grandson. They opened the gifts and played with Kevin for a few minutes then vanished out the front door just as quickly as they had arrived.

They didn't bring a gift for Steve, or even ask to see him. For that matter they didn't even acknowledge the fact we had a new baby. Through the years the relationship never changed appreciably. To this day our two daughters usually refer to the Togstads as "Kevie's" grandparents.

The next day was the greatest surprise of all. We awakened early with the babies. Sherrie felt nauseated and asked if I would mind helping with the bottles. I didn't mind and went about getting the kids their breakfast. Sherrie was sill feeling ill when I finished and told me that this was the way she had felt a few months earlier for almost nine months.

"No!" I shouted. "Tell me you are kidding."

"I'm kidding," she mused, then added, "but I think it's true."

It didn't take very long to determine that baby number three was on its way. Sherrie was terrified to tell her parents the news. Relations were poor to say the least, and the reaction to this bit of information would make the Los Angeles earthquake look like a Sunday School picnic.

Sherrie is an only child, and her parents are definitely not into the multiple progeny concept. The entire family situation was becoming a basic nightmare. My parents were Seventh-day Adventist, and lived only a few miles to the east of us in Palm Springs, California. They were non-smokers and non-drinkers. My in-laws, who were Catholic, lived in Canoga Park, California, about the some distance in the opposite direction. They both smoked and drank, and found it very difficult to have a good time without alcohol.

Myself, I had developed the habit of having an occasional drink with some of our friends. With others I claimed to be a teetotaler. Because of my upbringing I didn't want my folks to discover my vices. This kept me on edge when my parents were with us around our non-Adventist friends.

The life of the double standard can be a very difficult place to be. I loved and trusted in the Lord, but didn't want to walk the walk. The frustration of this way of life began to take its toll. I was beginning to feel the pressure from all directions. The gravitational pull between our two families was beyond belief. Both sets of parents wanted us to come to their homes for every imaginable occasion. Each occasion held a separate standard for me. Drinking with my in-laws was all right unless of course my own parents were there, at which times I became a teetotaler. Then I lived in the fear that someone would mention that I smoked and drank. The situation was becoming very unnerving to say the least.

I was a practicing physician at the Glendale Adventist Hospital and had an image to uphold. My peers were all ten to fifteen years my senior and members of the country club. They were all well established on the social ladder of success.

I was expected to play golf, join a club, and mingle with the all the "right people." Somehow we just weren't fitting in. My wife was pregnant, and we already had two children under a year of age. We were pushing strollers while they were driving golf balls. I was working day and night in order to establish myself in a community that I didn't want to be a part of in the first place. Something was dreadfully wrong with the picture. Something had to give or I was going to blow. I refer to this time period as "my life in an eggbeater."

Sitting on the L.A. freeway at rush hour with a gentle breeze blowing carbon monoxide into my window, the most logical thought I have ever had hit me. Of course, why hadn't I thought of that before!

I battled my way through the thick traffic and headed for home. My heart was pounding and my thoughts were racing so fast my head was reeling. I was so excited that I literally ricocheted into the house shouting, "Honey, honey come here! I have the answer to all of our problems." Sherrie stood and looked at me as if I had just lost my mind, and possibly I had, but it all seemed so terribly perfect to me.

"Well don't just stand there with your face hanging out," she said. "Tell me."

"It's all very simple" I explained "Let's join the army and move to Europe."

"What do you know about the army?" she asked.

"Absolutely nothing," I replied. "But I do know they have doctors, and I'm one of those." I was so excited I felt like jumping out of my skin. I wanted to stand there and scream, but managed to hold onto my professional dignity by a thread.

"It will all be so easy. Just sell everything we own. Pay off all our bills. Pack up the kids. Kiss the hospital goodbye. Say goodbye to our family and friends, and become an anesthesiologist in the United States Army. Then we'll move halfway around the world. How completely fundamental. Why didn't I think of it months ago? It's an absolutely brilliant idea!"

Sherrie looked like a statue, just standing there with her mouth wide open. Her eyes looked like they were going to pop out of her head. There was a long painful silence. Then she said quietly, "Sure, why not? I really didn't have much of anything else planned for the rest of my life anyway."

2

New Found Freedom

It was mid-November in Germany and the reds and the yellows of the autumn leaves were just starting to fade as fall was working its way toward winter. It was an unusually beautiful day for that time of the year.

I stood at gate number three of the Frankfurt airport watching a TWA 707 make its final approach towards the runway. On board, my wife peered expectantly from the window for the first glimpse of her new home. With her were Kevin, Steve and our new baby, Teri.

It seemed like forever since I had said goodbye to my pregnant wife at the L.A. airport two and a half months earlier. So much had taken place since we had made our decision to move to Europe nine months ago. The time spent between then and now seemed like a big blur. All the plans and actions to get us to this point were horrendous. Now everything seemed to be coming together. In just a few minutes the family would be together, and ready to start our new life. Glendale and the other life were half a world away.

It took an eternity for the plane to get to the gate. When the door finally opened Sherrie and the kids emerged looking as if they had just come out of Vogue magazine. Two young enlisted men were carrying the older boys and Sherrie had the new baby.

The trip must have been a snap, I thought. I just knew things would go smoothly.

Little did I know what really happened on that three day trip across the United States, the Atlantic Ocean, and a portion of Europe, with three children under eighteen months old. (That story will be saved for a future and more detailed book.)

The reunion was phenomenal. The thrill of seeing Sherrie, the two boys and the new little daughter was out of sight. What an experience! Steve had doubled in weight. Kevin was recovering from hernia surgery and wild as ever. The new baby didn't look like anyone I had ever seen before. Regardless, it was love at first sight.

In the two months I had been alone, I'd had opportunity to leisurely move into our temporary quarters. Everything was set up and ready to start housekeeping. All we had to do now was get home and let the jet lag run its course. From now on it was going to be an all new life.

And new it was. We had a new language and new money. There was no TV, which was a blessing. We had a radio but couldn't understand a word. Best of all were the new friends we acquired in a short time.

This was the life we had chosen. I had to remind myself why we were here. The need was to get away from the rat race of southern California, and the confusion of family frictions. We wanted our children to be brought up away from the social climate we had begun to resent. Moving to Europe seemed like a drastic measure, but we wanted them to learn Christian principles and we wanted them taught our way. I didn't want my kids to fall into the pitfalls I had fallen into. Geographical change seemed like a reasonable answer.

Although I was not practicing my beliefs as a Seventh-day Adventist, and Sherrie was a non-practicing Catholic, we wanted our family to be close to God. And I know God did take care of us through some very stormy times.

Our first Thanksgiving away from home was spent with American neighbors and could be considered pleasant and uneventful. I almost missed the aggravation that accompanied previous family get-togethers.

Christmas on the other hand took on a strange twist. Two days before Christmas while moving into our permanent quarters, Sherrie, Kevin and Steve, all came down with chickenpox. At first it appeared as if Christmas were over. However, not taking defeat lightly, I couldn't let this Christmas become another disaster like the last one.

With my three "pox patients" cared for and the baby under my arm I went to town and found a small out-dated Christmas tree. With only a minimal search I found a box of off-colored Christmas balls and a string of lights. I made a quick swing through the commissary and snagged a turkey, some potatoes and dressing, cranberries, gravy and pie. Christmas was in the making.

A call to one of our single nurse friends at the hospital got the party moving. He was to invite all the single personnel who had had chickenpox and had nowhere to go for Christmas to come to our house for dinner. Because! We were going to have Christmas!

The tree was trimmed. It looked as if it had been stolen from a refugee camp in Siberia, but it was colorful if you like chartreuse and purple. The dinner looked as if it would make the grade and smelled even better than it looked. At about five in the afternoon it began to snow, and at six o'clock, fifteen guests arrived.

Sherrie and Steve felt well enough to come out for dinner and open a couple of gifts. Everybody loved Steve. He played and put on quite a show in spite of his chickenpox. The entire setting was simple and spontaneous yet everyone had a terrific time. As I look back on that evening I can say we all felt the true spirit of Christmas.

From the very first, our stay in Germany was incredible. For the first time we began to feel a closeness that is hard to explain. We were our own little family unit away from the hustle and bustle of L.A. The social climate of Glendale and what we thought was interference by various family members seemed far away. The feeling of freedom and independence was incredible. I felt like a sponge attempting to soak up all of my new environment.

The military supplied us with a sweet little French girl from Tangiers to help with childcare. She was wonderful although she spoke neither English nor German. Of course that was fine, since I didn't speak German either. We drew pictures and made lots of hand motions. Very soon we had established a unique mode of communication. Years later when Monique had mastered the English language, we often commented on how well we had all known each other without speaking the same language.

We also had a Syrian lady who spoke only Syrian, and a German lady that didn't speak English. Each came in once a week to help with childcare. The children seemed to understand everything that was said to them in foreign languages. There was a complete lack of communication when I spoke to them in English.

Life revolved around our children, my new work, and the foreign culture we were thrown into. We learned to do our daily business using the hit-and-miss system with money and weights and measures.

The second week we were in Germany Sherrie went to the neighborhood market and ordered two tons of hamburger. The butcher thought it was funny and was good enough to give Sherrie a crash course in Grams verses Kilograms 101.

The world seemed to be filled with wonderful people, wonderful music, fantastic cities and villages as well as beautiful country sides and art. We studied language, and traveled extensively. Life was full. Everything seemed perfect.

Interestingly we lived across the street from the military church where both the Seventh-day Adventist and Catholic services were held each week. We didn't attend church often, but when we did it was usually the Adventist service on Sabbath.

Our military experience was one of the happiest and most influential periods of our lives. We had the privilege of seven years overseas: three in Germany, three in Hawaii, and one in Italy. From the time we arrived in Germany we were never separated and always traveled together. In all of our travels around the world we never had a mishap. I attribute this to God's loving care. There were several situations where I am positive that God intervened and saved us from tragedy.

One particular incident happened in Germany on a foggy night. We were out for the evening with another couple when we realized we were lost. The driver decided to turn around on a narrow, fog-obscured road. When our car was perpendicular in the road the engine died. Multiple attempts at starting the car failed. Suddenly out of nowhere we could hear the roar of an oncoming vehicle. One more twist of the key and our car made a lunge forward. The sensation we felt was as if the rear end of the car had been lifted and set over about ten feet to the side of the road. The other car flew past without incident. In my mind I know without a doubt God's angels were with us and lifted the car.

Toward the end of our second year of service in Germany, I was informed of an available position in an ob-gyn residency in Hawaii. I had a real interest in obstetrics. The thought of letting the Army pay for my training seemed like the right way to go. We could finish our three year tour in Germany, then extend our military time for an additional three years in Hawaii. It didn't sound bad at all.

I made immediate application. Sherrie filled out the paperwork. I signed the papers, and she mailed them. I received a letter of acceptance in about three weeks. There was only one minor mistake! The papers that were supposed to have been sent to army headquarters in Heidelberg, were sent directly to the hospital in Hawaii. This meant the extensive paper shuffling routine which is characteristic of the department of the army was eliminated completely. We were scheduled to be in Hawaii in exactly two and a half months. This not only came as a surprise but as a disappointment. We were looking forward to one more year in Germany. But the damage had been done. It was time to start packing.

The flight from Germany to New Jersey went as smoothly as could be expected with three screaming kids, a half dozen pieces of hand luggage, and a tearful wife, who didn't want to leave Germany.

After getting settled in our hotel room that evening I suggested we take the kids to the nursery and go to the officers club for a nice quiet dinner together. This idea was met with a flood of excitement. Especially the part about the children.

Dinner was peaceful and relaxing. I could see we really needed the time alone just to unwind. I probably drank a little more wine than necessary, but it did feel good. It was a beautiful evening so after dinner I suggested we take the long way home walking through the woods.

The minute we left the club the entire world began to detonate around me. Sherrie started in on me about my drinking, which I knew I deserved. All of a sudden I was being blamed for never helping with the children, which was not true. Then I was too strict in the way I handled Kevin. Strange, yesterday I had been too liberal. This was not Sherrie! She had completely lost it. She began to cry.

I stopped short and grabbed her. "What in the world is the matter with you?"

"I don't know," she sobbed, "I just don't feel like myself at all.

I'm so tired and feel kind of nauseated. I thought it was all the excitement of moving."

"You're not !" I shouted.

"I think so," she whispered. "At least that's the way it feels to me."

My voice started to soar. "Great! That's just great! We're halfway between Germany and Hawaii with three kids under three years old. Now you're trying to tell me we are going to have another baby. If that isn't a fine kettle of fish!"

The wine was beginning to rear its ugly head as I continued my lecture.

"How do you plan to make the trip across the Pacific on a ship if you are nauseated all the time? We can't even handle the kids we have. How do you think we are going to handle a fourth one? You can't expect me to take care of you and the kids on this trip all by myself. How could you let something like this happen?"

"It's not as if I planned it this way!" she cried. "There really isn't a whole lot I can do about it now either."

I was in a type of shock I had never felt before. I just couldn't believe we were going to have another baby. When I finally regained my balance I realized Sherrie was hurting badly. My being a jerk wasn't improving the situation. It occurred to me that I was on my way to Hawaii to study to be an obstetrician and had absolutely no idea about the mental flurry in a pregnant woman's mind.

I told her I was sorry for the way I was acting, and went so far as to say I thought having another baby would be fantastic. The last part was a lie.

3

Island Paradise

Hawaii and the sight of land were welcome after five days of uneven seas. The culture shock was severe. Nevertheless we surged forward and before long were barefoot, tan and appearing rather native. With the exception of Steve that is, who although extremely tan stood out like a lighthouse with his head of pure white hair.

Once settled we started taking the children to Sabbath School on a regular basis. This was no easy chore but rewarding. Not only was it good for the kids, it also served as an opportunity for Sherrie to learn Adventist teachings. Catechism had been stressed in her Catholic upbringing, making Bible stories a new experience.

Another example of God's protecting care happened on a Sabbath morning shortly after we arrived in Hawaii. On the particular morning in question I was to go to the church directly from the hospital and meet the family there. Standing outside the church I saw Sherrie waiting to make a left hand turn into the parking lot. There was considerable traffic which mandated a lengthy wait.

Steve, then four years old, saw me and leaped from the backseat of the car into the oncoming traffic and started to run toward me. Folk around me froze. Several ladies screamed! Without a thought I hurled myself into the traffic and ran to Steve. I grabbed him by the nape of the neck with my thumb and index finger and carried him to the edge of the street.

The screeching of breaks and the honking of horns was deafening. Yet, no one ever saw a car pass. The street was empty as if the oncoming cars had evaporated into thin air. Inside the church there were tears of thanksgiving. I knew God had delivered us from a severe tragedy.

Later in the day I attempted to pick Steve up with one hand. I was unable to do it. That experience left me with the perception that God had a special mission in life for Steve.

It was while living in Hawaii that Kevin was diagnosed as having hyperactivity syndrome, the condition that is nowadays referred to as ADHD (attention deficit hyperactivity disorder.) With the diagnosis came a markedly altered family situation.

It was as if we were living inside a cyclone. Kevin was out there somewhere whirling around at breakneck speed going nowhere. The girls seemed to have their feet planted close to the ground. Steve was drawn into the center of things in a type of vacuum. It became the situation that as Kevin went, so went the day. On a daily basis everything was directed toward Kevin. Steve on the other hand was just sort of there. He was not a leader and usually went with the flow.

From the time Steve started school he was an outstanding student. He had organizational skills that were unequaled by most of his peers. When he began his study he always looked through the entire chapter. Then outlined everything in his mind and went back and learned what he thought was pertinent. Almost without exception he brought home straight A's.

Kevin had difficulty in school. He was blessed with the ability to entertain, and entertain he did. He was always the class clown. A quality appreciated much more by his classmates then by his teachers. We could always count on a call from the principal about the second week of school, and it wasn't necessarily to tell us how well Kevin was doing.

The question became how to handle Kevin. Steve was left to fend for himself. It was always assumed that Steve would do well, and he always did. As a matter of fact when Steve graduated from the eighth grade years later he was honored as the only student who had never missed a spelling word while attending that school. I was very proud of his accomplishment, (especially since I can't spell even simple words without at least two or three attempts). When I told him how proud I was he blew it off with "So what, who cares anyway?" I'm sure I never gave him the feeling that I really did care. It was one of those things we as parents expect our children to understand without explanation. We assume they know how we feel. As a consequence certain attitudes often persist throughout life.

Oahu was a great place to live with small children. We made many lifelong friends. I learned to love the beach, as much I was learning to love spending many of my evenings at the bar in the officers club. Drinking had always been a social thing for me, but now little by little I could feel the pull of the addiction.

Let me explain to some of you that may not understand. The Seventh-day Adventist church takes a very strong stand on the use of alcohol and tobacco. Members in good standing just don't drink or smoke. Most of my friends considered me to be a member in good standing. Possibly more free thinking than some S.D.A.'s, but nevertheless a religious person.

My ability to maintain a double standard had reached the point of perfection. Morning could be spent in church with the evening extending into the wee hours in a bar. I avoided discussing my church affiliation when talking with bar friends and the subject of alcohol with my church friends. Two sets of friends became essential. I wanted to be a Christian. I also wanted the benefit of the pleasures the world had to offer.

Just one simple thought for those of you who are trying to lead your life by the double standard. It doesn't work well. Give it some thought. Pray about it and go one way or the other. It is impossible to serve more than one master.

In spite of my questionable format, by the time we left the Islands we were attending church almost every week, and one of my patients had been baptized as a result of my encouraging her to attend a series of evangelistic meetings. God does work in strange and mysterious ways.

After three awesome years in Hawaii, we had orders for a transfer to Italy.

Our last night in Hawaii, we threw a large cocktail party at our hotel for my fellow officers and their wives. It was a party of parties. The place was packed.

The following day we invited our church friends to see us off at the ship.

We boarded the ship in Honolulu with four children under seven years old, nineteen pieces of hand luggage and a fond goodbye to all of our Christian friends on the dock.

The band on shore was playing the strains of Aloha Ohe. The hula dancers were swaying as we followed the tradition of the Islands and threw some of our flower leis into the water. The legend goes that if your lei floats back to the shore, you will return someday. Steve was standing behind me with his little head peering around my leg. He was singing along with the band in his usual off key voice. It was one those bittersweet moments in life that you never forget.

As we sailed for San Francisco we could hardly see over the flower leis that had been placed around our necks. After we set sail, a quick trip to the bar completed a beautiful evening. With the exception of Teri coming down with chickenpox on board ship, Steve getting into my razor blades and bleeding on all of our belongings, and Kevin's attempts at disassembling the entire ship, the trip was uneventful. Cindi was still too young to be dangerous.

On the mainland we visited with friends and relatives. It was a welcome relief from the strenuous life as a resident. We relaxed for thirty day of bliss, obliterating all memory of the preceding three years of sheer torture while in the learning mode.

The day to say goodbye to family and friends came quickly. We boarded the big bird at Kennedy airport in New York City and, as they say, winged our way to Milano, Italy.

The memories of a magnificent vacation in the States reverberated in our minds as we converged on another adventure in a new world.

4

Lessons From Antiquity

Although we had lived in Europe previously, it was truly a new world that greeted us as we arrived in Italy. I don't know if you have ever pondered the question of how different Hawaii is from Italy.

Hawaii with the palm trees swaying to the melody of the deep blue surf, hula dancers with fragrant flower leis singing to the accompaniment of ukuleles, trade winds gently blowing to cool the warm humid air, beautiful blue skies, with large white billowy clouds and the brilliant green of tropical growth, combine to paint a picture of tropical splendor.

Italy on the other hand paints an altogether different picture of classic beauty. Seated at the foot of the snow-capped southern Alps, it is ensnared in antiquity. History abounds with every breath. The canals of Venice with Gondoliers singing Verdi and Puccini offer a charm found nowhere else on earth. Paintings of Michelangelo and Leonardo De Vinci and the all-encompassing Presence of the Roman Catholic Church are commonplace. The crucifix is displayed in every public place as well as on most of the people. Nuns, monks and priests in the habits of their orders rush in and out of the crowds. There are large cathedrals, with beautiful stained glass windows, available to everyone for prayer and meditation.

The mornings begin with the ringing of church bells. Evenings in the Piazza are graced by the playing of violins while tenors sing and pigeons converge in pursuit of morsels of food.

As the church bells continued to ring in the background I

became acutely aware of the firm footing the Catholic Church had established throughout the centuries of Christendom. The everyday lives of the Italian people seem to be completely immersed in their religious practices. The Blessed Virgin Mary is omnipresent, giving hope and comfort to all the worshipers continually.

The Pope appears to be as revered as God. The essence of St. Peter's Basilica, with its magnificent paintings, its altars, pipe organ and lavish accessories seems to reach toward heaven itself. I can see why the Church has such a tremendous grip on its people. The grandeur of the Church is without a doubt unequaled by any other church in the world. It gave me a feeling of inadequacy in my own Christian experience. I was impressed by the need of the pure simple Gospel of Christ.

In the midst of all this culture and beauty, Steve was always the star wherever we went. With his almost pure white hair and his bright blue eyes he stood out on the Italian hillside like a beacon. People would stop and talk to him on the street, or want to hold him. In restaurants the waiters would carry him from table to table as they went about their work. Steve was always able to throw a big smile, and truly seemed to enjoy the attention. He became mister personality. He was neither shy nor outgoing—he was just cute.

When we moved into our military housing, we learned quickly that we were the only Adventist family on the post. There was one military wife whose husband had been reared Adventist, but was no longer interested in any form of religion. She and Sherrie became friends and quickly decided to organize a Sabbath School for their children. There were six children in all and they met almost every week for a year.

The wife of a disinterested Adventist and Sherrie with her Catholic background made an interesting combination for teaching Adventist Sabbath School. The ladies ordered materials from the Sabbath School department, and probably learned more Bible stories themselves than the children ever thought of.

Looking back, it seems as if they were faced with an impossible situation, but God blessed their efforts and immeasurable good was accomplished. Once again God truly worked in strange and mysterious ways.

In spite of the effort to have spiritual training for the children, a large void was beginning to form in our own lives. The absence of a church family was becoming a real obstacle. Study of the scripture was becoming a thing of the past for me. My evenings off call were devoted to seeing how much wine I could consume before bedtime.

We no longer prayed before meals and God was seldom mentioned at home. On occasion we attended the military services on post, but that didn't hold much interest for either of us. I was beginning to feel that God didn't know we were around. He certainly did not appear to want to be a part of our lives anymore. How wrong we can be!

It's interesting that when we neglect God, we blame Him for not being around. In reality God was very much present in our lives. A chain of events began that I feel were directly instituted by Him and even though I refused to follow His plan for my life much of the time, He never abandoned us. Some of the events that followed were pure miracles.

In March of our first year in Italy we receive a letter from Adventist friends in Germany inviting us to attend the Adventist servicemen retreat in Bavaria. At first the thought didn't seem appealing at all, but the more I thought about it, the better it seemed. Religious retreats in the military meant an extra week off without taking official leave. And that was with pay mind you! You can see that my heart was in the right place. Nevertheless, after a short discussion we decided to go.

Going meant back to the closet with my drinking and smoking if I were to maintain my proper role as a hypocrite. In reality this was easy because of my previous training. All I had to do was not drink until after meetings and do all of my smoking in the bathroom, followed by a couple of good swigs of mouth wash. No problem, we would go!

The plan actually worked well for the first few days, until our friends dropped in unexpectedly one evening after the meeting. They were greeted by a cloud of cigarette smoke and the presence of an open bottle of wine.

They couldn't have been more gracious, but insisted on coming in to visit. It seemed to me they stayed for hours. The wine bottle kept growing larger and larger and the cloud of smoke became more dense. There was no way I could have been more miserable if I had tried.

Our guests exhibited the true expression of what a Christian should be. They didn't attempt to preach to me. It was almost as if there was nothing unusual. I'm sure a good sermon blasting the evils of alcohol and tobacco would have made me feel a lot better but it never came. We are still all good friends.

The retreat was a complete success. God spoke to our hearts in a way that brought unexplainable happiness into our lives. The association with Christian friends brought a passion for commitment to us that day as we drove through the Austrian Alps toward home.

It was a stormy afternoon and the snow flakes were the size of silver dollars. I was creeping along at a snail's pace when Steve woke up in the back seat and looked out the window and made the astute observation, "It could snow." This expression has been a family saying ever since, when something "stupid" is said.

Something else was said that day that set off the chain of events that would change all our lives. I mentioned it would be nice if we could move back to Germany where we would once again have church fellowship. We agreed that this would require God's intervention, and prayer would be an essential element if we were to be transferred. Military personal just aren't moved from one assignment to another in less than a year's time on their own request. We knew this would be a slow process, but felt it would have to be our goal even if it took a year or two.

The following month found us returning to Germany for an ob-gyn meeting. I knew that one of the high ranking officers in charge of physician placement would be there and that it might be possible for me to get an appointment with him to discuss our dilemma.

Sherrie and I discussed the situation on the way to the convention and decided we wouldn't mention moving to anyone until just the right minute. We decided to ask God to be a part of the decision making and committed ourselves to accepting God's will as our final answer.

When we arrived at the hotel Sherrie remained in the car while I went in to register. I reiterated to her once again not to mention moving to anyone, not even our friends, until I thought it was the right time. As I went into the hotel I said a short prayer asking God to be with me.

The registration line was long and I didn't see a soul I knew. I stood in line for what seemed like an eternity and just as I was approaching the desk, a gentleman stepped in front of me and asked if I would mind if he went ahead of me.

Are you crazy? I thought. Then I noticed the star on his shoulder. "On no, General, I'm in no hurry, you go right ahead."

Then without a thought I said, "Sir, you don't know me, but I know who you are and we are stationed in Italy and we don't have a church to attend. I think it would be great if you would help me get transferred to Germany." (Can you imagine not being able to find a church in Italy where there are one or two on every corner?)

The realization of what I had just said hit me like a bolt of lightning. I didn't know whether to hide or pass out. I didn't do either. I just stood there and looked stupid. He asked me what kind of a doctor I was, and I told him ob-gyn, which I thought might be self-evident since we were standing in line to sign in for an ob-gyn conference. I kept my mouth shut.

"I do know we have two openings coming up this summer if you would like to send in your transfer request" he said. I just stared at him. "Contact my office in Heidelberg when you get back to your post. We will see what we can do for you!"

I didn't even say thank you, but literally fled from the room. I jumped into the car shouting, "You will never guess what I just did!"

When I told Sherrie what had happened and that he was going to try to help us, she just grabbed me and held me and said, "I think God has His hand in this." We gave our prayer of thanks.

"What is our room number?" she asked. "I don't know," I replied. "I forgot to register!"

On returning to our post, I was informed that there were in fact openings available. But there was also an extreme shortage of family housing so orders were not being issued. We were told to anticipate at least a two year wait. My disappointment was so severe, I wasn't sure I was going to survive. I did survive, and I learned that life does go on after disappointment.

A month had gone by when I went to the post office and was handed a large brown envelope. The envelope was obviously very full, and had the return address of Heidelberg, Germany. I stared at the address for awhile. I just couldn't bear the idea of a further setback.

When I got up my courage, I opened the letter. To my amazement there in my hand was a full set of orders. In the military, a move requires orders for the entire family, including a set of orders for each of the children. All of the orders were included. The reporting date in Germany was to be in exactly thirty days. The packers were scheduled to start packing our household goods in two weeks. We were to be out of our quarters in three weeks. I just couldn't believe it, nor could anyone else.

We planned to drive our two cars to Germany in a caravan. The VW pop-top van would act as our living quarters. Sherrie would drive the Volvo station wagon which would house our carry-along possessions. The tent would function as an adult sleeping room. We planned a week of camping on the drive through the Alps, and possibly a day or two of camping when we reached our destination. We were told housing had become available, and that we could expect to be in our quarters almost immediately. God was without a doubt looking out for us.

The kids were particularly excited about the trip. Camping was definitely their bag.

The day came to vacate our quarters. We moved into the VW van and headed for a nearby campground to give this camping thing a hands-on trial. And trial it was. We weren't twenty minutes down the road when the thought hit me, "Where are all our passports?"

The last time I could remember seeing them was in the temporary file box in our bedroom before the movers left. I had specifically asked the movers, in my broken Italian, not to move that box. My guess was that no one had moved it. We drove on to the campground and set up camp, then I returned the thirty miles to the housing area. The Vilagio de la Pache, (Village of Peace), as the area was called, did in fact look very peaceful. For a brief moment I wondered if I really did want to move.

Once in the house I went immediately to the bedroom to get the box. The box was not there. Now what? It was late afternoon and I had no idea where the moving company was located. After several hours of searching I finally got in touch with the owner of the moving company. He said he could understand what I was trying to say, but it was apparent he didn't have a clue as to what I really wanted. He did tell me to come on down, and we would work on the problem. When I finally found the place, it was almost dark. About two more hours had passed since I had begun my search.

The gentleman tried to be helpful, but seemed to be having difficulty understanding my Italian. The less he understood, the more excited I got. Finally, he told me we could look into the large closed container that held our household goods. However, we wouldn't be able to open more than the two-foot by two-foot lid on the top. If I could see what I needed, fine. If not, I would have to wait until the goods were delivered in Germany. To try to explain that if I didn't get the contents of the box I wouldn't be in Germany was completely out of the question.

The owner opened the lid. There, right in front sat the box. I thanked the man, threw him a handful of lire, and was on my way. If the box had not been right there, by morning the storage container would have been on its way to Germany, and we would have been sitting in Italy without a country. God had done it again.

Sherrie was worried to death by the time I got to the campsite. To this day I'm not sure if it was me or the passport that concerned her most.

Vacationing in the Alps with the family was a dream come true. In our week of travel we had more fun than we had ever had as a family.

Sherrie drove the station wagon, and I drove the van. In the evening we would find a place to camp. We would start by putting the two cars parallel to each other with the tent between. We placed the stove on the table in the center and all worked together to make dinner. Peanut butter and jelly can be special when you are in the mountains in the fall.

It was cool in the evenings, so we bedded everybody in down sleeping bags. We read bedtime stories aloud until the last little eyes closed in contented sleep. There was always a candle lighted, and of course my faithful bottle of wine.

In my memory the coziness of those evenings will never be forgotten. In the morning the children were up and running at daybreak and it was off to the races for another day.

One evening we spotted a small one-ring circus in a valley near by. We decided to go. There was a small grandstand and the tent was filled with all sorts of animals, trapeze artists, clowns and all the other things that go along with a good circus.

By the end of the show the girls were falling asleep in my arms and Steve was sure he wanted to be a lion trainer. Even Kevin was captivated for the entire evening. I think it would be safe to say, "a good time was had by all."

Most of the people who attended the circus were Austrians from a small village in the area. They all wanted to meet the Americans who had wandered in. They treated us like long-lost relatives. It felt like old home week.

You may wonder how they knew we were American. In Europe you can always spot an American a mile away in a crowd. Sometimes that's good. Sometimes it's not so good. I often wonder if as Christians people can recognize us in a crowd?

The next three days we stayed in Heidelberg by the river, where we spent hours watching the barges hauling their wares up and down the river. The kids enjoyed waving at the people on the boats, and getting waves back. They thought it was funny to see clothes hanging on the back of the barges. I explained that these people lived right there on the barges. "That's their home." The kids still found the underwear hanging on the back of the boats to be hysterical.

We were able to walk the cobblestone streets, and visit the castle. We made picnic lunches and sat down by the river, where we could skip stones on the water, and try our luck at fishing with our crude hand-crafted poles. If it had been any more perfect we would have been known as the Brady Bunch!

It seemed as if God was leading us to the Promised Land. Two more days and we would be in Landstuhl, and our new duty station.

5

Land of Promise

When we arrived in Landstuhl it was already dark. I had never been in that part of Germany and it seemed very exciting. I went into the office and handed my orders to the lady at the desk. She spent a long time looking at them, and then excused herself and went into another room. She didn't come back for a long time and when she did there was a puzzled look on her face.

"Where are you from?" she asked.

"Vicenza, Italy," I said.

"Where did you get these orders?" she questioned.

"From the command center in Heidelberg," I replied.

Then she just sort of went crazy. She explained to me that there was a freeze on reassignments, and that no one with a family was to be sent to this area.

"And besides, you won't be eligible for housing for one to two years. On top of that you won't be able to get orders to bring your family here until then."

Looking me straight in the face she said, "And this is the good news. You shouldn't be here either."

For a short moment I wondered if she had any bad news to present. She quickly set my mind at ease with, "Don't even think about sending for your family! There just isn't any housing available and that's that!"

"What would you think if I told you that my wife and kids are sitting in the car in the parking lot?" I asked.

"I would tell you not to expect to get orders for any of them for at least a year, just as I told you before," she answered.

"The truth of the matter is, I have my entire family here with me and they all have bona fide orders from Heidelberg."

"No one on this earth could have done that!" she stated in a rather definite tone.

"You know, you may be right," I said. "No one on this earth."

Everyone in the car was tired and in a very silly mood. I didn't want to destroy the mood, but I just happened to have a great big bomb that I needed to drop at that particular moment. The kids didn't get the significance of having to live in a VW bus in the rain for the next one or two years, but Sherrie did! The tears appeared to be real, so I just stood there in the rain with my head bowed until I felt her major storm had passed.

"Don't worry, Honey," I whispered, "in a little while everything will be back to normal."

"That's what I'm afraid of," she cried.

With nowhere to go the only thing I could think to do was go to the hospital and look up my friend Dr. Stutz. He was an S.D.A. and at least he would be someone we knew.

When I arrived at the hospital he was on duty. As luck would have it he was in with a patient and would be busy for some time. I told the nurse I would wait. She offered me a cup of coffee. What I thought I really needed worse was a good stiff drink. I settled for the coffee.

While I was waiting, a young corpsman came into the room. I didn't want to eavesdrop, but I thought I heard him ask the nurse if she knew of anyone that was looking for a house to rent. I jumped to my feet and almost pinned him to the wall when I asked. "Do you know of a house to rent?"

"Yes I do," he said. "An architect in Kaiserslautern is moving to Brazil and wants to rent his house while he is gone. He doesn't know how long he will be away, but thinks it will be for at least a year. He wants three hundred dollars a month and that includes a man to take care of the yard.

"Have you told any one else about this?" I asked.

"No you are the only one I've talked to so far. I just found out about it myself fifteen minutes ago. I thought I would stop by work and see if anyone here needed a place to live."

"I've seen the house and it is real nice. It's completely furnished. The rent is a little on the steep side, but I think it would be worth the price if you don't mind not knowing when you will have to move out."

He finally stopped talking long enough for me to ask, "When can we move in?"

"Not for about four or five days." He smiled. "It seems to me that we all hit the jackpot tonight, I get a commission for finding a renter, and you get a house."

Dr. Stutz came out of the room and greeted me with, "I hear we have a major problem here."

"You know what Helmut," I said. "The whole world looks pretty rosy right now." And it really did.

The house was beautiful. It was a very modern home with a large stainless steel kitchen. The living room had floor-to-ceiling windows that were fully draped. There was indirect lighting throughout. And there were three bedrooms, one for the girls, one for the boys, and one for us. Compared to government housing we thought we had died and gone to heaven.

The yard man's name was Herr Dryier (pronounced hair dryer). He immediately fell in love with the kids. As soon as the early snow hit, he started taking them out on the hill behind the house for sledding almost every afternoon. Steve, the lion tamer, had very little courage when it came to racing down the hill on a sled, but he did it, and little by little Herr Dryier gained his confidence. They became the best of friends. It was a great place for kids. They loved the snow and the winter sports.

Skiing was probably the favorite family sport. Even though Steve was not the bravest guy on boards he did become a very good skier. He had beautiful form and excellent control. We began by having him ski between my legs, then little by little he was able to free himself of me until finally he made it down the bunny hill alone. You would have thought he had climbed Mt. Everest the way the other kids carried on. Steve just shrugged his shoulders and said, "What's the big deal?" A typical Steve reaction. A reaction with which I have never been able to completely cope. It seemed as if he always worked extremely hard to achieve something, then when he did succeed, he would just blow it off and say no big deal.

The other kids had been running the hill for days, but had absolutely no form or control. They had a wonderful time nonetheless. Steve on the other hand would work on every point to become perfect. He never seemed to be having much fun. However, he did miserable well!

Looking back, I think I always went the extra mile to make sure Steve was having a good time no matter what we were doing. I don't know if it was because he was adopted or exactly what it was, but I know that's what I did. I'm sure that he really did have a good time much of the time because he laughed a lot. But it seemed as if he really had a hard time expressing his happiness. There were times when I would get so frustrated when everyone was having fun, and Steve was just sitting there with a poker face, doing nothing. It gave me the feeling that he disapproved of everything we were doing.

The feeling that he was becoming withdrawn worried me. I began to see reactions that seemed inappropriate, such as his obnoxious laugh which came out very loudly at any place and at any time. Even when he was very young, I would try to talk to him about it, but it usually made him mad. His stock answer was, "if people don't like me the way I am that's their problem."

As he got older I tried to reason the point that it doesn't hurt to put your best foot forward. He always said that was hypocritical.

Although Steve had some idiosyncrasies, he was a neat kid. We did have some great times together. Always for his birthday we would plan a father-son time together. This was a custom I practiced with each of the kids. It was a truly special time for me.

The assignment in Germany seemed to be working out nearly perfect. The children adjusted to their new schools and loved the snowy weather. They were even excited about our new church. They seemed to enjoy the fact that there was a Sabbath School class for their own age group, and the boys didn't have to be in the same class with the girls. It took a bit of persuading to get Steve dressed on Sabbath morning, but once we were out the door he did well. In spite of himself, he actually seemed to have a good time once he was there. It did seem to be important to him, however, that no one be allowed to know that he was having a good time.

Near the end of our second month in Landstuhl, I arrived home to find Sherrie in tears.

"What's going on?" I asked.

"Your mother just called from the States and said that your father is in ICU in the Palm Springs hospital. They think it could be his heart. She seemed to be very upset and asked if you could come home."

My father was nearly eighty years old, and was as healthy as a horse. To my knowledge he had only had one tooth filled in his life. How could he be in serious trouble now? He did have emphysema when he was younger, but that hadn't bothered him in ages.

The thought that came to mind was, how in the world could my dad throw such a monkey wrench into the works when everything was just beginning to go so smoothly? And besides, how can I afford to fly back to the States after having just moved? And into an expensive home at that. Who would cover for me at the hospital?

Sherrie must have been reading my mind, because she said, "Sweetheart, it's your dad. He could be dying, and your mother needs you now."

Her words brought me to my senses, and I began to think about making arrangements to return to the States.

The kids were noticeably upset about my leaving. In part because grandpa was sick, but mostly because daddy was leaving. I tried to assure them grandpa would probably be OK, and that I would only be away for a very short time. Mother would be there with them. Steve, the worrier, was always sure that something dreadful was about to happen; he cried himself to sleep that night.

Sherrie started getting my bag packed, while I spent hours on the phone getting airline tickets and making arrangements for military leave. I finally dropped into bed a short time before the alarm was set to go off. It had been a stressful day to say the least. I was exhausted.

Emergency leave in the army takes precedence over everything else so by the following afternoon I was on a plane out of Frankfurt, Germany and on my way to Los Angeles, California.

43

6

God's Expanding Mercies

Traveling west across the Atlantic always seems like a race to catch the sun. On that particular evening the sun seemed to be bouncing on the horizon for hours. The brilliant reds and oranges of the sunset allowed restful thoughts of my own youth and the times I had spent with my father. The anxiety of not knowing his condition swept over me. I stared at the water so far below. I could see the fiords of Greenland in the distance. My little world in the sky seemed so remote from the cares of the world. How could it be that my dad was ill? He was always the one I turned to and he always seemed so strong. I felt alone, almost betrayed that he wasn't there for me right then when I needed him.

The stewardess announced that dinner was about to be served. Cocktails were available for one dollar each. There wasn't enough booze in the world to lift my mood, but I gave it my best shot. I spent more than a dollar and quietly fell asleep before dinner was served.

Only thirteen hours in the air and already it was last call for alcohol before landing. I had slept part of the way and drank all of the rest. My thought now was, why didn't I sleep more and drink less? I still would have to go through customs, find a rent-a-car, then drive through L.A. and all the way out to Palm Springs. And I was beginning to have conscious concern as to whether or not I would even be able to stand up, let alone drive.

For the first time I thought about my poor little mother who would be worriedly awaiting my arrival at her door. What a reunion! Sonny boy's home, and he's drunk. I felt so ashamed to be in this sort of condition. Here stood the strong support person completely out of control. I asked God to somehow forgive me and made some promises that I would never drink again if only I could feel better, and make it to Palm Springs.

I did make it to Palm Springs by about four in the morning. I pulled into the city park, and was able to sleep for several hours before I had to go to my folks' house. I felt, and I think acted pretty well by the time I met my mother. At least she didn't mention that my breath smelled like alcohol. She simply kissed me and told me how wonderful it was to have me home. She fixed me a great breakfast, then suggested a shower and a nap before going to see my father at the hospital. I felt like a little boy who had just been spanked.

The doctor was in the room when we arrived in ICU. He immediately alleviated my worst fears by announcing that they weren't sure exactly what was wrong, but he was almost certain that my father's heart was not the blame.

I was hugging my father with a sudden feeling of exuberance when my parents' friend and pastor, Carol, came into the room. We all sat and visited for some time. My dad joined in on the discussion and seemed to portray a sense of relief that he was no longer alone in the world.

Maybe this has been a worthwhile trip after all, I thought. Pastor Carol suggested that we have a word of prayer together. He gave a sincere prayer filled with hope and thanksgiving before saying "so long." Dad started to doze so I slipped out of the room without disturbing him and headed for home.

The next four days were spent doing time in the ICU ward (doctors don't do well just sitting in a patient's room). On the fourth day, Dad was transferred to the medical ward and allowed to be up and about. I felt a true sense of relief as I left the hospital for a brief period of rest and relaxation.

When I arrived home, my mother was in the kitchen cooking. No one had been home to eat for a week, nor would there be anyone for some time in the future. I guess cooking was just her way of doing something "normal." She seemed much relieved and more at ease than I had seen her in days.

"Oh by the way," she said, "Pastor Carol called today and asked if I thought you would like to play tennis tomorrow morning."

"What did your tell him?" I asked.

"I said I didn't think you played tennis," she replied.

My thought at the moment was that my only chance to escape into the real world had just flown out the window. "Why did you say you didn't think I played tennis?" I asked using intense restraint.

"Well I just haven't seen you play tennis in years," she answered.

Maybe that's because I haven't lived at home for the past twenty-five years, I thought to myself. I smiled and gave her a little kiss on the cheek. Some thoughts are better kept to oneself.

Carol and I did play tennis the following morning. It was great to be out in the land of the living and lose three games in a row. Maybe my mother was right when she said I didn't play tennis, or was I just playing with an exceptional player?

Pastor Carol didn't question me about my spirituality. We did talk much of the morning away and solved the majority of the world's more significant problems. He had to excuse himself to get some work done. He asked if I would like to come over that evening and just kick back.

"Sounds good to me," I said. "I'll see you then."

Back at the hospital the doctor met me in the lobby and told me my dad should be well enough to go home in a few days. I asked if I needed to stay much longer after my father was home. He assured me that the world would go on without me. I was free to leave. I felt as if I had just been released from detention hall in school.

The evening at Pastor Carol's house was worth the price of admission. We exchanged everyday conversation, and drank a can of pop. Then completely out of the blue he asked, "Do you pay tithe?"

"What do you mean?" I asked.

"You know, do you give a tenth of your earnings to God?"

"I'm not even a member of a church," I said without a thought. "Besides, Sherrie isn't an Adventist. There is no way I could ask her to relinquish ten percent of her money just for something I wanted to do. If I asked her to give a tithe, she might expect me to give a tithe to the Catholic Church, and I don't think I would feel right about that either."

"Just give it some thought and pray about it," he suggested.

I thought about it all right, but I didn't pray about it. I knew what I needed to do. I needed the money more than I needed a blessing.

The next few days went by rapidly and before I knew it, it was time to head back to Germany. Carol offered to drive me into L.A. to the airport and save a car rental. I took him up on the idea. Dad was at home and Mother seemed to have a handle on the situation. I was ready to fly the coop.

The drive in to the city seemed a little bit sad. I had had a good time in spite of myself. Carol seemed jovial enough, but seemed to be hung up about this "tithe" thing. I finally gave in and allowed him the benefit of the doubt. There really was no reason not to give it some thought. It probably wouldn't hurt to pray about it either. Paying tithe on my salary was another thing. There was no way we could afford to do it. At least not right now.

That boy is certainly persistent when he gets his mind set, I thought. No wonder he packs them in on Sabbath. Everybody is probably afraid to stay home.

The flight home was a rather routine trans-Atlantic crossing, except for the roar of the jet engines which seemed to keep saying, "tithe, tithe, tithe," in a rhythmic gyration. I buried my head in my pillow and tried to think about anything and everything else. The sound still kept ringing in my head. "You need to tithe, and you will receive a blessing."

My answer shot back, "I can't afford the money." The flight was becoming miserable. My mind just wouldn't turn off no matter what I did. Finally I came to a decision. I would give this tithing thing some consideration, but would definitely have to wait for the appropriate time and place to talk with Sherrie about it.

Naturally that would mean waiting until we were making more than the peasant's pittance we were currently trying to live on. Besides, I was pretty sure I knew what Sherrie's reaction would be anyway, so that would be that. The matter would be settled once and for all. Making a decision, whether right or wrong, always makes me feel better, so with that done I fell asleep.

At the London airport I took a running tour of the available gift shops to purchase the gifts for the children that I had failed to get around to buying during my two week stay in Palm Springs. Back on the plane it was only a short hop to the Frankfurt airport. I was almost home. I made it through customs without a hitch, fixed my flat tire in the parking lot, drove thirty miles home and there they sat. Three beautiful little kids in a row on the curb, waiting for daddy. What a picture. Sherrie told me they had been sitting there for several hours. We did the hug and kiss thing. Then went to the part they were really waiting for. The gifts!

When the kids were finally busy with their own things, I had a moment to spend with Sherrie. She wanted to know all about my folks, and how my dad was feeling, and what was it like in the States. Then she asked a most distressing question.

"Have you ever heard about tithing?"

"What do you mean by tithing?" I asked.

"Tithing is when you give a tenth of your earnings to God," she answered.

"I know what tithing is!" I raised my voice. "But what does that matter to you?"

She started in on a rather in-depth account about how everything she had found to read in the house since I had left was about tithing. All week she had been concerned about talking to me about it, but really felt this was something we should be doing.

For a minute I thought my mind was playing tricks on me. It must be the jet lag. A little rest should fix that. I asked one more time slowly, "What did you ask again?"

"I just wanted to know if you have ever heard about tithing?"

"That's what I thought you were asking."

I explained about the conversations Carol and I had had on the subject. It's a strange sensation when you know you have had no communication with one another yet you have been tormented with the same questions. We sat down that evening and wrote our very first tithe check.

The following morning I received a phone call from the finance department of the Army. The gentleman on the other end of the line apologized and told me there had been a mistake on my travel voucher. They had shorted me in an amount just a few cents short of what we had paid in tithe. There truly is a God and miracles do still happen.

7

Guilt, Responsibility, Success, and Failure

New Year's Day, 1974 we returned to southern California with the children for a two week visit with the grandparents. It didn't take long for us to become aware that we were greatly missed. The kids had a terrific time with both sets of grandparents. The relationship with my in-laws was so improved you would hardly have known it was the same people.

One afternoon I took my father for an appointment at the hospital for his routine blood work. Sitting in the waiting room he looked at me and said, "Son, when are you coming back home? You know your mother and I are not as young as we once were and we really need you closer to home."

Until this point the thought of returning to the States hadn't even entered my mind. Life had been so free of cares, particularly family cares. Coming home didn't even seem like an option.

I mentioned my father's comment to Sherrie that evening. She admitted that her parents had put the same question to her the week before. This brought some serious decision making close to home. We had been gone for nearly seven years and had only seen our families three times during that period. The kids were growing up in a hurry and deserved to see their grandparents more often. I knew that with my father's recent illness, and with my rank, reassignment would not be difficult.

Then there was the question of whether we should stay in the military or return to civilian life. Should we return to southern California, or go elsewhere? All of a sudden I was being challenged with real world problems again. There was the question of responsibility to our children and our parents. This time we did make God a part of the decision making. I asked God to help me find a place to work, and a place to live. Two simple requests—simple for God that is!

A few days later my father and I went back to the hospital to get his laboratory reports. I was waiting in the hospital lobby and reading the bulletin board when a gentleman came up beside me and started talking. I discovered that he was a doctor there at Desert Hospital. He also told me that he was an ob-gyn doctor. The conversation began to get interesting when he divulged the information that he would be looking for a third associate in a few months. He explained that he wasn't sure that there would be enough work for three doctors, but was in hopes the practice would continue to grow. God seemed to be answering my prayers before my very eyes. This has always been a hard thing to understand. It would seem that the times my attention was directed least toward God, His help was pointed most toward me.

When we returned home to Germany I put in a request for a compassionate reassignment. The request was granted. I would be sent State-side, but would have no say in where I would be stationed. The final assignment was for Colorado Springs in late April. The only decision left was whether or not to remain in the military. The deciding factor would be whether or not I was asked to join the group in Palm Springs.

We arrived at the Colorado Springs airport on Easter Sunday 1974. There was snow on the ground and everything looked extremely bleak. We had been told that Fort Carson was nestled in the mountains and had the appearance of a Bavarian village. To this day I fail to see the similarity. It was cold and the wind was blowing. I can remember the feeling that all I wanted in life was to be back in our comfortable home in Kaiserslautern.

It is interesting to note that a short time before we were to leave Germany, we received notice from our landlord. The notice stated that he would be returning from Brazil the week after Easter. He realized this was short notice and hoped this would give us enough time to make other living arrangements. God had really timed our move close this time.

Shortly after arriving in Colorado Springs I was accepted into the ob-gyn group in Palm Springs, California. Everything was beginning to fall into place. I was due to be discharged from the army in October, and the only thing left was to find a house. That came in just a few weeks. A friend called from Palm Springs; he had found a house he thought would meet our needs. I flew out to see the house a few days later. It was a nice four bedroom home with a pool and a playhouse for the kids. To my astonishment, the playhouse had two girls' names over the door: Cindi and Teri. One look and I knew this had to be for us.

We moved to Palm Springs in November. Sherrie and I were baptized together into the Seventh-day Adventist Church shortly after we arrived. I was asked to become an elder in the church and a member of the board. My ob-gyn practice was busy from the beginning. It was all coming together smoothly.

Out of necessity at this point I became what you might term a certified closet drinker. Giving up alcohol was no longer an option. The dependence had taken its grasp. Public drinking was out of the question. My folks lived up the street, my partner at work was a staunch member of A.A. (he later became a cofounder of the Betty Ford Center), and I was an elder in the Adventist Church. It seemed the situation was worse than before we had gone to Europe. I wanted to be an Adventist Christian and I wanted to stop drinking, but I couldn't do either.

I was spending less time at home, less time with the children and often went into the delivery room smelling of alcohol. However, I never missed work and I made sure to always be sober before going to church.

My friend, Pastor Carol, had more than one occasion to call me on the carpet. One evening that comes to mind was when he had asked me to have the prayer for a Christmas program at the church. It happened that was the same evening as the office Christmas party. I intended to drop in on the party for just a few minutes, and then make it to the church on time. In my mind there was to be no drinking, absolutely none. I made myself a promise, "no drinking!"

When I finally arrived home much later and very drunk, I literally fell into the entry hall. I really can't remember what actually happened that night, but I do remember how ashamed I felt, and how coolly I was treated at home the next day.

At work everyone thought I was a hilarious drunk and found it funny that I had gotten so plastered. Everyone, that is, except my boss. He called me into his office. The conversation hinged heavily upon the evils of alcohol. This was a subject that I really didn't need to hear; after all I had been educated in Adventist schools. I'm a physician and know about these things. Didn't he think that I was smart enough to know if I had a drinking problem or not? The more I thought about it, the madder I got.

That's what happens to people when they get involved in things like A.A., I thought. They become fanatical. Now I would have to stage my drinking to make sure that I wasn't seen by anyone at work or church or by my folks. I was becoming a slave to my habit as well as to the community. To tell the truth the bottle was becoming my closest buddy, one of the few things in life that I could really rely upon.

News travels fast in a small town and before long I was asked to resign as an elder of the church. My reign as head cherub was short-lived as the result of an unconverted heart. I voluntarily had my name removed form the church books.

In addition to the drinking situation, I was having a difficult time adjusting to life in the United States after being away for seven years. This was something that I had not counted on while we were overseas. It's still not clear to me if the country changed, or if I did. However, things were different that was for sure. It seemed to me that no one else in the world could understand my feelings. I tried to bury my unhappiness with booze and that didn't seem to help any more either.

Just before Thanksgiving of our first year in Palm Springs, I received a call from my boss asking me to meet him for breakfast the following morning. We exchanged small talk for the majority of the meal. Then he made a strange remark.

"I feel so badly that you aren't able to feel welcome at your own church anymore. I know how I would feel if I couldn't feel at home in my church." I was stunned at the remark and wondered where he was getting his information.

He went on to say, "It really breaks my heart to have to let you go, but you realize you are the new guy on the block and there just isn't enough work for three of us right now." It hit me like a ton of bricks. I'm being fired, I concluded. You can't tell me it's because there's not enough work to go around. All of us are working our heads off and he is trying to tell me there isn't enough work. I was insulted and humiliated. It seemed so unfair. There wasn't much more to be said so I thanked him for breakfast and all he had done for me and headed home.

Telling Sherrie was going to be hard, but it had to be done. She was backing out of the driveway as I arrived. I spilled out the news to my completely bewildered wife.

"I thought things were going so well," she said, crying. "Why in the world would they fire you?"

"I don't know, but that's what they have done," I answered. "At least they told me I wouldn't have to leave until I could find another position. They even went so far as to tell me I shouldn't have any problem finding work right away."

Unemployed and without a church family, I was devastated with no idea where to go or what to do. Sherrie stood by me all the way. Although I'm sure she suffered greatly, I don't remember her ever complaining. My pastor friend Carol was also a great support and has remained a lifelong friend.

Through a physicians' placement firm I found an opening in New Mexico. Heading for Los Cruses, I stayed overnight in Phoenix, Arizona the first night. On the night-stand when I awakened the following morning I found a Phoenix magazine and in it was an advertisement for an ob-gyn position. I called that morning, and made an appointment for that afternoon. I was hired on the spot.

I called Sherrie and asked her what she would think about moving to Phoenix. She told me her family had spent vacations there when she was a child, and she had liked it then. It seemed she was happy with the idea.

I signed on with the HMO the following morning. Life was great. Once again I was on top. Now I was going to be gainfully employed and able to care for my family. Better yet I could drink openly without fear of being chastised.

I would keep the subject of my church affiliation to myself. In my mind the church had done me wrong and if no one knew of my connection with it, all the better.

I never knew if alcohol played a role in the decision to terminate me from the Palm Springs office or not. I do know this was the lowest point in my life. With the exception of writing this chapter, I have tried to put it completely out of my memory.

8

Desperation's Web

It was only eight years and four months after leaving Glendale, California that we moved into our Squaw Peak home in Phoenix, Arizona. Yet a lifetime had elapsed. Our move was two days before Christmas and the day before Steve's ninth birthday. I went out to buy a small Christmas tree while Sherrie and the kids attempted to isolate the Christmas ornaments from the maze of boxes the mover has placed haphazardly about the house.

On Christmas Eve we decorated the tree and sat between the boxes, eating our carry-in-dinner. This was the house that was to be our home for the next fourteen years. The home in which we would experience love and joy and the pain and heartbreak that accompanies the rearing of a family.

In that brief moment in time, life seemed to be without blemish. Looking back on that evening with the closeness of the family unit, I praise God that in His great wisdom He doesn't allow us to know the future.

Christmas day we were invited to have dinner at the home of one of the HMO doctors. He said there would be a few of their close friends and thought it would be a great way to become acquainted in the community.

When we arrived at his home, I wondered where the parade was. There were cars and people everywhere. When we finally found the host he greeted us and suggested that we introduce ourselves to the other guests. We were the only strangers. Everyone else seemed to know everything about one another.

I mentioned to one lady that we were new to the area. She thought that was nice, because in her opinion there is no place in the entire world that compares to Phoenix. She had lived there all of her life, and so had her husband. Her conviction seemed to be that we were fortunate to have finally found our way into this neighborhood before it was too late. She never inquired as to what planet we had come from.

One person did ask where we had spent our last Christmas. I told her Palm Springs and the look of "name dropper" appeared on the faces of everybody around. I didn't even dare think the words Paris or Rome, which were more commonplace to us than Palm Springs.

The kids were invited to the play yard, where I saw them standing and watching while the other children played together. After dinner we all divided up into tables of four and six to play table games. We were the odd number, so weren't included in the games. At this point one of the guys asked me what I did for a living. I told him I was a physician.

"You mean an M.D.?" he asked.

"Yes," I said. "I'm a medical doctor at the HMO."

He then proceeded to introduce me as the only "real doctor" in the room. There seemed to be an air of disapproval. However, everyone nodded appropriately. I discovered later that most of the folks there were physician's assistants, chiropractors or psychologists. All of which are outstanding professions. For some reason the M.D. was definitely looked down upon.

After watching the other guests play games for a while I found Sherrie and alluded to the fact that it would be better to be miserable at home with our own family than to be lonely in a crowd. She agreed and we thanked our host and quickly retreated to a more user-friendly environment. We left unnoticed by a soul.

Home never looked so good. Even with its myriad of boxes and the disarray of furniture it was more inviting than the establishment from which we had just come. For the first time since leaving the service I was aware of how much I missed the close-knit fellowship that had been afforded us in the military. Once at home I began to feel better. With a certain amount of deliberation I was able to drink myself into oblivion before falling into the quiet escape of my bed.

The loneliness I was feeling was beyond description. We had no family or friends in Phoenix and I was immediately propelled into my work in an unprecedented manner. There were long days of seeing patients, surgeries and the delivering of babies at any time of day or night. The ob-gyn doctor that was promised to help me cover call never materialized. I was on call twenty-four hours a day and seven days a week.

The feeling of being drawn into a dark abyss swept over me. Depression was setting in. The despondency I felt was a completely new phenomenon to me. I knew I had none of the necessary tools with which to fight back. I was developing a longing for the warm and comfortable cocoon of the military while learning to detest the competitive climate of the civilian world. Even alcohol didn't offer relief. I was getting so despondent that on occasion I would begin to cry for no apparent reason whether I was alone or in a crowd.

Regardless of the inner turmoil, life had to go on and duties had to be fulfilled. The first of the new year meant getting the kids enrolled in school. I took the boys and Sherrie took the girls. When the paperwork was finished the boys and I stood in line to meet the registrar.

The registrar was an imposing, well-nourished young lady who seemed to excel in rude and fell remarkably short in tact. Looking at Steve's paperwork she quickly asked me about his family history.

"I don't know anything about his family because he is adopted," I replied.

"You mean he isn't your son?" she asked.

"Yes, of course he's my son, but he's adopted," I answered. "But we were never given a complete family medical history."

"Do you have his adoption papers?" she asked.

"No, but I do have his birth certificate and it has our name on it," I answered again.

"Do you have anything that has his real name on it?" she inquired.

"His real name is Mack," I replied with a certain amount of condescension.

Steve was beginning to show a degree of agitation and I think the registrar possibly caught on to the fact that things were not going well. She dropped the subject, organized the papers and pronounced Steve enrolled.

When we got home, I thought it would be a good time to talk with Steve about his natural parents. Stepping into his room I asked how he was doing.

"OK," he said.

"Steve," I asked, trying to approach the subject gently, "what does it mean to you to be adopted?" He sat for a long time and just stared into space. Then he answered.

"It means that my mother didn't want me so she gave me away!"

His answer almost broke my heart. "You know son," I said, "your mother was only sixteen when you were born and it may be she loved you so much that knowing she wouldn't be able to care for you, she wanted you to go to a family where you would be well cared for."

He didn't even give it a moment's thought when he came back with, "If she had wanted me she would have found a way to take care of me."

"But Steve," I replied, "it takes a lot of money to take care of a baby and a lot of work too."

"So what?" he almost cried. "She didn't want me so she gave me away. If I were sixteen I could take care of a baby. I'd get a job and earn some money, no big deal."

I could see I wasn't making a real breakthrough so went on to the next subject. "Would you like to find out about your birth family sometime?" I asked.

"Why?" he asked. "If she didn't want me then, she wouldn't want me now."

"But don't you think you would ever like to at least see your birth mother? Maybe just to see what she looks like? Or maybe you might have other brothers or sisters." I was fighting a losing battle and I knew it. I just told him if he ever wanted help in locating any of his natural family I would do everything that I could to find them.

"Yeah, yeah," he mumbled. "If I ever want to see my old lady I'll let you know. If she were any type of woman she would have come looking for me a long time ago."

His lack of respect for his birth mother concerned me, but I rationalized that he was just too young to understand right now. I would simply reinforce the idea of getting to know his natural parents from time to time. It would surely all come out in the wash.

Feelings of defeat became monumental. My life was in shambles. I was terribly unhappy and felt that my children were also. Reflecting back on all the miracles that God was supposed to have done for us to have gotten us to this point I wondered where God was now. If this is God's doing, why am I so unhappy? Why are the kids becoming so uncontrollable?

I concluded that if it had been God that brought us here He wouldn't have just dropped us and left us to fend for ourselves. Here we were all alone in Phoenix. Locked into an eighteen-month contract and it appeared I was going to have to do all the work by myself. No relief seemed to be in sight. Every time I asked when help would be coming I got the same answer: "We are looking!"

Settling into my work was difficult. I did the best I could, but the depression became so overpowering at times I knew I wouldn't withstand the pressures. When there was a little time at home all I wanted to do was sit in my room alone and submerge my sorrows in the bottle. The kids were with me much of the time, but I wasn't with them. It was becoming difficult for me to concentrate. Eating didn't interest me at all. Many times Sherrie would make a nice meal and leave it in the oven for me to eat when I got home from the hospital. I would take it into our room and eat a few bites and the rest would go on the floor for Sophie, the family dog, to eat.

If the kids did come in and want to spend time with their dad, I would offer a penny throw. The point of the penny throw game is to take a handful of coins, line the kids in a row and throw the money in the air. Whatever you grab in the scramble is your take. As the kids raced off to their rooms to count their money, I would pat myself on the back and think "what a neat dad I am." It was a great experience for everyone. It allowed the kids some fun. It helped me alleviate some of the guilt that parents often feel when they spend too little time with their children. It was an amazing conscience-appeaser.

The big black hole was getting deeper. All I was doing was working and drinking. Kevin continued to be in trouble at school much of the time. No one seemed to know how to deal with his situation.

On the suggestion of one of his teachers, we enrolled him in a once a week counseling session. After our first meeting the counselor asked to have the entire family come for the next visit. This went over like a lead balloon with Steve. He insisted it wasn't his problem and he wasn't going to go.

When I explained to him that he was going to go, and that was that, he became catatonic and just stared at me with the "I hate you" look.

"I'll go if I have to," he said, "but you can't make me answer any questions and I won't."

He did go and each visit was worse than the previous one as far as his contribution was concerned. He just sat there stiff as a board and peered straight ahead with those piercing blue eyes as if to say, "Just try and make me enter in. Go ahead just make me!"

Steve was beginning to show a stubborn streak that defied all authority. I particularly noticed it in regards to his attitude toward women. He displayed a chauvinistic attitude from a very young age. Authority of any type was difficult. However, if it came from a woman it became an impossible situation. Especially when it came from his mother.

9

A Dream Turns Real

About six months after our arrival in Phoenix, life was at its lowest ebb. Talking to my friend Carol on the phone one evening we discussed the difficult adjustment he was experiencing after his marriage plans deteriorated. He had recently moved to New Mexico to work in the family business which was a far cry from being a pastor. The old saying that misery loves company came into play in a big way. Carol listened as I poured out my heart. He said he could empathize, though he wasn't sure my method of handling the situation with booze was necessarily in the best interest of all concerned.

Nevertheless, a great plan was formulated that evening—a plan that would once again give a goal and some direction to life.

The idea was to pool resources. Get a place for Carol to live in the country. It could be a place where my kids could have animals and also work on the weekends to earn spending money. It would be like having a vacation home except it would be in the same town. The name of the project was to be "The Ranch."

The picture that I was formulating in my mind was something like this. We would buy two or three acres of land about ten miles out of the city. A triple-wide mobile home would be put on the property. A beautiful black lagoon pool with a conversation area and waterfall would grace the enclosed back yard. I envisioned a bridge across the center of the pool, with palm trees and flowering shrubs on all sides. The outside of the enclosed area would be entirely covered by lawn. On the extreme back portion of the lot would be a small shed for goats, chickens and a lamb. Adjacent to the shed would be the horse corral.

There would be a variety of weekend occupations for the kids to choose from. Each child would be expected to do his share of the work. After the normal working hours and training sessions there would be fun activities like swimming, horseback riding, barbeques, baseball, volleyball, etc.

Carol would have his own home and would be willing to maintain the stock and property during the week. All of this would be close enough to the hospital for me to be with the kids and take call at the same time. It seemed too good to be true.

I called a family counsel with the kids and told them about our brainstorm. They were ecstatic with excitement. Each had their own idea of what animals they were going to have. Kevin wanted a goose, Steve, a half dozen snakes, Teri wanted puppies and Cindi wanted a pony. They all wanted to have their birthday parties by the pool and invite their friends for swimming parties and barbeques.

We had a great time that evening. Sherrie even expressed the opinion that it would be great for the kids and I go to "The Ranch" without her some of the time to give her a little peace and quiet alone around the house.

Life took on a new dimension that night. For the first time in months there seemed to be a purposeful structure to our family. I could picture working together as well as playing in the pool and going horseback riding. It sounded like a little piece of heaven. It was going to be right in our own back yard. Now all we had to do was make it happen!

The dream did materialize in a little less than two years' time. Carol spent long hours slaving over sprinkler systems, lawns and planting trees, as well as setting up his mobile home.

On weekends we invited friends and neighbors in for barbeques by the pool. The kids had birthday parties as well as slumber parties and picnics. It reminded me of my favorite childhood book, *The Swiss Family Robinson.*

There was a black lagoon pool with a waterfall. There were cats and puppies. A goose named Sir Charles, and a pony named Fancy that could be harnessed to a two-wheeled cart. Carol saw to it that there were also peacocks and ducks, two horses and a pigmy goat named Sir

Galahad. The lamb, called Lamb Chops, came later as the menagerie continued to grow.

There was an old car on the back of the place that the children converted into a fort. They pleaded with me not to discard it. However, as all wrecked cars go, it went!

Much of the project was completed by the time our first Ranch baby was born. Carol called early one Sunday morning to let me know that the big event was about to happen. We got the family together in record time and headed for the Ranch. We arrived just minutes after the delivery.

The baby goat was just making its first attempts to stand as we walked into the shed. The girls both cried with excitement and Steve even exhibited a degree of emotion. The mother goat looked just as amazed as our kids did as she washed the new arrival in order to make it presentable for "The Ranch." With only a short discussion the kid was given a name. The official, as well as original, name from that time on would be "Billy."

We spent most of the day at the Ranch. There was a family camaraderie that I hadn't felt in a long time. I didn't do any drinking all day and felt truly happy without any alcohol. We even allowed Billy to come into the house for the evening, under the somewhat disapproving eye of my in-laws who had recently moved from Los Angeles to Phoenix to be near our family.

In the early days the Ranch was a happy place. We still talk about the good times we had there. The kids even seemed to enjoy working for a living. Steve, as might be expected, was our best worker. Kevin had the most fun and there was always someone to defend his every action. Regardless, we always had good times and I had the satisfaction of knowing something constructive was being done for our children. It also gave me the opportunity to do some serious drinking in a less conspicuous environment.

About this point in time, Steve came to me and said he wanted to learn a musical instrument. Having always played myself, I was very happy to have him show an interest in music. I asked him what instrument he wanted to learn and he informed me it would be the guitar. That was one instrument I knew nothing about other than the fact that it had a lot of strings. Although I wouldn't be able to help him with his guitar I felt if that was what he wanted, that was what he should go for. I asked why he chose the guitar and he told me that he wanted to be a rock-and-roll star. Once again I had to admit I knew nothing about rock-and-roll but was sure I could learn.

We went out a few days later and bought Steve his first acoustic guitar. He took to the strings like a duck takes to water. He spent hours sitting and strumming his guitar. Like so much of what Steve did, he attacked the guitar with a vengeance. We started him in lessons at the local music store and made sure he was able to get there for his instructions each week.

Everything went smoothly for a month or so and then one evening he told me he didn't want to go back for his music lessons anymore.

"Why?" I asked.

"They want me to play songs and I want to play rock, not their stupid little songs!" he answered.

"Why don't you at least learn the basics such as the notes and timing? Then you can learn to read music so if you ever want to learn another instrument you will have a good foundation?" I suggested.

"No way man," he said. "I'm not going to learn no other instrument and I'm not going to learn no songs! Jimi Hendrix didn't have to learn all that junk and he's the greatest rock star there has ever been."

"I don't think I have ever heard of Jimmy, what did you say his name was?" I said.

"Hendrix!" he shouted.

"You don't have to shout at me," I said. "I'm standing right here in the same room with you!" I raised my voice to match his.

"Anybody that knows anything about music would know Jimi Hendrix. He's the greatest star ever," he added. "I guess you're just too old to know much about real music. You think that old long-haired stuff's music. I'm not going to waste my time on that junk."

His face was getting beet red and his eyes looked glassy. His arms were whirling around his head like airplane propellers. It was apparent that contact with reality was slipping away. I dropped the subject.

I could see that rational thinking was no longer on the agenda for the evening's discussion so I left the room before my natural instincts led me to pulverize him. He had a way of bringing that feeling out in me and I hated myself for it. He was always able to get the best of me. From a very young age things were always black or white with Steve. There was never a gray area. Nor was there any room for negotiation.

As time went on, the guitar became a very dominating element in Steve's life, as did the influence of Jimi Hendrix. The role model of a great musician sounded like a good thing. But I just couldn't make myself believe what I was seeing and hearing constituted either a great role model or a great musician. A war zone was established as I laid the cards on the table. The fact that Jimi Hendrix had long hair and wore an earring was a turn off to me and something I had been fighting Steve about for a year or more. The type of music I was hearing was so foreign it was difficult for me to call the sounds that spilled out of Steve's room anything but a lot of noise.

"And worst of all," I said, "he's a pothead."

"What's so bad about smoking pot?" Steve asked. "You smoke cigarettes and they are a lot worse than smoking pot any day! They'll kill you. And besides it isn't the drugs that's the problem, it's the person that's using them. That's what the problem is."

I knew he was right about the cigarettes, but I couldn't understand his thinking on drugs. The statement, "don't blame drugs, it's the person that's the problem!" always baffled me. The only redeeming factor was that at twelve years of age. I knew Steve was too young to think about using any type of drugs. Fortunately, I thought, at least I have a few years before I will have to cross that bridge. Besides, he has always been a good student and he's honest.

There really was a lot to be thankful for without getting too upset over the type of music he was listening to. It's probably just a phase, I decided, and in a short time he will out grow it and we will be back on track again. I'm not sure what the definition of the word "phase" is when it pertains to teenagers. I do know it is something that usually grows rapidly out of proportion until it blows up and mushrooms creating some degree of devastation.

10

Missing Coins

As summer arrived the kids had all completed their respective grades in school and had done fairly well. As custom would have it Kevin's marks in citizenship were on the low side of normal. As a matter of fact there was a growing concern among his teachers and counselors over how to manage the coming year.

We had done the consulting routine and the Special Education classes that were available. Nothing seemed to be working. The principal of the school told us they would give him one more chance the following year. If there was not a marked improvement, we would have to pull him out of school and make other arrangements.

My frustration level was running high. It seemed we had tried every form of correction available. I suggested the possibility of sending Kevin to a military Academy. The in-laws went straight through the ceiling when they heard that idea. They informed us that there was no way this would ever happen. They had known some folks who sent their child to a military Academy and they felt the discipline was too stringent.

Yeah, I thought, that's exactly what I had in mind.

The grandparents had altogether different ideas. First of all they already thought we were much too hard on Kevin. They went so far as to tell him they would never allow us to send him to a military school regardless of what he did.

Steve was once again pushed into the background because all he did was do all of his work and bring home straight A's. We did try to give Steve his due praise but it always seemed to fall short of what he really deserved. The problems always rang louder than the applause.

The beginning of the summer brought other concerns. There were more times when items around the house were missing. Most of the time it involved loose change. I questioned the boys about what had happened to the missing goods. Kevin immediately confessed that he had been the culprit. Steve assured me that he would never take anything that wasn't his. He looked me straight in the face and said, "I promise I will never take anything that isn't mine." There was no reason not to believe him, so I did.

For Sherrie and the kids, the hottest portion of the Phoenix summer was spent in the motor home on the beach in California. Now that I was back in the field of anesthesiology and no longer associated with the HMO, I had more free time and was able to join the family for long weekends every few weeks. There is no way to express the feeling of freedom I felt as I began private practice in the summer of 1978.

Although my work situation had improved, my drinking had not. With more time away from my family and less time on call, the stage was set for a true alcoholic to present his finest performance. And perform I did. In order to be in the operating room all day and to drink much of the night, I had to be one of the finest actors imaginable. In fact my act was so good that whenever there was a function where drinks were being served, I would always decline the offer of alcohol and opt for the apple juice or something similar. Even my own brother's wife had no idea I ever drank. The nurses at the hospital were wonderful about enabling. They were always there with breath mints or a cup of coffee if the occasion should call for it.

One evening before leaving for a long weekend at the beach, I surpassed my quota of alcohol. Arriving at the airport the following morning I felt like death warmed over. The only way I was going to make it to the beach was to have a drink or two before I got on the plane. Then there was just about time for two more drinks during the flight. When I arrived at the motor home I was still feeling miserable. The only solution was to have another drink. Just as I was getting comfortable with a tall one my dear mother-in-law walked in.

"No big deal," I thought, "she's a lush herself."

She didn't say a word to me but I heard her tell Sherrie, "I think it is a serious situation when a person has to get drunk before noon."

She sure has her nerve, I thought. Then I slept the rest of the day and night away. During the evening there was a problem with the water heater in the motor home. Apparently a small fire broke out. Sherrie and her father extinguished it. There was no damage to the motor home, but the damage that was done to me by the time everyone got through with me the following morning was mortifying.

This was the first challenge I had received from any of my family regarding my drinking. Frankly I felt they were being a little unreasonable. Nothing was hurt and so what if I had gotten a little drunk? After all I had been working hard and needed a little relaxation.

It was intended that we all have a long weekend together. However, this was by far the longest weekend I had ever experienced in my entire life. I did very little drinking the rest of the time and had Sherrie drop me off at the plane two hours early Sunday afternoon. It was very peaceful sitting alone at the airport bar for a few short ones before flight time.

Apparently the boys were no better than their father had been. Reports filtered back to me claiming the boys had been sipping a bit of ale themselves and had generated their own agenda with the security guards. Also there was tampering with their mother's purse. Some of the family finances seemed to have dwindled. It didn't seem possible that the boys could be stealing when they promised me they wouldn't. I chose to ignore the accusations. The tincture of time would take care of all ills, I concluded, and let it go at that. The brain plays some mean tricks when it's lathered in alcohol.

With summer over and everyone back in school, things began to slip easily into a normal daily routine. The boys had been duly counseled regarding their extracurricular activities of the past month. We came to an understanding that gave me a sense of security that everything was going to be fine. I wanted to trust the boys and felt that their youthful pranks were nothing more than just that.

The following week, Carol came to me with troubling news. There had been a jar of loose change in his closet at the Ranch. He estimated that there were probably about three hundred dollars in it. It was missing. Only Kevin and Steve would have had access to that room.

"I don't want to accuse your boys, but I can't think of any other way the jar would turn up missing" he said.

My first thought was that he must have misplaced it. "Let's go in and look for it," I suggested.

"I have turned the whole house upside down and it just isn't anywhere to be found," he replied.

I questioned the boys together about the money. "Has either of you seen a bottle of money in Carol's closet?" I asked.

"No" was the unanimous answer.

"Steve, are you sure you didn't see the money?" I asked again.

"No, and why won't you believe me?" he pouted. "You always make me feel like some kind of criminal. Can't you trust me when I tell you that I didn't have anything to do with the stupid jar? Here let me swear on the Bible." He ran to find a Bible. "Maybe this will make you believe me for once. Why do you always think I'm telling a lie?"

"OK, Steve," I said. "If you say you had nothing to do with it, I believe you." Steve looked noticeably angry and a little hurt.

"Besides it's usually Kev that swipes everything in sight anyway," he threw in for a bit of spice.

"Cool it, Steve," Kevin replied. "You're just mad because you got caught and want to get me in trouble too."

"What do you mean got caught?" Steve shouted. "I haven't done anything to get into trouble for in the first place, so just shut up!" The battle was on when they left the room.

I knew I had just been hog tied as I stood alone in the room having accomplished absolutely nothing. The boys were probably in the other room laughing. "Man did we ever pull the wool over Dad's eyes. Smooth move man, give me five."

It's one thing to have your kids outsmart you. It's an altogether different thing to have them out maneuver you when you just stand there and let it happen. I felt overthrown. I was so angry that I wanted to stomp into their room and rip their arms off, but at the same time I wanted to have faith in them and believe they were telling me the truth. In my heart I knew they were both lying.

11

A Cry for Help

The years of excessive alcohol use were beginning to take a toll on me physically. I was developing a noticeable tremor in my hands. Any purposeful small movement made my hands shake. It was becoming obvious to members of the staff, as well as making my work more difficult. Simple things, such as loading a syringe, would on occasion become a major undertaking. Starting an I.V. was like hitting a moving target. My handwriting was almost illegible. I could hardly lift a cup of coffee to my mouth without spilling it. Life in general was becoming unmanageable.

At Thanksgiving that year my folks came to Phoenix for the week. Several times during their visit the subject of drinking was brought up, always in relation to other friends or relatives. My paranoia was skyrocketing. I was sure they were directing their remarks toward me. Lifting my fork at the dinner table made me fearful that they would notice the trembling. I for sure didn't want to write anything in front of them.

A good stiff drink would solve the problem, but then they would smell the booze on my breath. Hugs or kisses were out of the question for fear of being detected. I was sure they thought I was acting strange. The feeling it gave me was that I was looking over my shoulder the entire time they were there. Guilt makes such a miserable companion.

All my life my mother had used the expression, "the guilty flee'th, when no man pursuith." I don't know if it is a saying she just made up or if it is actually in the Scriptures, but when she said it to me at the Thanksgiving table, she could have cut out my heart with the carving knife and it wouldn't have hurt any worse.

Above all I didn't want them to find out I was a drinker. I so respected my parents' beliefs that the thought of disappointing them would have killed me. The entire week was spent in a living inferno. After they had gone to bed in the evenings I would go to my room and drink myself into the void of forgetfulness. I had major concerns that my boys were lying to me. Yet I was living a brazen lie in front of my own parents. The apple does in fact fall close to the tree.

My livelihood was dependent on my being able to use my hands, yet the only way I was able to stop shaking was to have a little vodka. The nurses were handing out the breath mints more frequently. Several times the remark was made that maybe I should cut back on the coffee. The world was coming down on me and I knew it. There was nowhere to run.

One afternoon in early December the chief of surgery stopped me in the hall and asked to have a few words with me. We went to the lounge and sat down for a short heart-to-heart. His concern was that I was possibly consuming an excessive amount of alcohol and that it could be interfering with my work. He assured me this was not a reprimand but a friendly suggestion. I let him know I didn't see that my drinking was a problem. I did assure him I would make note of his suggestion and do better in the future.

There has never been panic to match the feeling I had that afternoon. Everything I had worked for my entire life was on the line. I knew I couldn't stop drinking because my hands would shake so severely that I wouldn't be able to function. If it was known that I was still drinking after a warning, I would be called on the carpet and most likely be faced with disciplinary action. I couldn't tell Sherrie what had happened. After all why worry her? I had never been in trouble and I had always been able to do good work.

Then it began to make me mad. It really wasn't anybody's business in the first place. All I knew at that point was I needed something to make me relax so I could work out a solution to an expanding problem.

After visiting my friendly liquor store I headed for my haven of relaxation, the Ranch. There is no way of knowing how much I drank that night, but apparently after I passed out Carol called Sherrie and told her, "Well, he did it again." He threw a blanket over me on the floor and left me to sleep it off. The next few days never happened as far as I can remember although I apparently worked every one of them. In about three days I was able to get hold of myself and made a firm commitment. No more drinking!

For several days I did stick with my commitment. Rapidly the tremor in my hands became more severe. The realization hit home that I wouldn't be able to continue performing my everyday duties with such a low blood alcohol level. Something had to be done. The key word was "quickly."

I decided to keep a glass of vodka in my car which would allow me to run out between cases and drink just enough juice to steady my hands. That was the answer and it worked well for a short time. I felt comfortable in the operating room and yet never really felt drunk. Sherrie and I even took the kids to pick out a Christmas tree. I was steady enough to expedite the setting up of the tree and help with some of the decorations. This was going to be a great Christmas after all.

December 22, 1978 was "a night to remember." That was the night my ship sank! I broke my vow to myself and bought a half gallon of vodka and headed for the Ranch. That was the night Carol finally lost all desire to enable me. The more I drank the less tolerant of my behavior he became. He let me know that the Ranch was part mine so he couldn't ask me to leave. However, if I insisted on continuing my present lifestyle, he was leaving town. He supported the idea that I was a lousy father and an even worse husband. In no uncertain terms he told me "how the cow ate the cabbage."

"I thought you were my friend," I pleaded.

"I am your friend," he said. "If I weren't a friend I wouldn't even care, but you are destroying my life and everyone else's lives too. You don't spend any time with your kids or your wife. All you want to do is get drunk and I am getting sick and tired of watching you bomb out night after night. You don't seem to care about anybody but yourself."

I thought I would have another drink before he started his closing arguments, but he hardly took a breath when he informed me that I had already wrecked Christmas and it wasn't even here yet.

After listening to his short address I went about proving the insanity of the alcoholic mind. I started to destroy all of the gifts under his tree. For some reason I stopped before I damaged anything. After abandoning that little project I proceeded to go into the bedroom and pulled all the clothes from the closet. I faintly remember running through the house like a madman wanting to obliterate everything in my path. Mercifully, the events of the rest of the evening have been captured by a form of a hypnotic coma.

When I awakened the following morning Carol was sitting in the big chair in the living room staring at me. All he said was "Get help."

"I can't," I said. "I have to go to work."

"Get help," he repeated. This time he seemed to have lost the compassion I was accustomed to hearing.

I think I was crying when I asked, "Who will help me? You won't and you're supposed to be a friend."

"Call A.A.," he said in a very unpleasant voice. "Call A.A. and do it right now!"

"But A.A. is for alcoholics and I'm not an alcoholic. I may have a drinking problem, but I'm not an alcoholic." I was begging.

He dialed the phone and handed it to me as he walked out the door for work. The lady on the other end of the line sounded pleasant with the exception of the multitude of silly questions she asked. I told her I was a doctor and was probably not in need of what they had to offer. She suggested I might need all the help I could get. As soon as she could make necessary arrangements she would have a recovering alcoholic come and pick me up.

Then she asked the dumbest question of all. "When did you have your last drink?"

"That depends on how long it takes someone to get here to pick me up," I answered as I laid the phone down and headed for the kitchen to pour an "encore" in honor of my last great performance.

12

The Darkest Hour

Alone on my back in the darkness I was vaguely aware of the activity in the room around me. There was the shuffling of feet and an occasional soft evidence of speech. An overwhelming compulsion shrouded me to lie perfectly still. To even move so much as a finger, it seemed, would send me into a state of convulsiveness. If I were to open my eyes, I would vomit for sure. Every inch of my body was in pain. I dare not move!

My head was pounding and my mind was racing to figure out exactly where I was and why. There was a brief recollection that this was a hospital, but which one and why I was there was unclear. I knew for sure that I felt terrible and that it had to be either Christmas day or the day before Christmas. The sensation of spinning was getting worse.

If only I could have a drink, I thought, I know I would feel better. I need to move, but know I can't. I began to panic. Am I going to have D.T.'s? I wondered. I had taken care of enough patients at L.A. County Hospital with D.T.'s to know that was not something I wanted to have happen to me. Just don't make a move, I kept telling myself. Just don't move a hair.

Without warning out of the distance came a melodious voice croaking my name. "Keith, open your eyes, it's time to wake up and get ready for the day."

"Keith," came the voice again, "you have to wake up!" This time the tones reverberated about the room and suddenly it was perfectly clear what was happening. This has to be a dream and we are all in Dickens's *A Christmas Carol*. This must be Christmas Present and that is Nurse Scrooge who persists in calling me by my first name. In a few minutes Tiny Tim will wish us all a Merry Christmas and I will wake up and go home for a great turkey dinner with my family.

The idea of a dream came to an abrupt halt when Nurse Peterson, RN, arrived at my bedside to introduce herself.

"Keith" she belted out, "I am Nurse Peterson, the RN in charge." I wondered what the "R" stood for. She certainly seemed rude and a bit rowdy for so early in the morning and my guess would be that if I were to open my eyes, she would be rotund. "Keith," she repeated, "you must wake up dear, you have a busy day ahead of you!"

"My name is Doctor Mack," I answered, "and I don't really want to get up right now if you don't mind."

"But I do mind," she said as she continued to explain my day to me. "You are in the detoxification unit at St. Luke's Hospital, and the reason you are here is because you want to get the alcohol out of your system and get over your drinking habit!"

I wonder where she got that preposterous idea? I asked myself.

"This unit does not come equipped with rank, so you will be known as 'Keith' during your stay with us" she continued.

This must not be Dickens's *A Christmas Carol* after all, I reasoned. I must have just flown to somewhere *Over the Cuckoo's Nest.*

My mind was clearing and I was slowly beginning to realize how and why I had gotten myself into this predicament. Little by little things were coming into focus. My mind started to race. This must be a ward full of psychos and I don't think this is really what I want to do, at least not right now. My body still refused to bend and I felt as if I were on the verge of a seizure.

How can I explain that this has been a horrible mistake and that I am really not the type of person for this category of treatment? Alcoholics are usually the people who live on the streets and beg for food and sleep in parks of the inner cities. Besides, who has ever heard of an alcoholic that has a good job and owns his own home? These really aren't my type of people. I know for sure that I don't want to be on a first name basis with any of these derelicts. The thought of sitting in the dining hall with them would make me sick!

What do you suppose the staff here was thinking when they put me on a ward like this? If anything, I was the one who should be giving the treatment. So I think I will just ask the nice RN to give me my clothes and I will get dressed and be on my way, thank you very much!

When I finally built up enough courage to open my eyes and present my case to nurse Ratchet, I looked into the face of the most compassionate and caring angel I have ever seen. She gave me a little smile and all she said was, "We are all here to help you! So now then, let's get started."

My first appointment was for personal evaluation. I was ushered into a small office where a rather large lady overwhelmed a very small desk. She seemed pleasant enough as she asked me to have a seat.

"And you are Keith," she started in.

"Yes, I am Dr. Mack," I corrected her.

"Well then, Keith" she continued. "Let's get started." This woman not only has an eating disorder, she doesn't hear well either, I thought to myself.

She was talking too fast for me to follow her line of conversation. Out of nowhere she made the comment, "I'm an alcoholic also so you can feel free to be straight with me."

What does she mean by the term "alcoholic also?" I wondered. I really don't like the idea that everyone is trying to get me into this alcoholic category! There may be a little excess involved, but there is no way I will ever be labeled as an alcoholic.

"Now Keith," she reiterated, "the purpose of this session is to determine the degree of your problem and to establish a mode of treatment that will fit your needs. I have a list of questions and all you have to do is answer yes or no. Try and be as honest as possible. If you should need any explanation just interrupt and we can go back as many times as we need to."

I really felt confident that I would emerge from this little quiz unscathed, even though she was attempting to present it much like an oral board examination in surgery.

"Now, for question number one. Have you ever had a blackout when you were drinking?" she asked. "A blackout is when you don't remember what happened after you have had a few drinks."

"Yes, I have," I answered.

"More than one?" she asked.

"Yes," I replied. "As a matter of fact I had a real humdinger the very first time I ever had a drink."

Her eyebrows flew to new heights as she asked the second question. "Do you ever drink before five in the afternoon?"

"Of course. And in the morning if I feel like it," I remarked, feeling a little stressed.

"Now for question number three," she smiled. "If you were to go to a party and the host asked if you would prefer apple juice to an alcoholic drink would you ask for apple juice?"

Now there's a no-brainer, I thought. I laughed out loud. She put a check mark next to "no." She gave me a look that would indicate that in her mind the next twenty five questions would be superfluous, but suggested we should continue as a matter of course.

When we finished, she looked me straight in the face and said, "Well you pass. You have met all the criteria that would classify you as an alcoholic and we have just the treatment that will help you if you are willing to work the program. Your stay with us will be about four to six weeks if you adjust well to the program."

She kept talking but I couldn't make any sense of anything she was saying. There was a ringing in my head and I was sure that I had misunderstood what she was trying to say. Well, whatever she meant by it, she was wrong.

She thinks I'm an alcoholic and I think she's fat and it would be my guess that neither of us is going to make any changes. The only redeeming factor is that in the morning when I wake up I will be sober whether I like it or not and she will still be fat. This whole thing is beginning to get too ridiculous, I thought to myself.

I knew now that anything I said out loud would do nothing but slap me with another diagnosis. Wouldn't it be great if all we had to do in medicine was ask a list of stupid questions and have a diagnosis and a treatment plan? I wonder who thought up that bunch of questions in the first place? I might be a lot of things, but being an alcoholic isn't one of them and nobody's going to ever convince me that I am! I almost laughed out loud at the thought.

My tour guide arrived at the door and I was informed that I

would be given a walking tour of the facility. This was accompanied with a complete list of pre-flight instructions.

"The exit signs are over the doors at both ends of the hall and the window in the middle of the hall. There will be no smoking in the lavatories or the hallway. Designated smoking areas have been provided. You will remain in your room at all times unless you are on your way to a scheduled appointment, the restroom or the day room. Meals will be served in the dining hall. You are required to eat all meals and that includes breakfast. There will be some turbulent times during your stay with us but if you will push the button immediately beside your bed an attendant will assist you."

I wondered why she skipped the part about using the mattress as a flotation device in the case of an emergency. Oh, yes, and the part about an oxygen mask dropping out of the ceiling when it got really rough. A grain of sarcasm was apparently beginning to germinate in my mind.

"Our next destination will be a two-hour steps meeting. We are a little early," my guide advised me. "So I will take some time and explain about the twelve steps of A.A. In reality the steps are the backbone of the entire program," she said, "and they can be worked at any rate you feel comfortable. The first step is the most difficult for most people."

I really didn't want to give in to their silly program, but my curiosity got the best of me and I asked, "Would you mind telling me what the first step is?"

"Sure," she said. "It says that we admit we are powerless over alcohol and that our lives have become unmanageable." In my mind I wondered why that would be so hard. If I were an alcoholic, I think I would want to admit that I had a problem and do something about it.

Already it was beginning to seem to me that everyone was trying to make a lot out of nothing. As far as I was concerned all I wanted from the program was a little rest, to get sober and to get on with my life. This program was not going to become a career to me and I was sure working the steps wouldn't be for me either!

The room was starting to fill. It looked as if all the street people were still out on the curb. Particularly impressive, was the chairperson of the meeting. He was dressed in a highly-starched expensive looking shirt and slacks, groomed to the hilt. His hair was cut short and he was clean shaven. Even his smile was impeccable. My first thought was, what is he doing here? Then I realized he was one of the instructors. I was surprised however, at the other folks who were present. Not at all the type of group I might have expected.

Everyone took their seats and the chairperson called the meeting to order. Then everybody began to repeat, "God, grant me the serenity to accept the things I cannot change, the courage to change the things I can, and the wisdom to know the difference."

The chairman began with, "Hi, my name is Allen and I'm an alcoholic." The entire group chimed in with "Hi, Allen."

That's amazing, I thought. How could someone that looks like that be an alcoholic? (I later learned that he was pilot doing around the world flights for a leading airline.) Allen went on to explain that this was a steps meeting and tonight we would be talking about the third step which says, "We made a decision to turn our will and our lives over to the care of God." He continued, "For those of you who may be new and may not have been here yesterday, the second step says, "Came to believe that a power greater than ourselves could restore us to sanity." This step confirmed my impression that we were dealing with a bunch of psychos, and strengthened my conviction that I was in the wrong place.

Allen went on to tell us that this was an open meeting and that anyone with a desire to learn about the steps was welcome. That explains why these people are here, I thought. They just want to learn about the program and aren't alcoholics at all. That came as a relief to me. It would be a real shame if these folks were part of the club and admitting they were powerless over alcohol and insane on top of that. This whole thing was taking on an air of being too weird. If these are the first three steps, I could just imagine what the next nine must be all about. It was like a fairy tale: you go to a meeting, work on a few simple steps, and then live happily ever after.

A plan to get out of there was beginning to form in my mind, but there didn't appear to be any way to escape. I would have to sit through this meeting, then check myself out of the hospital ASAP when I got back to my room. I was good with that idea and was sure I could make it through two hours of pure nonsense and then take my flight.

There were about fifteen people in the room and we were each going to have our own few minutes to tell about ourselves. Whoopee, I thought sarcastically. Now I too can be in the loony bin of this distinguished assembly. What a privilege!

To my surprise, as we started around the circle, each person introduced himself as, "I'm so and so and I'm an alcoholic." The guy next to me had a lot of spiritual things to say about the program and how the only way he personally was able to succeed was to "let go and let God." He went a step further and quoted a text from James 1:2,3 which says, "Dear brothers is your life full of difficulties and temptations? Then be happy, for when the way is rough, your patience has a chance to grow." In essence he was saying that God wants us to take heart when we have troubles and that we should be happy with all of our problems.

Neat quote, I mused. But I bet it isn't really in the Bible.

My heart started to pound as my turn got closer. I knew that I had the opportunity to skip my turn if I should choose, but I didn't want folks to leave the meeting with the idea that I could be an alcoholic. So for clarification, I would have to give a brief dissertation on why I was at the meeting. Everyone was looking at me. I could feel myself starting to sweat. My mouth felt dry and nothing was coming out. The heads were starting to nod as if to say, "Well?"

"Hi," I whispered. "My name is…"

"We can't hear you," someone said from the other side of the group. I got a burst of courage and belted out, "My name is Dr. Mack."

"This is Keith," Allen announced. "This is his first meeting."

I was beginning to feel more comfortable when I said, "My name is Keith and I hate to disappoint you all, but I am not an alcoholic and shouldn't be here in the first place." Then I went on to tell them what I thought about the whole program and its steps. The term 'drunks' came out several times during my short talk, which I ended tactfully with, "You all say you are a bunch of drunks and yet treat this place like a church, with all that God stuff! Give me a break!"

My speech was followed by a moment of silence. When the silence was broken, the entire world caved in on me. There wasn't a question in the world as to whether anybody present thought my remarks were in any way cute, amusing or even clever. My flippant attitude was examined with a fine tooth comb. To the majority, it would appear, this was considered serious business and making a joke of it in order to appease my own apprehension was not the method of choice for handling the situation.

The remainder of the meeting was devoted to explaining to me exactly how much I needed the program and that in the minds of most of those in attendance, there was no question that I was an alcoholic. We closed the meeting by standing in a circle holding hands and repeating the Lord's Prayer.

So much for church, I said to myself and retreated to my room for a little peace and quiet. All hope of rest went out the window when I opened the door to my room.

"Hi, my name is David and I am your counselor," was the greeting from the man standing by my bed.

"And I bet you are an alcoholic too," I responded, with a sarcastic inflection.

"Yes I am," he said. "And you will find that most of us that work in this unit are alcoholic by trade," he added with a little chuckle. "My job is to see that you are lined up with a program that fits your needs. Why don't we sit down and I can give you an outline of what we will be expecting of you. It is my guess that you don't know much about the inner workings of A.A."

"You're right about that," I replied, "but no one here seems to understand that I am not an alcoholic and don't belong here in the first place. So I guess you can understand when I say that I am not interested in your program. All I want to do right now is get out of here!"

David stood up and headed for the door. "That's it?" I said, "you're not going to try and hold me here against my will?"

David stopped and turned, "You know, Keith, we didn't invite you here. You are the one that called and asked for help. If you don't want help let's not waste my time or yours either. This treatment is only for those who are willing to turn their lives over to God and to honestly work the program."

"Well I do want to get sober," I argued. "I could do with a little drying out period even if I'm not an alcoholic."

"You don't get it do you Keith?" David continued. "This is a serious treatment program and I'm not sure your nonchalant attitude would cut it if you were to stay. If you should decide that you want what we have to offer, let me know. Otherwise, pack your bags and don't let the door hit you on your way out!"

I didn't bring a bag when I came in, I thought. But maybe that wasn't the point of the conversation.

Sitting alone in my room with nothing but my impulsive opinions, I wondered how I had managed to win so many friends and influence so many people in such a short time. Nobody wanted to do it my way and no one understood that my problem wasn't all that severe. There was a knock on the door and Nurse Peterson let herself in.

"How are things going?" she asked.

"Not well at all," was all I could answer. "Not well at all."

"Would you like to tell me about it?" she asked. "I am a pretty good listener."

This seemed like a good time to spill it all out, particularly to someone who wasn't an alcoholic. "You know that I have had a drinking problem and should dry out for a while until I can get my act together. But I'm not one of them," I concluded.

"By one of them you mean you are just an everyday drunk and not a full-blown alcoholic," she said.

"That's not exactly the way I would have put it, I guess, but maybe it is one way of looking at it," I said. "This place is so confusing. I'm not sure what I really think anymore. All I do know is that I'm not one of them!"

"You know Keith, some of us aren't all that bad when you get to know us." Nurse Peterson smiled. "Particularly when you are able to get past the first big step of admitting that you are powerless over alcohol and that your life has become unmanageable. From that point on you can let go and let God. Tonight's meeting will give you a lot of insight to help you get started. I will be at the meeting and will walk you through it."

All that came to my mind to say was, "You're one of them too?"

"Yes," she answered, "and I wouldn't be surprised if so are you!"

During the afternoon my physical condition began to deteriorate.

My entire body started vibrating to the extent that I felt like I was going to fly apart. My head started to throb, my stomach was churning and I was certain I was going to vomit. I tried to walk, but was hardly able to stand.

"What is happening to me?" I asked the aide.

"You are detoxing," he told me. "I'm here to make sure we don't have a convulsion."

"Do you think I am going to have D.T.'s?" I asked.

"Your reflexes are really brisk, so I am going to stay with you and make sure we don't have a seizure. We won't be going to our group this afternoon either," he added.

I liked the way he used the term "we" and "our" as if he had a concept as to what I was going through. He did sit at my bedside most of the afternoon . There was a time during the afternoon that I thought I would die and, as they say, there was a time I was afraid I wouldn't. Slowly but surely I felt better as the afternoon wore on. The shaking did subside somewhat. In my mind I knew this was an experience I never wanted to repeat.

Lying there in my bed I wondered again how I had gotten to this point in the first place. Had I done anything so wrong? Why had it progressed to this state so rapidly? Now I was sure that what I needed was to get out of the hospital, go home and get on with my life. This was not the place for me.

13

Back to Class

That evening, Nurse Peterson came to the door to escort me to my first A.A. meeting. The room was full when we arrived and I suggested the two empty seats in the back row as opposed to the two seats in the front row. She led me to the front row! The group consisted of patients as well as normal-appearing people who had come in from the outside.

I was surprised that the majority of those present did in fact look very normal and not at all like your everyday alcoholic. This confused me even more. Nothing in this place fell into the stereotype I had pictured for alcoholics or Alcoholics Anonymous. I wondered what this meeting was going to be about and how it was going to get me over my drinking habit, which by the way, I really had no intention of getting over in the first place. The next two and a half hours gave me many answers to my questions.

The guy that seemed to be in charge stood and welcomed the group to the meeting. "Hi, my name is Bob and I'm an alcoholic."

The group called out, "Hi Bob."

Then Bob added, "And a merry Christmas Eve to each of you."

That was my first thought about Christmas. The thought gave me a severe pain in the pit of my stomach. Why had so many Christmases been problematic? This was the one time in the year that everything should be all happiness and at that particular moment I was feeling anything but happy. I wondered in my mind if I was hurting my family by being away at Christmas. This was my first thought of family or home since I had been picked up at the Ranch.

The leader continued by asking us to repeat the Serenity Prayer. I listened to the words. The fact that "God" was the first word impressed me. Then there was the idea of being able to accept the things that could not be changed. I could go along with that because I knew there were a lot of things in life over which we have no control. The next sentence, however, gave me no little concern: "The courage to change the things I can." What in my life could be changed? I wondered.

The next sentence gave me to understand that I needed enough smarts to know the difference between accepting and changing. That's a pretty heavy little prayer, I concluded. What I really do need right now is serenity, or peace of mind as I would call it.

The chairman continued the meeting by stating that he was going to read from Chapter Five of the Big Book, "How it Works". The Big Book must be the Bible of the alcoholic, I assumed. They talk about God all of the time and yet they have their own Bible. I just don't get it!

The leader looked like a normal, well-groomed person. I wonder where I got the idea that all alcoholics were directly from the gutter?

Bob started reading, "Rarely have we seen a person fail who has thoroughly followed our path. Those who do not recover are people who cannot or will not completely give themselves to this simple program, usually men and women who are constitutionally incapable of being honest with themselves. There are such unfortunates. They are not at fault. They seem to have been born that way. They are naturally incapable of grasping and developing the manner of living, which demands rigorous honesty. Their chances are less than average."

This didn't seem very hopeful to me, but I would hear him out this once.

"Our stories disclose in a general way what we used to be like, what happened, and what we are like now. If you have decided you want what we have and are willing to go to any length to get it, then you are ready to take certain steps.

"At some of them we balked. We thought we could find an easier, softer way. But we could not. With all the earnestness at our command, we beg of you to be fearless and thorough from the very start. Some of us have tried to hold on to our old ideas and the result was nil until we let go absolutely.

"Remember that we deal with alcohol, cunning, baffling, powerful! Without help it is too much for us. But there is One who has all power, that One is God. May you find him now! Half measures availed us nothing. We stood at the turning point. We asked his protection and care with completed abandon."

This entire meeting was beginning to remind me of my early training. Most conspicuous was the fact that A.A. was preaching that a person had to be completely honest with himself and at the same time turn his life over to God, completely. Wow, I thought. That part of the meeting does make sense. But what about the steps? I didn't have to wonder for long.

The chairman continued, "Here are the steps we took, which are suggested as a program of recovery:

1. We admitted we were powerless over alcohol and that our lives had become unmanageable.
2. Came to believe that a Power greater than ourselves could restore us to sanity.
3. Made a decision to turn our will and our lives over to the care of God.
4. Made a searching and fearless moral inventory of ourselves.
5. Admitted to God, to ourselves, and to another human being the exact nature of our wrongs.
6. Were entirely ready to have God remove all these defects of character.
7. Humbly asked God to remove our shortcomings.
8. Made a list of the persons we had harmed and became willing to make amends to them all.
9. Made direct amends to such people wherever possible, except when to do so would injure them or others.
10. Continued to take personal inventory and when we were wrong promptly admitted it.
11. Sought through prayer and meditation to improve our conscious contact with God, praying only for knowledge of His will for us and the power to carry that out.

12. Having had a spiritual awakening as a result of these steps, we tried to carry this message to alcoholics and to practice these principles in all our affairs."

Then Bob read that there were three pertinent ideas:

A. That we were alcoholics and could not manage our own lives.
B. That probably no human could have relieved our alcoholism.
C. That God could and would if He were sought."

I didn't sleep much that night and for the first time in years I spent hours in prayer. The phrase "God could and would if He were sought" kept resonating in my mind. The possibility that there could be some good in this program was beginning to filter into my mind.

14

The Trip Back Home

Routine was broken for Christmas day. Families were allowed to come in for a two-hour visit. A Christmas tree was set up in the day room along with a table with a variety of goodies to eat. The room was decorated by the patients and staff and really gave the feeling of Christmas, all things considered. Sherrie and the kids arrived late in the afternoon. I wasn't sure I really wanted to see them just yet, but there was no way to defect.

Sherrie greeted me with a kiss, but seemed a bit cool. I concluded she had spent too much time in the kitchen at her mother's preparing Christmas dinner. I apparently had no feelings at that time for anyone's emotions but my own. Kevin and the girls didn't seem very excited about seeing me, and headed straight for the dessert table with a little more than a "Hi, Dad."

Steve seemed to be tuned into the situation and wanted to talk. He said, "Mother says that if you hadn't come to the hospital, we would have eventually had to live in this part of town." He went on to tell me he thought that would be neat because if we lived in a poor area of town we wouldn't have to lock anything up. Because if nobody had anything, nobody would steal anything.

"Good thinking, Steve." I chuckled. "I'm sure poor people are a lot more honest than the rich ones."

He also brought up the fact that he thought it was great that I was in for treatment. Then he made a statement that gave me some concern. "I think it would be good if you learn how to drink right."

"What do you mean by that?" I asked.

"I think people need to learn how to use drugs right," he repeated.

"Don't you think a person should just give up alcohol and drugs altogether?" I suggested.

"Na," he answered, "it's not the drugs that's to blame, it's the way we use them that's the problem."

His comment made me freeze. What did he mean by the statement "It's the way we use them?"

He is just a little boy, I thought, certainly he doesn't know anything about drugs. Sherrie came over and we had a chance to talk for a few minutes. She told me that I looked better than I had looked in a long time. I forgot to mention anything about what a jerk I had been or that I was sorry if I had hurt her in any way. I did remember to ask if she could bring me my razor and toothbrush. "Oh yes, clean socks and shorts too," I said, with all the compassion of a truly concerned husband.

After they left, I wanted to kick myself all the way around the hospital, but I knew the harm had been done and trying to make up for it at this time seemed futile. My heart ached and for the moment I believed that I really did need to be right where I was. There was a lot of confusion in my mind as to why I would even have an idea like that because I was still certain that there was no way that I could be an alcoholic.

Steve's attitude toward drugs and Sherrie's apparent lack of concern for my well being, coupled with severe shakes and horrible itching, made for a most unpleasant night. The nurse told me the itching was part of the detoxification process and was to be expected.

"I don't care if it's to be expected or not" I said. "I want to know how to treat it!"

"It will start going away in a week or two" she answered.

"I won't have any skin left by then," I complained.

"Possibly not," she said, laughing, "but at least you will be sober and that's a plus!"

"The nurses really are nice here," I remember thinking before I finally rocked myself to sleep with my shaking.

Morning comes early when you don't sleep well, and although I felt less hung over than the day before, I felt terrifically tired. Nurse

Peterson was off, so Nurse Nightingale appeared with the joy of the morning flowing from her lips. Her first recommendation was that I get myself out of bed and skedaddle down to the dining hall. When I realized that she was a much bigger person than myself I was out of bed and on my way to breakfast.

Part of the treatment was good nutrition and although breakfast is not my favorite meal of the day, I was able to get a few bits down, which pleased the staff beyond belief.

I dreaded the thought of going to the steps meeting after my previous fiasco. Somehow I had the feeling that I was not the most popular man on campus. Once again I knew that I was trapped with no way of escape. That was getting to be the story of my life lately.

Remembering that in the reading of the steps the word "humbly" was used on at least one occasion, I chose to use humility as my plan of attack.

Humble I was. Looking at the group made me feel like I had just arrived from a third world country stark naked. Nobody spoke or even gave me the time of day. It was rather obvious that I had overstated my point at yesterday's meeting. This morning nobody could have accused me of being frivolous or even friendly for that matter. I walked in and took my seat without a glance at anyone in the room. This was not the way I was accustomed to being treated, though there was some notion in my mind that I deserved everything I was getting. Not only did I feel humble but I was beginning to feel very inferior.

The Serenity Prayer reminded me that there are things in the world that can't be changed. Being in the steps meeting was one of the things that I wished I had the courage to change at that very moment. Several of the members told their stories, but most of it just seemed like words blowing in the wind. I couldn't seem to make myself care about anyone else's problems. My pity pot was getting about as full as I could handle. About the time I thought I was going to have to get out of there, I realized everyone was looking at me and it was my time to speak. I said a prayer and started.

"My name is Keith."

"Hi Keith," everyone vocalized.

I had come that far so thought there had to be something to say, but what I wasn't sure. I started in with the fact that I felt very ashamed for the way I had acted toward my wife on Christmas day. I told the group that I was probably doing her an awful disservice by being in a place like this when I wasn't even an alcoholic.

When my comfort level reached a new plateau, I went on to tell about Steve and his comment about drugs. I expressed my concern for him even though I knew he was much too young to be involved with drugs.

For some reason it felt good to be talking. I began telling the group about my drinking history. The more I talked, the more desperate I became. I was finally talking so rapidly I'm sure no one could understand me. The tears started to flow down my face and I didn't feel any embarrassment at all. I just went on talking and talking. I felt afraid to stop. I knew what I had to say but the words wouldn't come out. I prayed to God, "Lord, help me to have the courage to change the things that I can. Please Lord. Please, Please!" Then I realized that I was begging out loud to the entire group. "Please Lord," I whispered, almost under my breath, "please."

The group remained in silence while I sat for what seemed an eternity with my head bowed and tears rolling off my face. Then I looked up and said, in what felt like a resounding voice, "Hi, my name is Keith and I'm an alcoholic."

"Hi Keith, welcome home!" came the reply.

Step number one was behind me. Now I knew that I was powerless over alcohol and could ask God for His forgiveness. No human power could have done this for me. The promise that God could if He was sought was fulfilled for me that morning. The serenity was overwhelming.

Recovery didn't happen instantaneously. The road of rehabilitation was unending with moments of wonderful success interspersed with miserable failure. Strength was gained from the phrase found in the Big Book: "We are not saints. The point is, we are willing to grow along spiritual lines. The principles we have set down are guidelines to progress. We claim spiritual progress rather than spiritual perfection."

Walking out of the hospital in early February seemed like a dream. Saying goodbye to my new found friends and support group was a soul shaking experience. As the sliding doors closed behind me

I realized for the first time that now I was alone. This was the moment of truth that would require me to put into practice all the learning that had been pumped into me during the last month and a half. The feelings of fear and elation swept over me all at the same time. I was free. I couldn't look back. There was only one way to go and that way was up.

15

Reality Strike's Hard

The first few months after treatment were fantastic. I was welcomed back to work with enthusiasm by everybody. Sherrie was happy to have a husband again, and the kids seemed to enjoy having a father even though some of my attitudes may have been altered somewhat.

We bought a boat and made plans for some water skiing trips to the nearby lakes. Everyone seemed to be on line except Kevin. It seemed that his attention span was too short for the required learning. On the other hand, his ability to entertain and disrupt the entire class continued to be above average. It was recommended by the school board that he would benefit from attending a private school with a special education program rather than returning to the public school system.

Finding the right school was not an easy matter. We finalized on a small private school in Scottsdale that had a faculty that seemed to care. By the time summer came to an end all the plans for the following school year were in order. Life's biggest problems seemed to be behind us. I was sober, Kevin was enrolled in a school that gave promise of making him an academic success. The other kids all seemed to have a good outlook. We spent quality time together with boating, skiing, barbeques and just plain having a good time. God was back in His heaven and all was well with the world.

All did go well for the next year. Kevin graduated from the eighth grade, not necessarily magna cum laude, but he did in fact graduate! You have heard the phrase, "calm before the storm." That's exactly what it had been. The fall of 1979 saw the beginning of a new world for all of us.

Kevin was enrolled in a Christian Academy and the other three were transferred to the private school Kevin had attended the previous year. There was a noticeable change in the boys. Steve, who had always been fastidious about his grooming was taking on a new look. When I asked him about his appearance he told me he wanted look like a rock star, and the one he wanted to emulate in particular was Jimi Hendrix. I had already conceded to the idea that Steve was going to have long hair, but the complete lack of personal hygiene posed a real concern to me.

The day Steve came home with an earring just about did me in.

"Steve," I hollered, "what in the world were you thinking when you went and got your ear pierced?"

"You wanted me to be a Christian," he shouted back. "So I thought a little gold cross in my ear would let the world know that I am a Christian."

"That's a bunch of malarkey and you know it," I yelled. "You wanted to have your ear pierced and just put a cross in it to make me think you were doing something good. I'm not stupid! You just want to look like that rock group, and I don't like it."

The war was on and I made it plain that the earring was not going to be worn as long as he was living in my house, and that was that. The fact that the hair was dirty seemed less important now that the earring had arrived.

"Why are your eyes so red all of the time?" I asked him.

"Probably because I study so much," was his quick reply.

In closing I threw in a parting remark. "About that stuff you call music, keep it down!"

"Good night, Pops," came his sarcastic reply.

The little boy attitude in Steve was rapidly declining. His room was becoming cluttered with posters of all the top rock stars and their bands. Skulls were the artifact of choice, and a bong that I was assured was only for decoration was placed on his night stand. Despite what I considered a low-life environment, his teachers assured me he was the top student in his class, and his citizenship was phenomenal.

There wasn't much time to worry about Steve because of the

chaos Kevin was producing at the Academy. To get his grades much lower would have required extreme effort. His marks in citizenship were just slightly lower than his grades. Rumor had it that he was actually seen in class on several occasions. My only hope was the fact that he was at least passing in some of his subjects.

Looking forward to next year with both boys in the Academy, I had hope that the influence of Christian teachers would rub off on them. Presently at home there was evidence that their moral values had not reached a point of excellence. The situation had advanced to the place that everything in the house was under lock and key. Missing money was a common occurrence and nobody had the slightest idea who could have taken it. Talking with the boys was of little value. Kevin would always tell me exactly what I wanted to hear. Steve would lie to me with such conviction that I would believe him even though I knew he wasn't telling the truth.

Discovering that the boys were smoking shouldn't have come as any surprise to me, allowing that I was still smoking myself. For some reason I gave into the idea and allowed them to smoke at home but nowhere else. I also made it clear that I did not approve of their smoking and yet made no effort to give up the habit myself. I knew from experience that the double standard wouldn't work, but was encouraging it in my own children.

Shady looking characters began to haunt our home. Rapidly the music was becoming acid. The smell of "pot" permeated the house. Instead of groups of young people sitting and watching the game on TV, there were groups of hoods sitting and getting stoned and just staring at the walls.

One evening I walked into Steve's room to see him sitting in candlelight with the rock music blaring in the background. Smoke was pouring from the bong.

"Can you see the walls melting, Dad?" he asked. "Just look at how they are melting. Isn't it great? They are melting into the floor! Can't you see it, Dad? The walls are melting, isn't it great?" he kept repeating.

"Steve," I said. "This is a serious situation, and it's going to have to stop!"

"Yea, Dad, this has got to stop," he slurred. "The walls are melting into the floor and I gotta get some sslleeepp." He slouched over, knocking the lighted candle to the floor, and lapsed into a state of unconsciousness.

Until that point I had known we had a problem, but was truly not aware of the serious level it had reached. Sherrie and I sat up half the night discussing how to handle the situation. It was apparent both boys were not only smoking cigarettes, but probably using drugs. I couldn't believe this was happening to us. All of our friends' kids were playing sports and receiving honors for their academic achievements. Our kids were running with a subculture, doing drugs and watching the walls melt.

Why hadn't I noticed all of the danger signals before it was so late? Why hadn't I put a stop to all this a long time ago? Now it had gone so far it almost seemed as if there was no turning back. Talking to the boys didn't do anything. I was overwhelmed, heartsick and defeated. There was nowhere to turn.

We called several drug rehab centers during the next few days, only to receive the same answers. "He is too young, or unless he wants to come on his own accord there is nothing we can do for him."

The question I liked the very best was, "Are you sure your boy really has a problem?" The fact that he is stoned three-fourths of the time might be a clue, I thought.

There just didn't seem to be help anywhere, yet all I ever saw on TV were stories about kids and drug problems. There has to be help somewhere, I reasoned. The big question is where?

I went to the hospital where I received my treatment only to be told once again that there was nothing they could do for someone Steve's age. There was no program at the Academy that would even come close to our needs. There just was no way out.

My attempts at being more strict and laying down serious ground rules backfired and drove the entire subculture underground. The family would go to bed at a reasonable hour only to be awakened in the middle of the night by a room full of hoodlums doing drugs.

None of his cronies admitted to having family, yet I knew they had to have folks who were just as concerned as we were. I even attempted to follow some of the kids home without any success. Steve became very defensive of his buddies, not wanting me to have any idea who they were or where they came from. I tried to ban them from coming into our home only to find they were sneaking in as soon as my back was turned.

A chance for action came one evening when a big party was going on in the back of the house. I knew all the kids were getting stoned. We debated about what to do, then called the police. We asked them to come to the door as if they had been informed by another source.

The police were more than willing to cooperate and arrived in about an hour. They were directed to the back of the house where five boys were sitting with Steve in his room. All were stoned to the hilt. The officers talked to the boys individually for about an hour.

"At last we have help," I told Sherrie. "Now something will be done!"

When the officers came out of the back room, they had one of the younger boys with them. We were informed that he had marijuana on his person, and that they would take him to his parents.

"What about the others?" I asked.

"None of them had any drugs in their possession, and they all denied using anything this evening," the officer answered.

"You can see they are all stoned, can't you?" I said, my voice cracking.

"They're all stoned all right," one of the officers confirmed. "But you can't hold a person until you catch them in the act."

"How much more 'in the act' can you get?" I could feel myself getting angry. "They are all stoned. The room is filled with pot smoke. And you are telling me that there is nothing you can do unless you catch them in the act?"

"Yes sir," the officer replied. "This young man is the only one we can do anything about, and then only if his parents will give their consent." The officer went on to tell us how he could understand our concern and that he was sorry there was no more he could do at the present time.

"What can we do?" I begged.

"There really isn't much a parent can do until the child is willing to seek help," he explained. "Probably the best thing that could happen is if your son should get into some minor trouble with the law. Then there would be legal recourse for detaining him."

All of this was beginning to seem mythical to me. Here we had a group of boys who were obviously stoned and using drugs and the officer was telling me there was nothing that could be done.

"Where can I go for help?" I asked.

"Your church would probably be a good place to start," he answered.

"My church doesn't even know that the problem of drugs exists," I stammered. "It's not something that even happens in our church. Everyone is too concerned about whether the kids are eating meat or going to shows to worry about drugs. The subject just isn't even discussed."

I could feel myself blaming the church for all the problems we were having. The law wasn't willing to help. The church had its head in the sand and I was paddling upstream on the river of severe frustration with a broken paddle. My boat was filled with a bunch of stoned kids and was sinking.

I was angry at the world. Where is God when I need Him? I asked myself. I don't think I ever took into account the fact that I really hadn't spent much time in prayer asking for God's help.

"I really wish that we could help you more," the officer added very sincerely, "but this is out of our jurisdiction."

As the officers left, Steve burst out of his room and started accusing us of everything from manslaughter to child abuse.

"You had better show your mother and me some respect," I shouted. "You could just find yourself out on the street, young man!"

"Yea, you think you could throw me out of the house? I'm only fourteen years old, and there ain't no way you're gonna throw me out. There are laws about such things you know."

I wanted to take him in my arms and tell him how much I really loved him and that the way he was going would only lead to destruction. But he was too angry, and much too stoned for reason. There was another side of me that said, *pulverize* him. I sent him to bed and tried unsuccessfully to get some sleep myself.

That night I did pray that God would grant Steve the same privilege that He had given to me with the twelve-step program. I claimed the promise of Matt. 22:21 that says that whatsoever we ask in prayer believing, will be given to us. Steve is a good boy and I know it, I thought to myself. I just know God will take us through this thing. I determined that night that Steve would be the center of my prayer life, and that "God would if He were sought."

Steve graduated from the eighth grade that year with honors and was accepted into the Academy for the Fall semester. Not to worry, he's just a kid, doing kid things. I thought. Getting him into a Christian school should be the answer. In my mind, a Christian environment would remove the threat of rock-and-roll and the drug scene. ("Too soon we get old, too late smart.")

16

The Brief Reprieve

The summer was planned with precision. The girls would go to the beach with Sherrie. Kevin would attend summer school to replace failed classes and Steve would go to camp. When the boys' sessions were finished we would all join the girls in California and finish the summer vacationing in Yosemite and the "big trees" area of Northern California. The main objective was to keep everyone busy in a supervised and drug free environment.

We chose Orme School for the boys because it had both an outstanding academic program and summer camp activities. The first snag came when Kevin failed to meet the academic standards for admission. Steve was admitted without a hitch. Steve was anxious to go to Orme for the high school prep and camp activities, so he was enrolled.

With Kevin's slightly less than minimal grade point average a ranch school near Orme was able to provide the necessary missing classes. It was settled. Everything was in place and ready to be set into action.

As soon as school was out Sherrie and the girls left for California. Kevin was next, when I dropped him off at the bus station for his trip to the ranch school. Steve was home for an additional week and had to be driven to camp.

Sunday morning Carol joined us for the drive to northern Arizona. Steve seemed excited as we arrived at the school. We helped him unload his gear and were about to say the final goodbyes, when he stopped short and went for his backpack.

"Here give this to Uncle Carol," he said, handing me a small bag. "Ask him to keep it for me until I get back."

"What's in it?" I asked.

"Just a bag of grass," he answered, "and I wouldn't want them to find it in my things."

"Why didn't you give it to me?" I asked.

"I thought you would get mad if you knew I had it," he said.

"You are right about that," I said. "Surely you knew I would find out about it sooner or later anyhow, didn't you?"

"Sure, I knew you would, but not until you were out of here," he replied.

In my mind I was ecstatic with the concept that he wasn't riding back with us that afternoon. How could anybody that is apparently so smart be so dense? I wondered.

At home alone there was a peaceful bliss I had forgotten even existed. The quiet was almost deafening. The fear that the next phone call would be from the principal or the police department was gone. I felt that I surely must have died and gone to heaven.

It's hard to imagine the peace of mind that comes from knowing that everyone is in a safe place and well cared for. This was to be *my* home for the next few weeks. I could sit up half the night and read if I wanted or eat my meals directly from the can. I could run through the house naked and drink milk out of the carton with the refrigerator door open.

All of this would be considered acceptable behavior for a father at home alone. Dishes wouldn't need to be washed. Dirty clothes were predestined to go to the cleaners. I was genuinely looking forward to this hiatus from responsibility that had just been placed before me. I didn't need a drink, I was drunk with freedom! What a fortuitous month of rest laid ahead.

A phone call from Sherrie the next day assured me that everything was going well with the female half of the household. The nagging cold she had had before she left home had worsened slightly, but she was convinced it would get better quickly during her stay with my folks in Palm Springs. She intended to spend a few hours a day in the hot desert sun, which she knew would kill any bug that even attempted to invade her body.

The bug proved to be more stubborn than had been expected and by the end of the week bed rest became a last resort. My parents were able to take care of the girls so there was plenty of time for rest. In just a day or two Sherrie was feeling much better. On Sunday morning she felt well enough to continue her drive to the beach. My father was not convinced that she was as well as she thought and asked her to at least be checked by a doctor at the hospital emergency room before leaving. She agreed and had an X-ray of her chest which was read as clear. Against all of my parents' badgering to have her stay for a few more days, she packed the motor home and headed down the freeway in order to arrive on time for her reservations at the beach RV park.

According to the girls the trip was without rival. As far as Sherrie was concerned there is very little about the event that she remembers at all. In recounting the event, the girls said that she appeared to be confused and unable to read the map. On one occasion she ran off the freeway and removed a portion of the oleanders growing in the median.

Teri told us, "All of a sudden there was a big noise and flowers were flying all over the windshield. It looked like we were driving in the middle of the forest. Then Mother jerked the steering wheel and we went across to the other side of the road. It was real scary, *real scary!*"

Cindi tells it another way. "I was old enough to know how to read the map, but nobody would pay any attention to me, so we got lost. Mother didn't feel well and was trying to drive and read the map at the same time, but nobody would listen to me! Anyway it didn't seem all that bad. But it was a little scary."

Myself I believe God appointed one of His angels to take over the controls of the motor home that afternoon and take my family safely into the port.

Although access to a pay phone was difficult, Sherrie was able to make contact with home several times during the week. Each call confirmed that she was feeling better. Her chest was apparently clearing and breathing was requiring less effort. All in all she seemed to be getting well.

Early on the morning of the fifth day the phone rang and a little voice on the other end whispered, "Hi honey, it's me and I don't feel so good." There was a long pause, then she continued, "I'm having a real hard time breathing and I feel weak, and I'm scared. I don't know what to do!" She was crying and I knew things were probably worse than they sounded.

"Have you talked with a doctor?" I asked.

"No it's all I can do to talk to you. And besides, I don't know who to call," she gasped.

"Get to the emergency room at the hospital as quickly as you can," I told her. "Leave the girls in the motor home until you get back. They'll be all right. I'll call the managers of the park and let them know that you have gone to the hospital and ask if they would check in on the girls from time to time. Call a cab from where you are and tell the girls where you are going. Tell them to call me collect if they need anything. Now you get going right now," I ordered. Then I added, "I love you."

"I love you too," came the weak, almost inaudible reply.

The forty dollars designated to sustain the girls during Sherrie's absence seemed phenomenal for such young girls. The warning from their mother that accompanied the money was even more impressive. "Not one penny is to be spent for anything other than food and I mean good food. Keep all of your receipts for me. This is all that I have to leave you so make it last." With that she threw them both a weak kiss and the taxis sped down the street.

The girls were all alone for the first time in their lives. There were two meals they knew how to prepare and could afford: macaroni-and-cheese and potatoes. They passed the test with funds to spare. As far as I know, to this day that was the only time that either of them has been able to adhere to a budget of any type.

The hours that lapsed seemed like days, then a call finally came from the hospital. The lady on the phone informed me she was my wife's physician, and that Sherrie had been admitted to the intensive care unit of the hospital.

"Your wife is very ill," she began. "She has a very severe respiratory disease that resembles Legionnaires Disease. You may have read about the epidemic that hit the Legionnaires in Pennsylvania a few years ago. They all became extremely ill, and many of them died."

I stood staring into the phone with disbelief. This woman has a real way with words, I thought. Yesterday everything seemed so much better, and now I am being told that my wife may be going to die. The voice on the phone was still talking when my mind tuned back into the conversation.

"You really need to get here as soon as you can. I will keep in contact with you and let you know if there is any change in your wife's condition," she rattled off in a very matter-of-fact manner. "Just feel free to give me a call at any time if there is anything I can do for you." There was an abrupt click on the other end of the line and she hung up.

There was no place to start. The boy's respective schools had to be contacted and bus tickets purchased for their return to the city. We would need airline tickets for the three of us to fly to California once the boys were back in town. Then of course, there were the girls who were only twelve and thirteen years old, all alone in a motor home in Los Angeles at the beach. Sherrie was in intensive care with a disease I knew nothing about other than the fact that a lot of guys had died from it in Pennsylvania a few years back. As fate would have it this was my long weekend on call at the hospital to boot. I was no longer drunk with the feeling of freedom, and my anxiety level had just hit a six on the Richter scale.

A sincere prayer went up to heaven as I asked the Lord to not only give me strength, but to protect my entire family in each of our separate situations. God answered my prayer!

It took several days of juggling and planning until the boys finally arrived at the bus station just two hours before our flight was scheduled to depart for California. I noticed immediately that neither of them had been exposed to a shower or a laundry during their time away from home and wondered if I should redirect our airline tickets toward steerage class. However there was more significant business to be considered at that moment so I promptly dismissed the idea.

Kevin immediately asked about his mother's condition and wanted to know how bad it was. Steve's main concern was that he had had to leave camp early. I heard him say to Kevin, "She probably isn't going to die anyway so what difference would a couple more days have made?"

My mind was already in overload so I didn't even dignify his comment with a reply. On the flight while Kevin slept, I was surprised to find that Steve *was* concerned about his mother's well-being. He asked repeatedly if she could really die, and if she did, what would happen to us? It warmed my heart to realize what a macho man he wanted to be in front of his brother, but what a little boy with major concerns he was to me.

In her hospital bed Sherrie was the same beautiful lady she had always been. To look at her there you would think she was the picture of health. It was interesting to watch a new nurse walk into the ICU room then quickly retreat only to return in a moment or two.

"I thought I was in the wrong room," one of the nurses exclaimed. "You look so pretty and healthy I just knew I had to be in the wrong room."

As flattering as it may have seemed, it wasn't at all pleasing to Sherrie. She had the feeling that everyone thought she was just putting on. Her doctors assured me that her illness was very real although she was showing signs of improvement. They explained to me that she had likely experienced some brain damage as a result of low oxygen concentrations in her blood over a period of days. I was told that the changes in her personality would be subtle and probably only notice-able to those of us who knew her best. Otherwise I could expect a complete and rapid recovery.

Progress was slow, but each day showed a degree of improve-ment. Finally the day of her release came and we left the hospital for a few days stay at the nearby home of a friend. The kids were bored out of their minds following the long hospital ordeal and were difficult to contain. Happiness happened when I went to the door one afternoon to see Carol standing there. Greater happiness happened when I looked out and saw his van with the boat behind it.

"I thought you and the kids might need a little fun in your lives," he said, smiling. "So here is a little surprise."

It was more than a little fun. While Sherrie recuperated at our friend's home the rest of us spent hours out on the ocean jumping the swells and racing the tide. The hot sun and the cool ocean spray injected a new spirit of well being into each one of us. We laughed and sang and just plain hooted and hollered. What a feeling of exhilaration swept over us!

Sherrie was getting stronger by the day and we knew the worst was behind us. It was time to get on with life.

To my knowledge there had been no using of drugs by the boys during our time at the beach. Most of the summer was over and I felt that many of the problems of the last year wouldn't surface again. I was getting anxious to get home and start putting things back in order. Getting everyone back into school struck me as a secure shelter after the storm.

One afternoon toward the end of our stay, Steve stood up on the bow of the boat and shouted at the top of his lungs, "Sex, drugs, and rock-and-roll!" to a group of young ladies in a passing boat.

"What are you shouting?" I yelled to him.

"Sex, drugs and rock-and-roll," he yelled back. "That's what it's all about, you know Dad, sex and drugs. What else is there to do when you are young?"

"Steve," I called back to him, "you may think that's funny, but I think it's serious and not something to be joking about!"

"Who's joking," he asked. "I'm serious about it. There really isn't much to this world anymore than some good drugs, sex and rock-and-roll." The girls on the other boat gave a wave of approval as if to agree with what he was saying.

"See, Pops, you just don't dig today's world. It's not like it was in the old days when you were a kid. This is the real world."

I gave him a tongue-lashing while he sat on the bow of the boat with a defiant grin on his face. Then he said in a low whisper, "Yea man, it's sex, drugs and rock-and-roll!"

"Steve," I asked, "have you been using drugs while we have been down here at the beach?"

He had a smirk on his face when he replied, "Oh, Pops, get real!"

Steve and I sat up late that evening in an attempt to establish the importance of building strong moral values while you are young. The evening concluded with the observation that because of my advanced age I most likely had no concept of what goes on in the "real world."

"Steve," I explained, "you may not realize it, but I have experienced some of life myself. You could benefit from some of my mistakes if you would only listen."

"Yea, Pops, I know you think you know something about life, and I am sure you probably do. But you don't understand about the world today. Kids and the world just aren't the same as they were in the old days when you were young. You didn't have the good things like rock-and-roll or drugs, and you didn't even talk about sex. What a dull world! In those times a 'party' meant cake and ice cream. What a bore! You thought popping popcorn was the social event of the year. Kids of your day were kept in the dark and had no way to *feel* life. You didn't even have TV to show you how things really were." When he finally finished I thought I had heard it all.

"You're right," I told him. "Somehow I wish you could feel the joy of being a kid like I felt when I was your age. It was great!"

"Well maybe I can tell that to my kid someday," he answered, "but I still don't think you have a clue about today's world. You can argue all night and you won't change my mind one bit!" With that the conversation ended and once again I felt I had lost.

17

Mr. Mom

Surrounded by pillows in the motor home bed, Sherrie appeared to be comfortable but weak. It was good to be on our way home. The doctors had given her a clean bill of health as well as a release for home. The only requirement at this point was for her to get plenty of bed rest.

Everything seemed to be going well until mid-afternoon when we stopped for a short rest. I fixed Sherrie a bowl of soup which she ate without any hesitation. She told me she was feeling pretty well and didn't want anything else to eat.

While I was taking the dog for a short walk, Teri came running to me in tears.

"Why are you being so mean to Mother?" she cried.

"What are you talking about?" I asked.

"Mother is in the motor home crying because she is hungry. She said she asked you to get her something to eat and you said she couldn't have any food." Teri continued to sob. "Why don't you want her to eat?"

I took Teri in my arms and told her, "Sweetheart, I just gave your mother a bowl of soup and she ate the whole thing and said she didn't want anything more to eat." We talked about her mother's illness briefly and then went back into the coach.

Sherrie was still crying and insisted that she couldn't get out of bed and that no one would get her anything to eat.

"Don't you remember me giving you a bowl of soup just a few minutes ago?" I asked.

Her reply flew back, "I haven't had anything to eat since I left the hospital and if you think you are going to starve me to death you have another thing coming." We all just stood paralyzed, unable to believe what we were hearing. "Why are you doing this to me?" she pleaded. "I'm so hungry why can't I have just a little something to eat, please?"

I held her for a few minutes and explained to her that she was very sick and possibly didn't remember things as well as she normally would but it wouldn't be too long before she would be well again. With that she stopped crying and in a few minutes was asleep.

Back home again we were greeted by Sherrie's parents. It only took a glance from Sherrie's mother to realize that we had a very sick patient and that she would need a mother's full-time care. We agreed that Sherrie should go directly to her parents' house for at least the next few days.

The kids helped unpack the motor home with the idea of "batching it" for awhile. In my wildest fantasy I would never have dreamed that the few days would grow into three and a half months.

The next few days were complete havoc. I started back at the hospital the second day home. The house was in shambles. There was no food in the refrigerator. I was still up at one in the morning doing everyone's laundry. I quickly began to understand the plight of the single parent. There were not enough hours in the day to get even the everyday necessities done, let alone take care of any of the frills. Getting food into the house became a monumental achievement. Then getting it into a form compatible with eating was an even greater art.

Referring back to my college course, Organizational Skills 101, a plan had to be put in order. It would have to be short, sweet, and effective all at the same time. I came up with five simple, yet understandable steps.

Step number one would allow each child one day a week to do his or her own laundry. Instructions as to the use of the washer and dryer would be given on a individual need-to-know basis. Failure to comprehend could result in damage to clothing as well as to the person performing the procedure.

Step number two would require each child to detail his own

personal living area and to stand inspection daily.

Step number three would require Teri to go to the grocery store with me to pick out the ingredients for one major dish. We would then go home and prepare a meal that would hopefully last for several days. (Tuna casserole and meat loaf became hot items.) Cleaning up after dinner would be the responsibility of the others on a rotating basis.

Step number four stated that there would be only family members in the house at any time that I was not at home.

Last but not necessarily least, there would be no smoking, drinking or drugs in the house at any time.

The program was presented, posted on the bulletin board and voted upon by the entire group. All five steps were agreed upon unanimously with the exception of Steve's dissenting vote when it came to general housekeeping, which he contended was a woman's job. He was overruled and the program was implemented post haste.

As necessity became our new mother of invention, we reinvented the wheel. When the wheels began to turn, the family machine functioned smoothly. There were however, always a few minor squeaks. The major voice was that of Steve, who continued to fight the idea that he should be required to do a woman's work. He excelled in laundry and cooking, but as for housekeeping, "No way man!"

Teri was a wonder in the kitchen and a flop in the laundry. She could see no logical reason for sorting clothes according to color. So as not to make waves she did continue to wear her army green, previously pink jumpsuit, with pride.

Kevin was ingenious. He was able to have one of the others do his laundry on a regular basis with only a minimal bribe. The dupe was usually Cindi. He did an excellent job of avoiding any cleaning whatsoever and was never guilty of being in the kitchen before or after dinner. In all fairness, he did always offer to help just before he vanished into thin air.

Cindi was always there to help in spite of the fact the boys kept her in tears most of the time with their constant harassment.

We hit a major hurdle when it came time to outfit all the kids with new clothes for school. A light went on in my head that said, why not let them do it themselves? And that is exactly what I did.

We all went to the bank together and drew out what I considered would be enough for a starter kit of clothing. Everyone receive the some amount. We then went to the shopping mall for a four hour shopping excursion. There was an extensive briefing before the shopping began.

Nothing but clothes suitable for the Academy were to be bought. Everything had to be tried on for size, there would be no returns. Look for the sales. No food except for one drink and a sandwich at lunch time. A receipt was to accompany every article of clothing. The girls would do their thing and the boys would do theirs. Then I threw in a closing incentive.

"The one who gets the best value for his or her money will get a ten dollar bonus from Dad." Then they were off and running.

When I returned four hours later, there were four exhausted little shoppers waiting for me at the curb. Their arms were loaded with packages. Nobody had the slightest interest in eating. All they wanted to do was to get home and try on clothes and see who was eligible for the bonus prize.

I was amazed at the time and thought that had gone into their choices. They had some values that boggled my mind. A dad in need was proud indeed. I thanked them all for being such great troopers in this time of stress and made the choice that all of them had gotten the best value and therefore they would each receive a ten dollar bill. Who says you can't buy a kid's love?

Sherrie's progress was slow, even with her mother's excellent nursing care. Our visits were obviously tiring to her and for that reason kept short and infrequent. I knew the kids missed their mother, but the subject was seldom discussed. The routine was set and working as well as could be expected and when the weeks stretched into months, we managed. It was nearly Thanksgiving when Sherrie finally felt strong enough to return home.

Homecoming was a very special day. Each of the kids arrived home at a different time which allowed them time alone with their mother. It was a happy afternoon. Sherrie seemed well and more than ready to take over her position as mother of the brood. Myself I jumped at the opportunity to relinquish the position of Mr. Mom and become just plain old Dad. It had been a long three and a half months. It was over and we had actually reached our goal each day: survival!

It quickly became evident that the position of mother had been reestablished. It wasn't necessarily an easy transition. Teri began to act out and was showing signs of depression. Most of the time she just moped around the house. When I asked her what was wrong she would shrug her shoulders and say, "nothing." This went on for several days until one day I mentioned it to Carol. He started in on me in a way that about knocked me off my feet.

"Can't you see what you are doing to that poor girl?" he began. "For the past three and a half months she has been your right hand man and now without batting an eye you have pushed her aside without so much as a thank you. Poor little thing. I can't blame her if she acts hurt and depressed. Why don't you go and have a talk with her and let her know how you feel and that you really still need her."

Carol continued, "The two of you went shopping together for groceries several times a week, came home and worked together in the kitchen preparing the food. The key word here is 'together.' She had her dad all to herself. Now she no longer has you and her mother doesn't need her help either. Would you like it if your father did that to you?"

I did all that?" I asked. "I guess I thought she would be relieved to be out of the kitchen and have some time to do her own things again."

Teri and I had a nice long talk that evening. The wound wasn't entirely healed in one short session, but recovery was in sight.

Whether or not having their mother at home again caused the boys conduct to plummet is not certain. What is for sure is their behavior did deteriorate rapidly. Old friends started frequenting the house again as did the smell of pot. There were late night parties and the volume of the music skyrocketed. It was the holiday season and I could see the situation slithering out of hand. Something had to be done and quickly. This Christmas was not going to be ruined by anything or anybody if I had any say about it! Everyone was going to have a good time whether they liked it or not!

Christmas was planned totally with the boys in mind. We rented a cabin in the White Mountains near a ski resort. My idea was to get the family together away from the influence of undesirable friends. In my mind a geographical change would change old habits. It did help and with only a few lesser incidents we had a wonderful week of skiing and a great Christmas.

Quality time on the slopes in the clean drug-free situation proved to be flawless. Steve had become an accomplished and very controlled skier. He made each turn to perfection and with deliberation. He worked so hard on perfecting his style that it was almost painful, but beautiful, to watch. He seemed happier on that trip than I had seen him in a long time. He actually enjoyed time with his mother and seemed to put the fact that she was a woman out of his mind. It was great to see them having a good time together again.

Kevin and Teri ran the hill with speed and little thought about form. Cindi was beginning to show signs of becoming an excellent skier, which she has maintained all of her life. When chemicals were not involved we had an almost perfect, fun and loving family. This was one of those Christmases.

18

Final Diagnosis

Shortly after the first of the year Sherrie began to show signs of severe fatigue. I attributed most of it to the stress produced by the actions of the boys and the prolonged recovery of her previous illness. As the boys' situation worsened, so did Sherrie's. She was spending long hours in bed once again and started complaining of severe headaches that felt like hot oil flowing through the vessels on one side of her head.

One morning she awakened with her left eye completely dilated and non reactive to light. The left side of her head was throbbing, and she felt sick to her stomach. This gave cause for considerable alarm and I immediately called the Neurological Center for an emergency visit.

The boys were completely uncooperative. I finally told them that I couldn't deal with them that morning so they would have to wing it on their own. They thought that was great and promptly went back to bed.

During the next few weeks Sherrie underwent a large battery of tests at the Neurological Center as well as at the University of Arizona Medical Center. The symptoms were perplexing to the doctors, and a catch-all diagnosis of "migraine syndrome" was slapped on her. We returned home to watch her sleep.

It was suggested that there could be undue stress in Sherrie's life and that if that could be done away with her condition would improve. We gained all of this information for only ten thousand dollars and a month of testing. I was frustrated with the diagnosis and insisted she be reexamined in order to come up with a more definitive diagnosis. For only $10,000 more and two more months of testing we received the diagnosis of "migraine syndrome associated with chronic fatigue syndrome." I decided while there was any money left I would learn to live with the diagnosis and lay off the testing for a while.

Sherrie's condition didn't improve and much of her time was spent in bed. I spent long hours in the operating room and the kids were left to provide for themselves much of the time. The home situation just wasn't improving and I was confused as to what to do about it. There were too many hours of work, but I couldn't slow down and still pay the medical and private school bills. (We definitely had too many kids, however the thought of getting rid of some of them was only a fleeting fancy.)

With Sherrie getting sicker by the day and no one knowing the reason my feeling of hopelessness soared. In my mind I knew that God was still watching over us and He wouldn't allow more to come down on us than we could bear. In all honesty I was beginning to feel that He was pushing it a smidgen too far.

One afternoon near the end of the school year I received a phone call at work. The familiar voice on the other end of the line launched the conversation with, "Hi, this is Mr. Russell, principal at the Academy." This was not an unusual call at first, but as he continued the discussion began to deteriorate.

"I'm at your house right now," he continued. "Your wife appears to be very sick and is having a difficult time communicating. The girls aren't at home and Kevin is with me and he is very drunk."

"He is what?" I shouted.

"Drunk," he repeated.

"You mean like with alcohol?" I asked, not being able to put things together in my mind.

"Yes," he said again. "He is drunk as in booze, and completely out of control. He seems to think the entire incident is hysterical. He keeps falling down and I wouldn't be surprised if he gets sick in a few minutes. I don't think Mrs. Mack is in any condition to take care of the situation and I have to get back to the school as soon as I can. What should I do?"

I called Carol and with only a brief explanation he said, "I'm on my way."

"What a friend," I told him. "Thank you!"

Kevin was *not* invited to finish the school year. Staying home all day was out of the question so he would have to find work. Carol came to the rescue for the second time. He suggested having Kevin come to the Ranch each morning and work at all the necessary jobs that needed to be done around the place. He assured me he could keep him busy. All I would have to do was drop him off at the Ranch on my way to the hospital and pick him up in the evening. It sounded like a plan.

When Kevin sobered up he was surprised to find that he was no longer enrolled at the Academy but didn't show much concern. The idea of working struck him as a tad foreign, but amusing.

Kevin started work the following morning. Carol had a list of things that needed to be done while he was away doing his own business. Kevin set about his work with great enthusiasm as was evidenced by all the stain that was on the floor and walls of the area under the ceiling that needed to be painted.

Carol returned home to find Kevin sitting under a tree eating a sandwich, oblivious of the fact that there was still work to be done. Work was a difficult concept for Kevin. It didn't take long at all to realize that having an occupation just wasn't for him. He did continue to put his time in at the Ranch for the remainder of the school year, but not without hazard. His creative ability to produce mass destruction was exceeded only by his innate lack of concern for what he had done. My screaming availed nothing.

My frustration at not being able to control the friends who came into the house and the availability of drugs and alcohol was overwhelming. There had to be help somewhere but once again the same old question came up, where? I read every piece of literature I could find. It seemed the problem was always the same. Unless they do something illegal or are willing to seek help for themselves, nothing can be done.

Friends would tell me not to allow the kids to do drugs. I fully agreed but once again the big question, how? Nobody seemed to understand that telling a sixteen-year-old "no" isn't always the solution. We didn't give them any money, so they stole what they needed.

We insisted they work and hold down a job. They would leave for work in the morning and return in the evening, usually stoned. I took away privileges, no one seemed to care. They were grounded at home for a while and not allowed to have their friends over. They solved that problem by climbing out the window or sneaking their friends in after we were asleep.

God was my only refuge. I prayed and I prayed. I began to feel like the prophets of Baal when Elijah told them to call louder, possibly their god was asleep. Yet I knew God wasn't asleep and that He was hearing my prayers. Panic was beginning to set in. I was desperate. I began to grasp the concept I was going to lose my boys if something didn't give. How I was losing them I wasn't sure. All I knew was it was happening. I was scared.

"Lord," I begged, "help me with my boys. Give me the knowledge and the understanding to be able to help them. And above all, Lord, give me the faith to trust you completely." I prayed this prayer over and over again yet the situation only seemed to worsen.

God did answer my prayer. One afternoon Steve arrived home with a pamphlet about a Christian youth group that was going to all parts of the world helping in the building of church schools. It was a nondenominational group and would be sending early teens. Steve was ecstatic about the idea and asked if I would be willing to help him raise the money to go.

Thank you Lord, I said in my mind. Thank You.

The deadline for applications was only a few days away so we would have to make tracks. We phoned directly to the headquarters in Florida. There were only a few locations left, but there were in fact still some openings. Steve did the paperwork over the phone while I listened. He had all the qualifications required and the excellent grades that were a must.

Confirmation of his acceptance arrived in just a few days. He was given an assignment in Korea. The flight would originate in New York, flying east to Korea and returning west to arrive in Los Angeles, completing an around-the-world trip. He was to leave in the middle of July and return the first of September.

Due to the short notice there wouldn't be time for Steve to raise the money so we would have to pay the fee. The money would certainly be worth the experience. Actually I would have paid double for the peace of mind I was expecting.

The paperwork was completed and the money sent. All that was left was to get his bags packed and the necessary requirements for overseas travel completed. In less than six weeks he would be on his way.

I spent a lot of time in prayer and meditation, thanking God for His unbelievable answer to my prayers. Getting Steve away from his drug using friends could be his only salvation and God had just handed it to us on a tiny slip of paper.

The next few weeks were busy. A new passport was necessary. Booster shots were needed for the Far East. Airline tickets would be purchased for the entire group and given to Steve in Florida. We would have to arrange for his transportation to Florida and from L.A. to Phoenix. It was going to be a whirlwind for awhile but so worth it. There is no way to picture how happy I was about the entire adventure. God had not only answered our prayers but He had answered them in a manner that far exceeded my expectations.

Most of the preparations were finished two weeks before Steve's departure. He seemed excited when he came to me with the declaration.

"Now, Dad, don't get agitated but I'm not going to go to Korea."

"You're what?" I shouted.

"I'm not going to go to Korea," he repeated.

"Can you give me one good reason why not?" I lashed back.

"Yea," he said very calmly, "I've been talking with Steve Koner and he tells me there isn't anything to do in Korea."

"Has he ever been to Korea?" I asked.

"I don't think so," Steve answered, "but he says he knows. He asked me why I would want to go way over there when there is so much to do right here in Phoenix."

"What is there to do here?" I screamed.

"Parties and concerts and just kicking back," he replied.

"We are talking about a six week trip around the whole world. Do you know how many kids your age would give their eyeteeth to go on a trip like that?" I was begging him to be logical. "Steve, don't do this. Don't throw an experience like this away just to sit at home and kick back."

"Don't take it so seriously, Dad. It's only a few months out of my whole life. Who cares anyhow?" He was almost laughing. "You always get so serious about everything. I just don't want to go all the way over there with a bunch of kids that I don't even know. Steve Koner says it would be real boring. So I've decided I'm not going."

"Don't you think you should give it a little more thought?" I asked. "You can't just take one person's opinion about something this important. Please give it some thought. There is still time to reconsider."

He looked me straight in the eye and whispered, "I just don't want to leave Phoenix when there is so much going on here. They will give you your money back if you ask them, so it shouldn't be any skin off your nose."

I stood for a minute in stunned disbelief. God, I wondered, where are You now?

"Well, Steve, it's your choice. You know I can't force you to go if you don't want to," I told him. "But I don't want you to come back to me in a few years and ask me why I let you do it."

"Ok," he said, "that's a deal." With that he turned and left.

Once again I realized the need for a geographical change. The summer would have to be restructured in order to attempt to eliminate some of the drug traffic and undesirable friends from the boys' lives. This would mean getting out of town for awhile even though getting out of town was not always an easy matter for me. The summer was turning into a nightmare as well as this emergency that had to be dealt with immediately. There was no way we were going to "hang out in Phoenix" for the rest of the summer.

We planned a two week water skiing trip to Lake Havasu. Remembering how much fun we had snow skiing made this trip very appealing. The realization that the boys were out of control made me dread the idea all together. I tried to let go and let God, adding the petition, "Please God, come with us and keep a special watch over the boys." Then I added, "Be with the rest of us also."

The trip started off well. Steve and the girls loved to ski and Kevin enjoyed long hours sitting by the lake with a fishing rod in his hand. The weather was extremely hot and the water was cold. Skiing was the best ever. I felt good about the idea that I had taken off work for a family time like this. We were all having such a great time. Sherrie even seemed to be so much stronger than she had been and actually spent some time skiing. We were all sunburned, eating well and playing hard. I began to wonder if maybe I had been overly concerned about the boys. To my knowledge there hadn't been any drugs used during the entire two weeks. What a blessing this vacation had been. It seems to me that God always knows when a person has been pushed to the limit. Then He provides a break in life like the one we were having.

The night before we were to leave for home I was awakened by a phone call. The gentleman on the line said, "Do you know where you son is?"

"Yes," I replied, "asleep in the other room."

"Maybe you should check and see," the restaurant manager continued. "I think I have one of your boys here with me. Apparently he and some other kids have broken into the restaurant bar and stolen some liquor. He says his name is Kevin and he looks pretty drunk to me."

"I'll be right there," I told the manager, then threw on some clothes and headed for the confrontation. When I saw Kevin and another kid sitting on the lawn, drunker than drunk, I blew! I don't remember exactly what I did at that point. I do remember kicking Kevin repeatedly as he stumbled toward the motel room. I threw him into his bed and in doing so discovered Steve hiding under the bed.

"What are you doing under the bed?" I screamed.

"Just sleeping," he said in a fake sleepy voice.

"I bet you are just sleeping, how come you have all your clothes on?" I asked.

"We're on vacation," he answered with a very snide voice. "Why do you always accuse me of doing something wrong every time Kev gets into trouble?"

"Who's accusing who?" I said. "All I asked was why you are under the bed sleeping with all of your clothes on. It was only a simple question!"

I could feel myself losing it so I threatened them both within an inch of their lives and headed back to my own room. When I sat down on the edge of the bed Sherrie didn't even ask. My red face and shaking body indicated that I was not at all pleased with the way things had gone.

I met the management along with several other rather irate parents the following morning. The restaurant manager was very nice about the incident and explained that they would not be pressing charges and would write the entire event off as a childish prank.

19

The Kansas Experience

Kevin had become incorrigible and Steve was racing along right behind. There is no choice something has to be done and done quickly, I was beginning to think like a broken record. Sherrie and I spent hours talking about what to do. She told me that her folks had friends with a child like Kevin and they had sent him to a military school. She wasn't sure how he had done but had in mind that things improved. My thought was if Kevin was out of the house for a year or so we could work on a little regrouping.

I started making calls to the different military schools around the country. Kevin didn't meet the academic standards for most of the schools until I came across one in Kansas. They said he could be enrolled on a six month probationary status. To me it didn't matter what his standing was, the fact that he could be enrolled at all made me want to sing.

As usual we were doing everything on the spur-of-the moment. Due to the shortness of time most of the matriculation had to be accomplished over the phone. The final verification arrived the following week. Now came the hard part—breaking the news to Kevin. We took him into the kitchen that evening and his mother and I sat down to explain the situation.

When we had finished painting a very detailed picture, he looked at us and asked, "So when do I go? It sounds good to me." He got up to leave the room, then stopped and said, "By the way, where is Kansas?"

As luck would have it my in-laws arrived that evening for their once-in-a-lifetime visit. Kevin met them at the door with a mood of excitement.

"Guess what, Grandma," he blurted out, "I'm going to go to a military school in Kansas starting next month."

I got the feeling we had just announced the bombing of Pearl Harbor. There is no way I could ever describe the look on both of their faces. What followed is easy to describe. There was no way that a grandson of theirs was going to be subjected to the treatment that flourished in a military school. In fact it was pointed out that their friend sent their son to a military school and he didn't like it at all.

"Did your friend's son get any benefit from the school?" I asked.

"Well he finished high school and never got into any trouble after that," she admitted. "He wasn't happy there and there is no way that our little Kevie is going to a place like that. I will take him home with us before I will allow that to happen!"

One thing I could say for my mother-in-law, there was never any question on where she stood when it came to Kevin.

"I'm truly sorry that you feel that way," I told them. "However, all the arrangements have been made and he and I will be leaving for Kansas in two weeks."

In the discussion that followed there was no room for cognitive thinking. No matter what I presented as justification for sending Kevin to a military school, I was shot down. It even got to the point where I became the culprit for the entire decision to send him away. They were convinced Sherrie would never do anything so radical to "poor little Kevie."

But the evening ended with the certainty that Kevin was going to go to Kansas to a military school. Not all concerned were happy although an understanding had been reached. Then for the benediction I suggested that I was sure they would see it our way if they would only give it some thought (not the best suggestion for my closing argument).

After they left Steve proceeded to amplify matters with his comments.

"Steve Koner knew a guy that went to a military academy and

the other kids beat him to a pulp the first day he was there. He hated the place and finally escaped."

"Thanks Steve, we all really need your input about now. Please keep your comments to yourself!" I ordered.

"I'm only telling you the truth about what happened," he said. "They literally beat him to a bloody pulp for no reason. That's the way they do things in those schools. It's just like the government. They have all the power and you have nothing so you just learn to take it. You know how the government is taking all of our freedom away out here! Just you wait 'til you see how they do it in there. It's like a prison for good people who have never done nothing wrong. It's sick, if you know what I mean."

"Steve," I demanded, "keep your comments to yourself or get out of here."

"Yea," he countered, "I'm just telling you the truth so you won't be a sucker, Kev."

"Steve!" I yelled.

"I'm out of here." When he got to the door he stopped and turned back, then he added, "Sucker!"

"Don't let him get to you," I told Kevin, "He's just mouthing off."

"Yea you just have to understand where Steve is coming from," Kevin said.

Now Kevin has never been known for having a lot of ambition but when it comes to sensitivity he is a master. The one aptitude with which he has been greatly blessed is his ability to be smooth. As a matter of fact we have always said that he could sell ice cubes at the North Pole and turn a profit if he wanted to. He learned at an early age to tell people exactly what they want to hear. Then do exactly as he pleased. To him it is a great big game which he has turned into an art form. I knew that what I was about to hear would hold an element of importance. I asked him to go on.

"Well, Papa-San," he started in, "you know that Steve is afraid, don't you?"

"Afraid of what," I asked.

"He is afraid of everything. You know how we always kid him about not eating off of someone else's fork for fear of getting leukemia. Well to him that's no joke. He really believes that if he eats after someone else he will come down with some sort of a dread disease."

"Are you putting me on?" I asked. (With Kevin it is necessary to distinguish between fact and fiction.)

"Believe me, Dad, he's scared to death about everything. Have you ever seen Steve play baseball?"

"No I guess I haven't," I answered. "Why?"

"Because he always sleeps with a baseball bat under the bed," he replied. "And he doesn't even own a mitt. Get it? He's really scared of getting beat up."

"I guess I have never given it too much thought," I admitted. "But why does he want to hang around with all those gang type guys then?"

"Because he is a little skinny guy himself and he knows they will protect him. That's one of the reasons he does drugs with them so they won't turn against him. You notice he likes to hang around with me," Kevin boasted. "That's because I'm tall, muscular and strong.

"And what about his attitude toward God?" he continued. "He really thinks God is out to get him too. So if he does one thing wrong he is going to get zapped."

"Now that is ridiculous! What about the fact that he lies, steals, smokes and does drugs? Isn't he just a little scared that he will get zapped for that?" I questioned.

"I guess he feels that if he's going to get it anyway he might just as well take the full ride." Kevin shrugged. I could tell he wanted to keep talking so I just sat and listened.

"You know the way he treats Mother? It's not because he has it in for her, he just really doesn't like women in general because his mother didn't like him and gave him away."

"That's not the reason she gave him up for adoption," I butted in. "She loved him very much I'm sure, but she knew she couldn't take care of him the way we could."

"Yea, I know all of that stuff," Kevin agreed, "but you are never going to get Steve to believe it. He is afraid to get close to any female for fear he will get dumped again. He wants to be a big man so he can't let himself be subservient to any woman. That means not doing a woman's job like housework. In his mind all women are inferior because his real mother was inferior."

"Is there more?" I asked.

"Sure, lots more, Papa-San. He's scared that the government is out to get him. He thinks that all the walls in the house are bugged and that wherever he goes he is being watched. And that if he says the pledge of allegiance to the flag, he is worshiping the government. The reason he won't open an account at the bank is he is afraid the government will steal all his cash. Bret told him that the government is probably poisoning our water and that the authorities are out to start a nuclear war any day now. He believes everything that anyone tells him, unless it's you of course."

Kevin had one closing remark. "This is the main reason he uses drugs. It helps make the pain of all his fears go away!"

Maturity seemed to be running high in Kevin that evening. It was easy to feel proud of his understanding about the military school and his insight into Steve's complex makeup. I felt confident that having him away in boarding school would be the best thing for him. It would also allow me more time to build a more concrete rapport with Steve. I thanked God again for the remarkable way He had answered our prayers.

Preparations for Kevin's departure were complete. Two nights before we were to leave, the grandparents came to our home for a farewell dinner. The evening went well and the goodbyes were said with only a few tears.

I went to bed that night confident life was coming together in a favorable fashion. I awakened the following morning to the grim reality that Kevin had taken his bags and run away from home.

There was no word from Kevin until late the following day when we received a phone call in which he asked us not to worry. He told me there was no way he could go to a military school. He had decided to stay out of school and get a job. He would find his own apartment and start supporting himself. I asked him if he had any money or anywhere to stay. He said no on both counts.

"How are you going to survive until you get a job?" I asked.

"Just don't worry about me," was his answer. "I'll be OK. I'm sorry but I just can't go to a military school. I love you both." There was a click on the other end of the line and he was gone.

It was several days before we received another phone call. It was from the in-laws. There was no hello or how are you. No explanation, only a request to help them get Kevin enrolled at a high school in their area. There would have to be some special arrangements made for him to attend a school in a new school district.

They had decided that Kevin would move in with them and Earl (grandpa) would tutor Kevin every afternoon after school until his grades reached an acceptable level. There was no question as to whether this was all right with us or not. This was the way it was going to be! It was suggested that it would be our responsibility to pay for his groceries. There was no goodbye or how wonderful it has been talking with you. Just a dial tone. After they hung up I stood and stared at the receiver.

"It's been nice talking to you too!" I mocked.

Registration at the high school was accomplished with only a few hours of meetings with class advisors, and an interview with a psychologist. There was a ton of paperwork that needed to be done in order to assure the admissions office that Kevin was really living with his grandparents and not with us.

It was explained to me, at great length, that each district received funds according to the number of students that live in its area. I really wasn't interested in how they acquired funds to cover their expenses until I was informed that we would be paying tuition because we were from another district. A financial statement would have to be filled out and accepted by the committee before we could be approved for self-pay. This could be done at my convenience within the next twenty-four hours.

The real corker came when the counselor informed us that Kevin would be placed in a special education class since he had been branded with the label "emotionally retarded." The registrar informed us that additional psychological testing would be necessary before they could determine where to place him. The testing would have to be done by a private psychologist and needed to be done as soon as possible.

"Oh yes," the lady behind to counter added as we were leaving, "there will be an additional charge for the special education class."

I acknowledged that they were right about Kevin's degree of maturity. Grandpa, on the other hand, made it plain that he would prove the school wrong after Kevin received a few weeks of his own personal tutoring. As I left the building I realized that going back to square one would have been a step forward.

20

The Lost Incentive

Another school year was in full swing. Kevin seemed happy in his new environment. Steve was tolerant of the Academy and the girls were as happy as clams at Camelback school without the boys.

For enhancement in the grade department I elected to offer an incentive program to our kids. The reward would be a week out of school in February for a ski trip to Aspen, Colorado. The requirement was to have all school assignments completed and at least a "C" in every subject. Even Cindi, who was cute but not necessarily scholastically inclined, felt the goal was not out of reach.

The proposition was discussed with Kevin's special education teacher who promised to use the trip as a tool toward forced learning. The goal was kept constantly in the forefront. With the special tutoring of his grandfather, Kevin was able to pull down an "A" on his very first math exam.

No one was too surprised because Kevin had always exhibited a good brain, crippled only by a lack of ambition. The grandparents were so proud they went out that very afternoon and permitted Kevin to pick out any new bicycle he chose. He showed exquisite taste in his selection.

With the advent of new wheels the afternoon study periods were abandoned. A city park where more than bicycles were being peddled became his favorite hang out. By the end of the first semester his grades had plunged to new lows. Kevin's teacher counseled him daily. Parent teacher conferences were a regular happening. The possibility of missing the Aspen trip was a constant threat. Nothing seemed to change the course that had been set.

Before Thanksgiving the grandparents told us we would have to take Kevin home from Friday night until Monday morning. It seemed he was disrupting their social life.

At the other end of the scale, the girls had both exceeded the requirement of a "C" and each had completed all of the required assignments. Steve, although devoid of all social skills managed to sail through the first half of the year with straight "A's" as was his custom.

As the date for the ski trip grew near, Kevin's teacher felt a conference that would include the grandparents and Kevin was crucial. At the meeting a simple conclusion was drawn. Kevin had not done the work. Consequently, he did not deserve to go skiing. The grandparents were furious. If we were going to take the others and leave Kevie at home they refused to take care of him. We would have to find other accommodations. Kevin was shocked and appeared to be on the verge of tears. I was heartbroken and sincerely wished I had never come up with such a ridiculous plan in the first place.

If I were to let him go, the others would feel betrayed. After all they had worked hard and deserved to be rewarded. Leaving Kevin at home would further tear down the already weakened relations we had with my in-laws. Taking him along would show that one does not necessarily have to face the impact of his own actions and what Dad says doesn't mean anything either. It was a no-win situation. The only answer was to stick to my word and face the music.

We did just that. We went, we skied, and we had a good time. But in the back of my mind was the nagging reminder that there was one missing. I kept beating myself with the impression that if I hadn't set the criterion we could all be skiing together. In my mind I knew I had done the right thing. In my heart I wondered.

Kevin's academic experience continued to deteriorate following our return from Aspen. The in-laws were completely unforgiving to us as well as intolerant of Kevin. The school no longer was able to cope with the problems that Kevin was displaying. It was obvious that other arrangements would have to be made.

The psychologist told us of a private school in the mountains of southern California. It was designed to teach the incorrigible. The environment was closed to outside influence and each student could progress at his or her own rate. Privileges would be earned in accordance with the student's behavior. The results of the training were reported as excellent. I arranged a meeting with the headmaster the following week.

The school was located near Lake Arrowhead in the San Bernardino mountains. It was housed in a beautiful old mansion that had once been the home of a Hollywood movie star. The setting was beautiful. It was explained to me that a student would not be able to enjoy the benefit of the area until his actions warranted it.

I was asked to sit down before the expense of such a place was brought to the table. Having me sit down was a merciful gesture and after only a brief recovery period I was able to resume the tour. Arrangements were finalized that afternoon and on the following Sunday Kevin and I left home for the school. Carol rode to California with us just in case Kevin should at any time decide to bolt.

Once Kevin was settled, the headmaster informed him about the structure of the school. When he heard he was in a school without visits for the first four months he began to cry. I held him in my arms in an embrace steeped in love. We were both crying too hard to speak. I gave him a big squeeze then left.

"I can't do this," I bawled to Carol when I got outside. "It just isn't fair to leave him all alone up here."

Carol didn't say a thing other than, "Come on we have to get back. You have just done the best thing that could have happened to that poor little boy!"

Sherrie and I made the decision on the school with no outside help. To our amazement my in-laws were relieved when we told them what we had done. The only question they asked was why they hadn't been let in on the plans so they could have told Kevie goodbye.

The rules of the school dictated that no family members were allowed to visit for the first four months. Then it was parents only for a four hour visit. The time between visits would get shorter with the progress of the student.

Leaving Kevin at the school left me with an empty feeling of relief. With the ambivalence came the sheer joy of knowing Kevin was protected from himself and the comfort that now full attention could be turned toward Steve. God had once again given me the serenity to accept the things that I couldn't change, and the courage to change the things that I could.

Having Kevin comfortably tucked away in his posh boarding school should have made life much easier at home. It actually did for exactly six weeks and then the next bomb fell.

21

Caught with the "Pot"

The day before final exams at the Academy a call came from the principal telling me that Steve and some of the other boys had been caught on campus with marijuana in their backpacks. The consensus of the faculty was fair. If the boys would come in and talk with the board and agree to adhere to the rules of the school, they would be allowed to return to the Academy in the fall. There would be no interruption in their education.

I felt that was a more-than-generous offer and told the principal I would discuss it with Steve as soon as he got home from school.

"No way, man," were the first words out of Steve's mouth. "If they were Christians they would accept me the way I am."

"But Steve," I argued, "you broke the rules. They are still willing to let you come back next year and they are going to let you take your finals tomorrow. I think they are being more than fair."

"I really don't care what you think," he contended. "They had no right to get into my backpack in the first place. They think they are government agents. The school and the United States government are all corrupt. They are all out to get us. No way am I going to give in to their political agenda. They are all crooks, just no good crooks.

"Bret told me that the government is out to get us and is probably poisoning us right now. They are all using us as pawns and getting ready for a nuclear war. This whole thing is a bunch of garbage.

"I think the Academy stinks and they are wrong. I told them they had no right to get into my backpack, but they did it anyway.

Communist countries have it better that we do! I'm not getting down and kissing their feet no matter what you say."

He finally took a breath and I asked, "Are you through?"

"I just don't see how they can think they are Christian and do things like this."

He started to go on, but I interrupted him and asked, "Do you think that maybe we should wait and talk about this later when you have had a little time to think about it?"

He threw his hands in the air and left the room mumbling something about a bunch of dictators that were out to get him!

With a strategy that was painfully designed to maintain sanity in a house filled with adolescents, we dove full bore into the summer. My exclusive attention was devoted to getting Steve past what I considered a major obstacle. His aim was apparently to drive me as close to the edge as possible without pushing me over. With that ground work understood we began.

I felt we needed to spend quality time together as father and son on a regular basis. Such things as day trips to the lake or dinner for just the two of us seemed to excite Steve's interest. He would talk about the plans for days and then not show up at the given time.

Several times I arrived home for our "quality time together," only to find Steve on the bed, stoned. Each time when he recovered he assured me he was sorry and it wouldn't happen again. So we continued to make plans in order to allow my resentment to build. On the rare occasion when the plans did materialize we both actually had a great time. At times like that I became aware of the closeness that can only be felt between a father and his son.

That summer we survived the family vacation to the beach and water skiing at the lake. Both went off without a hitch. These times away from home gave us an opportunity to discuss going back to the Academy faculty to clear the slate. I even offered to go with him as a spokesperson if that would help make him more comfortable. All my efforts to persuade him to bridge the gap were met with negative reactions. I begged. I pleaded. All to no avail.

"Steve," I appealed, "just go in and tell them you are sorry and will try and do better from now on. They will let you back into school and you will be there with all of your friends and everything will be hunky-dory."

"Dad," he would come back, "you just don't get it do you? In the first place I'm not sorry. Besides they are the ones that should come to me and ask for forgiveness. They got into my backpack without my permission. Any good Christian would know that. You should be smart enough to understand that yourself!"

With that we were off to the races once again. There was no way on this earth that the situation was going to be saved. He was not going to say he was sorry no matter what the benefit. In reality I'm sure he didn't see that he had done anything wrong whatsoever.

The conversation always ended with, "If they were any kind of Christians, they would accept me the way I am!" And with that the chapter was closed.

At the beginning of the next school year Steve was enrolled as a junior at the local public high school. All of his friends returned to the Academy after a short interview with the faculty. Steve remained proud that he had not given into the dictatorial pronouncements of the establishment.

Friends were hard to come by in such a large high school and Steve's Academy friends quickly drifted into their own worlds of endeavor. It was obvious that he felt very alone as he tore into his studies with a vengeance. As always he stayed high in all of his classes as well as high on drugs. It was amazing to me that he could do drugs and have any degree of mental retention.

His social graces were completely lacking as were his grooming techniques. The disarray of his long blond hair and a struggling partial beard, garlic and cigarette breath, dirty unkempt clothes, coupled with a small tattoo and pierced ear all screamed of an unhappy inner self. Yet his scholastic achievements were without reproach.

Six weeks into the semester Steve showed signs of being disillusioned with the education he had acquired thus far at the high school. I became hopeful that he would want to return to the Academy, if for no other reason than to be with his friends.

My hopes were quickly shattered when he went to the high school principal and informed him that the classes they offered were worthless. He suggested that he would be happy to take the examinations at the end of each course, but was tired of wasting precious time sitting and listening to "no good teachers hour after hour." Steve had a real way with words.

The principal apparently took exception to what Steve was saying about the staff and fired back, "If you think you are so smart, why don't you go and take a GED examination and get your certificate and have it all over with once and for all!"

That is exactly what he did. He waltzed into the GED examining office the following week with no preparation and took the examination on the receipt of a minimal fee. He received his certificate having obtained an overall average of ninety-six percentile.

Fifteen years old with only two years of high school behind him. Now he was a high school graduate. He was finished. In a single stroke of the pen he had wiped out two of his most important years for maturing into young manhood. Two years of developing invaluable social skills. Years he was never able to recapture.

I will not belabor my subsequent discussion with the principal. Suffice it to say, he was aware I had materialized in his office! I left no stone unturned.

22

Teenage Anarchy

Many of the events of the next couple of years have been drowned in the merciful elixir of time. Kevin was peacefully confined to his mountaintop resort and incommunicado for the first few months by order of the school. I had to battle the guilt that came from the joy of having him out of the house. Notwithstanding, I forced myself to accept his plight in life as an act of God and promptly put it out of my mind.

Teri was admitted into the Academy as a boarding student and was seldom at home except for an occasional weekend.

Cindi continued her studies at the private day school; due to hard times inflicted on a limousine company, she was escorted to and from school daily by a uniformed driver at minimal cost. This appealed greatly to her affluent nature as well as to her moneyed friends. She did admit to me one day that she had a friend whose family had only one swimming pool and didn't even own a motor home. I expressed appropriate concern for any person in such desperate circumstances.

Steve was the problem. With no structure and stripped of all the normal responsibilities of a teenager, his life literally disintegrated before my eyes. The discussions that transpired on the subject went smoothly and he agreed wholeheartedly that everything I said was right and that he was more than willing to abide by all of my requests.

In a nutshell I told him all the rules of the house would remain in force as long as he was living at home. He would be expected to get a job and give a portion of his income toward room and board. It seemed reasonable and simple to me and to my surprise it apparently seemed reasonable to Steve also.

In reality none of the above materialized. When asked about the job the same stock answer flowed out of his mouth.

"I'm looking and have put in my application. I'm waiting for a phone call to let me know when to start."

"Do you ever call to ask if they are working on your application?" I would ask.

"No," he would reply. "They told me they would let me know when they wanted me to start."

"But, Steve," I reminded him, "if you want a job you have to go after it and let them know you are really interested in working for them. By the way, how many applications do you have in?"

"Just one," was the reply.

"Steve!" I shouted. "You can't hand in applications one at a time and wait a week or two for an answer, then do it again in a few weeks. You will never get a job at that rate. You need to have applications in all over town and you should keep calling to see if they are being acted upon."

"That wouldn't be very honest now would it, Dad?" he snapped back in a somewhat sarcastic voice. "If I go in and ask for a job and tell people that I want to work for them and then go and tell someone else the same thing I would be lying to them both. I'm not going to be a hypocrite just to get a job!"

"You aren't being a hypocrite by trying for several positions at the same time. That's just good practice. It's the way it is done if you really want a job!" I maintained.

He came back, "There is no way that I am going to lie to people and be a hypocrite just to get a stupid job."

"What is so stupid about working so that you will have food to eat and a place to sleep?" I could feel my voice soaring as I tried to maintain my cool.

"So now you are telling me that if I don't lie to people and become a hypocrite you are going to throw me out of the house just because I can't find a job." He was angry. "I can't believe your attitude. You want me to be a good Christian yet you are trying to get me to lie and be a hypocrite just so I can pay you rent."

"No one said anything about paying rent," I whispered trying to conceal my anger. "The point of the conversation was how to go about getting a job. Sitting at home doing nothing day after day isn't one of the best ways. You need to get out there and hustle."

"So what you are trying to tell me," he said in a rather controlled voice, "is that I am lazy. Is that what you think? So why don't you send me away and lock me up the way you did Kevin? Then you could just forget all about me the same way you have done to him!"

"I don't think that you are lazy," I exploded. "And I never have. I am just trying to help you in the way you are going about getting a job. You can't just sit at home all day and expect an employer to come to you and beg you to let him pay you to work for him. It just doesn't work that way."

We both began to calm down and were able to discuss the subject in a more civilized manner but were never able to reach any firm conclusions.

In desperation I went to the head of housekeeping at the hospital and asked her to do me the favor of a lifetime and hire my son to work in her department. She was more than willing to help and said she would put him on just as soon as he turned sixteen.

That will be almost three months from now, I thought to myself. There was nothing to assure me that I could survive for that amount of time with any degree of sanity. He was still too young for drug rehab. He was too young to work, yet old enough to graduate from high school. Once again we were back at square one and that was getting a little old as far as I was concerned.

I got on my knees and pleaded with God for His guidance. Why had He apparently put the rest of life in its proper place and left Steve out there with nowhere to go but down? It became obvious to me that nobody was going to hire a fifteen-year-old without skills no matter what I did. The Ranch would supply some part-time work but was in no way the answer.

Any activity I suggested was out of the question as far as Steve was concerned. We would just have to sit it out for the next few months until he was old enough to get on at the hospital. The waiting period was grim indeed. Steve automatically migrated to a subculture of unemployed drug using high school dropouts. The situation became so severe that his previous low quality friends stopped frequenting the house.

During this period of time his regard for the establishment hit rock bottom. In his mind anyone with money or any finery was trash. He prided himself on the fact that he was too poor to have material possessions. His clothes came from the thrift shop. He refused to wear anything that was clean and didn't have holes. People in nice cars with air conditioning were referred to as "capitalist pigs." The term "mammon" was used for anything that was unsavory to his own taste.

He was convinced that the government was out to get us all. One of his favorite statements was that he wished he could live in a third world country where no one had anything, so he wouldn't have to worry about being robbed.

Although there wasn't much evidence of drug use at home, it was apparent that he was stoned much of the time. Worst of all, it was obvious that he was extremely unhappy. My heart bled for him. Trying to talk to him didn't get me anywhere. There was nothing to do but spend a lot of time in prayer and that is what we did. It was difficult not to get discouraged because the answers were so long in coming. My own faith was growing thin and I knew it, but I also knew that I couldn't give up.

"Please, God," I pleaded, "save my boy."

By the time the Christmas holidays arrived I realized that what little wit I had left had just about come to its end. A break in the routine was essential. Something was going to have to give.

Kevin's school had granted us a visitation for the day before Christmas and the day after Christmas. Students were required to remain at school with their "school family" on Christmas day.

We packed into a first class hotel at Lake Arrowhead two days before Christmas. My parents planned to spend Christmas Eve at the hotel with the other children while Sherrie and I visited with Kevin at his school.

That was also going to be Steve's sixteenth birthday—the day commonly referred to as "liberation day"—the day that he would become old enough to get a job. Old enough to get help from a rehabilitation center and, if the occasion should arise, old enough to be thrown out of the house.

For some very mysterious reason I had the misunderstanding that when a child reaches sixteen he also achieves maturity. That may be a common mistake among many parents. At any rate it isn't true. Maturity in teenagers is the substance of things hoped for and the evidence of things not seen. In this case I was confident that it wouldn't materialize in my lifetime.

The visit with Kevin went well considering it was only our second visit in six months. In fact things went so well the headmaster gave us permission to come back on the day after Christmas and take Kevin off campus for an hour. Kevin was very excited about this and didn't seem to mind the fact that he would be spending Christmas day away from our family.

Christmas Eve, the rest of us opened our presents in the hotel before going to the dining room for a special birthday dinner for Steve. It was an especially fun evening after the kids had had such a good day with the grandparents and we had such a good visit with Kevin.

In the dining room we had a stack of birthday presents for Steve. We had decided that since this was a special birthday, it would have to be celebrated on the actual day instead of on his half birthday in June as was customary. The waitresses gathered around the table and gave Steve best wishes on his sixteenth birthday. It was truly a refreshing evening.

One of the waitresses took me aside and told me they were going to come to the table and sing "Happy Birthday" to Steve at the end of our meal. I thanked her, then suggested that Steve was rather shy and I didn't think he would take it in good humor.

She said, "You can't let his sixteenth birthday go by without a little harmony."

"I know you are trying to be nice. However, I know it would embarrass the life out of him and make him very uncomfortable. I really don't want to ruin his evening. Thank you very much but I think this time we had better just skip the fanfare. Trust me!"

She said, "OK," and left.

We had a great dinner and when we were finished I asked for the check. Instead of the check, the entire dining room staff arrived at the table with a cake complete with sparklers. Everyone in the restaurant started singing "Happy Birthday." Steve looked stunned at first and then stood up and exploded.

"I don't have to take this garbage," he hollered, and stormed out of the building before the chorus could reach its brilliant crescendo.

The restaurant fell into a painful silence. I left the table in hot pursuit and attempted to intercept Steve in the parking lot. He was nowhere to be seen.

When I returned to the table, Sherrie and the girls had already left with the stack of presents. The waitress was near tears and fell all over herself to tell me how sorry she was. All I could say was, "I asked you not to do it!"

"I know," she cried. "I'm sorry. It just seemed like the right thing to do at the time. I've never had anything like this happen before."

"You have never sung to Steve before," I told her as I ran out of the room.

Back in our hotel room Sherrie was furious. She felt I had completely abandoned her. She explained to me (that's a husband's way of saying it was mentioned in no uncertain terms) that she was stuck with the bill, which drained all of her available cash.

"And! That was minor in comparison to the batch of uncomfortable explanations I was required to make to the staff."

My attempts to make amends fell remarkably short. Another beautiful Christmas Eve had been blown. Steve was nowhere to be found. When he did return a few hours later, all he said was, "I told you not to do it!" Then he went to bed. He appeared to be stoned.

Sitting alone I continued to whip myself for allowing the evening to be so botched. Then it hit me. This whole thing is about choices. I'm not the one that made the bad choice. I began to understand that although it is my responsibility as a father to instill proper principles, that is about all I can do. The choices had to come from his own conscious judgments. In this case he had made a bad choice.

It's finished and it is over. Nothing can be done to change the situation. All that could be done has been done, I reasoned to myself. Now let's call it a bad day and get on with it and try to do better next time

When I discussed my feelings with Steve the following morning he let me know he felt I was the culprit. I had made the bad choice. The responsibility for allowing the incident to happen in the first place was mine.

Rather than destroy an already compromised Christmas I chose to abandon the subject. The coward's way out is not always the best way. It is however often the quickest and almost always the easiest.

23

Hope Reigns Eternal

My motion to accompany Steve to his job interview for moral support was dismissed without consideration. I went along anyway! As we entered the tiny office of the director of housekeeping I felt as if I were in the palace of a maharaja. Steve looked as if he were entering the gas chamber. Mrs. Matthews greeted us by telling Steve how happy she was that he had chosen to apply for work in her department.

She continued, "I have had the privilege of working with your father for many years. He really is a great guy—so soft-spoken, kind, and easygoing. Nothing ever seems to ruffle his feathers. You are a fortunate young man to have such a man for your dad."

With each platitude Steve's eyes got bigger and bigger. I knew what he was thinking. This is not the man I know. I wonder where she got all that stuff?

The interview went fine and Steve was hired as a member of the housekeeping staff. My sixteen-year-old son was now gainfully employed. I breathed a sigh of relief as we walked out of the hospital. Another major hurdle was behind us.

Steve entered the work force with determination and from the start did an admirable job. He got on well with most of the staff and seemingly enjoyed his work. On his second day of work I asked him to join me at the snack bar for a bite to eat. While we were eating he informed me that he wanted to ask the little girl behind the counter for a date.

"Don't you think she would make a good girlfriend?" he asked.

"Well," I said, "having only seen her for the first time five minutes ago, and having never spoken to her makes it a little difficult for me to make a sound judgment. But given the question I would have to say she is the prettiest girl behind the counter, but not necessarily the prettiest girl in the room. Judging from her complexion she must be very young."

"You don't get it, Dad," he interrupted. "I want to ask her to be my girlfriend and to go with me. Not just someone to date."

"Don't you think it might be well to get to know her a little better before you ask her out?" I suggested.

"What's there to know?" he asked. "She can be my old lady."

With that remark still hanging in the air he jumped out of his seat to finalize arrangements with a girl he had never met. I sat in sheer amazement at his complete lack of finesse.

The world must have changed considerably since I was sixteen or I was terribly naive or both, I thought to myself and let it rest. It seemed like only a minute when he returned.

"Yeah, Dad, she says she'll be my girlfriend and we have a date for Friday night to go to the game."

"What's her name?" I asked. With that he flew out of the chair again in the direction of the counter. When he returned he answered, "Cindy, just like my sister."

"When do I get to meet her?" I inquired.

"Anytime you want," he replied. "She works here all the time so just tell her who you are. Don't tell her you're a doctor. I wouldn't want her to know my dad's a doctor."

Great! I thought. Now I can pose as an orderly in the department where I am the medical director. The thought hit me, if this is going to be a permanent relationship she will probably catch on in time. On second thought, who knows? I elected not to dwell on the subject and went back to work.

A high school diploma, a new job and a girlfriend doesn't always spell maturity. In the case in question it actually seemed we were losing ground. Rumor had it that Steve was doing a good job at his work of cleaning the operating rooms between surgeries, but I also heard it suggested that some of his actions were a bit immature for the setting. For example, running down the hall giving out his loud obnoxious laugh, or playing rock music so loud while cleaning, it could be heard three rooms away.

I was waiting for the supervisor to call and ask me to speak to Steve. The call came sooner than I had expected. The director of nurses asked me to stop by her office. She assured me it was a difficult task to tell me. Something would have to be done to get Steve to calm down. She had been receiving complaints from the surgeons about the unnecessary noise in the halls. I assured her I would make it my top priority to speak to Steve. I approached him that evening.

"Steve, I have gotten some complaints about your behavior in the operating room," I began.

"Yeah, Dad," he snapped. "I knew this wouldn't work with me working in the same department with you. Every time I do the slightest little thing they come running to daddy to have him give me a spanking. I am so sick and tired of the attitudes of those people up there. All they know how to do is gripe and complain. They think theirs is the only way to do anything. If they are so interested in having me work for them they should learn how to treat a guy."

"Steve!" I interrupted, "you are the one that wanted the job!"

"Oh no, Dad," he shout back. "You are the one that wanted me to get a job. Now that things aren't going to your satisfaction, you are trying to throw the blame on me. I'm not buying into that. If they are so interested in me working there they need to accept me the way I am."

"Steve," I said very softly. "All they are asking is that you calm down a little and not make so much noise in the operating suite. You are right. They should have come to you directly and left me out of it altogether. I will make sure I stay out of your business from now on." And I did.

The story is a bit muddled from here on for a while. Apparently things didn't work out too well for Steve in the operating room so he was "offered" a position on the night shift working in other departments that were less populated. This meant he would be home all day most of the time.

The house rules became a thing of the past. He smoked in his room all of the time and did drugs regardless of my requests and threats. His sisters were harassed to the point of tears much of the time. The girlfriend never came around so I am not sure just what was going on there. The bottom line was that things were just plain not going well and something was going to have to be done about it once again.

After much deliberation and prayer, Sherrie and I came to the conclusion that for the good of everyone concerned, Steve would have to move out of the house and into his own apartment. We would pay for his rent and it would be his responsibility to take care of all the rest. He was thrilled with idea and couldn't wait to get started.

At sixteen and a half years old Steve moved into his own furnished studio. His mother packed boxes of pots and pans, while he and I went to the grocery store for supplies to fill his refrigerator and pantry. I helped him throw some clothes and personal belongings into a bag and he was off.

After Steve moved into his apartment our home returned to a mundane routine of normality. The threat to the girls of Steve's weird friends was gone. The eardrum breaking sound of rock music was replaced with Cindi's melodious young voice dispersing strains of "Tomorrow, Tomorrow," at the top of her lungs throughout the house.

Teri felt comfortable in bringing her friends home for the evening. Kevin was showing some signs of progress at his school on the mountaintop. In time even the smell of pot was hardly detectable in many areas of the house.

After he moved into his own apartment, we didn't see much of Steve during the next year. The occasional visit was usually for the useful purpose of dropping off several weeks' worth of laundry. He usually was able to make it home for important holidays that were accompanied by some sort of a feast. The rest of the time his life was kept very secret and to himself.

My infrequent visits to his apartment were accompanied by severe bruising of my tongue as I walked through the piles of dirty clothes and dirty dishes. On the floor were the remains of uneaten food that was totally out of the confines of a proper diagnosis.

Any comment about the total destruction that lay before us was met with a loud laugh and a comment like, "Oh, Dad, let's be joyful and learn to overlook the insignificant details." His overuse of the term "joyful" annoyed me to no end as I smiled and tried to be joyful.

Steve continued to do good work at the hospital but his exuberant outbursts of "joyfulness" began to get on the nerves of the other employees. Once again any suggestion on how to improve his behavior was met with the same old commentary. "Oh, Dad, don't sweat the small stuff."

His attitude mandated that he be moved from one department to another until there was nothing left but the back door. From that point on I was never sure just where he was working or if he even had a job at all.

My monthly visit to the apartment manager's office to pay the rent was becoming increasingly more unpleasant. I was told of the late night parties that were reportedly going on as well as the excessive number of guests that came and went at all times of the day and night.

One night I made a point to stop by the apartment late at night for a personal view of the so- called festivities. To my surprise the lights were off and there was nobody around. There wasn't even a hint of any music or disorderly conduct.

In the darkness I spotted what looked like a body lying in the doorway. I froze in my steps.

"Steve," I whispered, "is that you?"

There was no motion as I bent over Steve's body. He was without a shirt and barefoot. His skin was like ice. I immediately grabbed for his wrist. To my relief there was a pulse. He was breathing. The smell of beer was almost intoxicating as I bent over him calling his name. There was no sign of movement for several minutes. Then at last a small moaning sound, then another, until he showed signs of awakening. I was finally able to get him into the house and onto the filthy sofa. I covered him with an even filthier blanket. At that point my intent was to let him sleep it off.

After I gave Sherrie a cursory explanation of what had happened, she lashed out at me. "My poor baby, we have to get him and bring him home right now!"

"Poor baby, my eye," I lashed right back. "The poor little baby has been out partying all day and probably most of the night and now he is drunk out of his mind. He needs to sleep it off. As for me and my house I'm going to bed and get some sleep. After all I do still work for a living and need my rest. If he wants to be a lush, he will have to do it on his own time."

The word, "Keith," coming from Sherrie's sweet little mouth at full volume was impressive. We went and got Steve and brought him home!

I was able to get him into a warm bath while Sherrie made sure the sheets were fresh to go along with the hot soup she was making for him. He lavished in his bath and ate several bowls of soup before his alcohol-soaked brain returned him to the necessary state of unconsciousness to sleep it off.

The following day he thanked us profusely for caring. He left immediately after announcing that he had just been thrown out of his apartment by a manager, "who wasn't man enough to accept him the way he is."

The visits became even more infrequent after that. I was never privy to his whereabouts but I do know that he moved in with his girlfriend for a while. He arrived home on Thanksgiving to have a "joyful day with the family."

We didn't see him again until Christmas Eve when he arrived home in time for dinner and to open his birthday presents as well as Christmas presents. There was a large "care package" that had been prepared by the entire family, including the grandparents.

During dinner I made the remark to Cindi, "You sure did wolf your dinner down."

She answered me with, "I was really hungry!"

Steve looked at her with a blank stare and observed, "You don't know hungry!"

From that remark I took it that finances had not been as readily available as might have been desirable. The evening was over and Steve left to return to his friends and a lifestyle that was too congested to yield space for his family.

That night I realized just how much I missed Steve. Both of my sons were gone at a time when they needed me and I needed them. It seemed as if fate had torn them from my arms, never to allow them to return.

24

The Grandparents
Take Charge

The holidays came and went with life remaining status quo until late spring. A phone call came one late afternoon. The caller's voice sounded stressed beyond belief.

"Have you talked with your son Kevin in the last few hours?" the voice blasted.

"No," I answered, "he's not here right now. He's at school in California."

"I know," came the indignant voice on the other end of the line. "This is the headmaster at the school. It appears your son has disappeared. We have searched the entire premises. He just isn't anywhere to be found! I was hoping he might have called you to let you know his whereabouts. It's several miles to the nearest town as you well know. There isn't anyway he could possibly make it all the way down the hill to the city. It's miles through woods and rough terrain. There just isn't anyway he could make it on his own. Even if he did make it to the city he doesn't have any money and he probably wouldn't know what to do anyhow!"

The headmaster's words of comfort grated in my head.

"When did you find him missing?" I stammered.

"Several hours ago," he answered.

"Why wasn't I notified sooner?" I shouted.

"We thought we could find him," the headmaster said. "You know we have never lost a student like this before. I don't even know how he could have gotten out of here without someone seeing him. You know we have never lost a student like this before.

This is the first time this has ever happened."

It was beginning to sound like a stuck record so I interjected the thought that it might be well to contact the police. The suggestion was received with a certain degree of enthusiasm just before he repeated. "You know this has never happened to us before, this is the very first time."

"Yes, I believe you did mention that!' I replied. In my mind I was thinking, You may not have ever had a student quite like Kevin before either!

The police confirmed that Kevin was in fact missing and that an all-out search had been launched to find him. The roads down the hill were being watched for any unusual foot travelers. The immediate area was combed in search of the missing student.

The headmaster called a few hours later to inform me they were convinced that Kevin had run away from school. I didn't even dignify the thought with an answer but merely thanked him and began to pray. I was begging God once again to take care of my son.

The feeling of guilt hit me like a tidal wave. I knew that God had to be thinking if I were any kind of a father this would never have happened in the first place. I should have kept Kevin home and been a good father instead of turning his care over to a bunch of teachers. The stress was overwhelming. I just knew he was either lost in the woods to be eaten by a wild animal, or he had fallen from a cliff and was lying injured and helpless to freeze to death in the night. Maybe could he have been picked up while hitchhiking, by some crazy and who knows what!

We decided it would be best not to worry the grandparents until we had more details. Nothing was mentioned. I knew we would be at fault for sending him to that dreadful school in the first place and I really didn't need any more guilt at that particular point in time.

Like so many parents, I had often thought about having one of my children disappear. Now the dreaded reality was here. There is no way to describe the empty, hopeless feeling that comes from not knowing where your child is, and trying to keep out the thoughts that rage though your head as you imagine the worst.

Days passed with no word. I felt I was going to go crazy. Calls to the school and the police were always met with the same response:

"We will let you know as soon as we hear anything new. We are doing everything possible to find your boy."

The encouraging thing was the police would ask without exception, "What did you say his name was again?" There was nothing to do but wait.

On the fourth day after Kevin's disappearance I received a phone call from Carol. "You will never guess who I just talked to," he began. "I talked to Kevin and he is at your in-laws house."

"How did he get there?" I asked. "Why hasn't anyone called to let us know he was there?"

"Apparently he called his grandfather from California and asked him to send an airline ticket. He told them he wasn't happy at the school anymore. The grandparents were not to call you because he knew you would be furious. The plan is to call you in a few days. He asked me not to call you either. Of course, I lowered the boom and told him I was going to call you right away. I imagine he is sitting over there shaking in his boots waiting for your call. If I were you, I think I would wait a little while before you call them so you can get a grip on yourself."

I did in fact wait awhile. About thirty seconds. My father in-law answered the phone and immediately informed me. "We would have called you but Kevin asked us not to."

Good, I thought. Just make sure we don't do anything to upset little Kevie. I was so relieved and so livid at the same time that I honestly don't have any idea what transpired in the conversation from that point on. At any rate Kevin was home safe and sound. At least safe. I thanked God for returning him to us without incident, and asked for a special outpouring of strength to keep me from committing mayhem.

Almost simultaneously with the return of Kevin came the return of Steve. I received a call from another of Steve's apartment managers suggesting that other living arrangements for Steve might serve the best interest of all concerned. In other words, "Your son Steve is being evicted in light of the fact that he has a serious problem conforming to the rules of the establishment. Tomorrow as a day of departure will be soon enough. Oh yes, and by the way, since he gave you as the responsible party you will be liable for any damage that might have occurred during his stay here." He thanked me for being so understanding and hung up.

Understanding, I thought, I didn't even say a word.

Having both boys back at home didn't pose a great advantage to an already dysfunctional family. New house rules had to be established quickly. First of all no one was going to live at home rent free and without a job. There would be no, and I meant no smoking, drinking or using of drugs in my house. None of this staying up all night and sleeping the day away or lying around the house all day watching television. Things were going to be different this time around or I was going to know the reason why!

Things were different. The boys left the house each morning and went out to "look for a job." Each evening when I got home I was greeted with the statement "We have been looking but can't find anything." The smoking and drug use went underground. When confronted they would both look me straight in the face and say, "Don't you trust us, Dad? You asked us not to do those things in your house so you know we won't."

The truth of the matter was that I knew they were lying to me about everything, the smoking, the drinking and the drugs. I knew they had no intention of getting a job in the near future. The problem was I couldn't catch them smoking or doing drugs. So, I set out on a witch hunt and caught them dead in their tracks. After sitting for hours peering through a crack in the drapes of their room like a school child, I captured them red-handed lighting up a joint and cigarettes.

The expressions on their faces were priceless as I walked into the room and announced that the flight was over and they had exactly twenty minutes to pack their bags and bail out. I told them I would sign them into the Holiday Inn for two days and in that time they had better find somewhere to go because they weren't coming home!

They laughed and made wisecracks all the way to the motel. To them the whole thing was one big joke. For the first time in my life I had absolutely no remorse as I drove out of the parking lot of the motel. After offering my fond adieus I asked God to take care of my boys once again as I realized, it can't get any worse!

The boys found a low rent cabin in a court on the other side of town. Steve went to work immediately in order to put food on the table. Kevin followed suit with some part-time work to aid in their meager income. There were rare collect phone calls. On occasion I would drop off a care package at their cabin. They seldom came to the house for lack of transportation, yet they never asked for money.

It was my prayer like the prayers of so many parents that this would be the wake-up call that would give them greater maturity with a better understanding of responsible living. I knew in my heart that they were both good boys down deep and that God would take care of them through these terrible teenage years. All would be well on the other side.

Toward the end of the summer Sherrie received an interesting phone call from our neighborhood branch of the bank.

"Your son and his bride-to-be were in today," came the greeting from the bank manager. "They asked us to cash the three thousand dollar check you gave them as a wedding present. Kevin opened a savings account and was going to deposit the entire amount. Then at the last minute, he decided to take half of the money to help with their immediate expenses. I gave him fifteen hundred in cash and deposited the remainder. I just thought I should check with you folks to make sure it was all right to do it that way."

By the time Sherrie caught her breath the long silence had already identified a severe problem. "This is the first I have heard about a wedding or even a girl friend for that matter," Sherrie began. "I for sure don't know anything about a check for three thousand dollars."

"Are you telling me that you didn't write the check or give your permission for Kevin to cash a check?" the bank manager asked.

"That's right," Sherrie answered. "I haven't heard anything about any of this until this very minute."

"This could be a very serious matter," the lady from the bank continued. "Would you like to cover the check so your son won't get into trouble?" she asked.

Sherrie was stunned. "Let me talk to my husband and I will call you back in a couple of hours."

The dilemma was overwhelming. If we covered for him he could avoid a felony charge, but if we didn't he could go to jail. The situation was solved when we received a second call from the bank stating that an anonymous customer had covered the check so no charges would be filed. The bank manager apologized for any concern that her call may have provoked and thanked us for being such good customers.

We never knew for sure who paid the three thousand dollars. The grandparents would have gotten my vote if I were asked. Feeling betrayed but satisfied once again that the worst possible had happened, I dropped into bed that evening for some much needed sleep.

The one a.m. phone call was from a police officer in Wickenberg, a small town fifty miles north of Phoenix. He stated he needed some questions answered about my son Kevin who was sitting there with him.

"Your son was driving through town at a normal rate of speed when I pulled in behind him. When he saw me he put the pedal to the metal and took off. I took after him in hot pursuit and the race was on. He missed the turn in the road and drove your Cadillac through a barbed wire fence and out onto the desert. Then he jumped out of the car and started to run. Being barefoot he turned around and gave himself up. My main question to you is did you give your new car to your son?"

"No," I replied, "I had no idea that he had my car."

"So you are telling me that you didn't give your son permission to use your car?"

"No," I said again. "As far as I know he has never even driven that car."

"Where is your car right now?" the officer asked.

"In my driveway," I told him.

"Would you mind going out and looking to see if your car is in the driveway?"

Obediently I jumped out of bed, pulled on my pants and headed for the garage. As I approached the driveway a thought struck me. If the officer has my son named Kevin in front of him and a new red Cadillac that is registered in my name in his possession, why am I walking to the driveway in the middle of the night? The driveway was in fact empty.

The events that followed over the next few weeks revealed that Kevin had been involved in a burglary a few weeks earlier as well as a trip to Las Vegas with a group of friends on a stolen credit card.

He was also charged with illegal flight from an officer and driving a stolen vehicle. All the counts granted him an eight month stay in the county jail.

Steve was devastated by the manner in which the establishment handled the situation with his brother. His feeling was that they had no right to put him away for such a minor offense and that if the government wasn't so corrupt, they would have given him a second chance. We sat up long hours many a night going over all the facts about the results of Kevin's actions. Steve never conceded the fact that the law had been broken and a punishment was necessary. In his mind his brother had been given a bum rap. The legal system was all wrong. Nothing was ever going to change his feelings on the subject and that was that!

The holidays were ruined. Without exception Steve would sit at the dinner table crying over his plate and missing "brother." Long dissertations on how corrupt the government really was always followed ad nauseam. In Steve's mind Kevin remained the victim rather than the perpetrator. I personally thanked God that Kevin was off the streets, sleeping in a warm bed and being well fed. As far as I was concerned the punishment was just.

Somehow in the heat of all the hurt, I was able to give up cigarettes once and for all. Sometimes there is some good that comes out of a traumatic situation.

Simultaneously with the problems of my immediate family my mother fell and fractured her hip. It soon became apparent that my parents were unable to care for themselves in Palm Springs. A move to Phoenix became a necessity.

Following the move my mother continued to deteriorate and in mid-January she became terminal. The home care nurse called me to come to my folks' condominium late one afternoon and told me she thought this was the day.

I sat holding my mother's hand as she lay in a comatose state until early morning when she finally breathed her last breath. Sherrie was home sick in bed and the kids showed no noticeable concern. My father had fallen asleep from sheer emotional exhaustion. I sat alone with my mother's lifeless body. Eighty-nine years of a beautiful life had come to an end.

25

Back on Track

A pattern was quickly set in Steve's life. His jobs were short-lived, low paying and usually terminated "because of the boss's lack of understanding." Living arrangements were also temporary. He shared an apartment with his girlfriend for a while then went to crashing at friends' apartments for days at a time until he was invited not to come back.

When Kevin returned home from his stay in jail, Steve started spending more time around the house but didn't move home permanently.

Kevin walked the edge for about three months until he crossed over and was arrested for breaking probation. He apparently got "high" by sniffing paint. He went to the grocery store and, with his finger in his jacket, held up a lady at the door and demanded money. She gave him all she had (about seven dollars) and he left. He returned in a minute or two and thanked her and disappeared again. Later he was apprehended and charged with armed robbery. The charge of armed robbery carried an automatic fifteen year sentence in the state of Arizona at that time. This time Kevin was in real trouble.

Steve was devastated once again and couldn't understand how "brother" could have allowed himself to get back in the same mess. The difference this time was Steve was beginning to see that Kevin was manufacturing his own destiny.

The surprise of my life came one Friday night as I was sitting in the kitchen reading and Steve arrived.

"Hi," I greeted him. "How come you're not working at the

bakery this evening?" In my mind I knew he had been fired but didn't want to ask.

To my astonishment he answered, "I had a long talk with my boss today and told him that I wouldn't be working on Friday nights or Saturdays any more because it is God's Sabbath and we have been commanded not to work on the seventh day of the week."

"Excuse me," I said, "what did you say?"

"I just told him I couldn't work on the Sabbath any more," he repeated. "I have decided to turn my life over to God and I want to go back to school and learn to be a preacher. I have quit smoking and drinking and haven't used any drugs for several weeks.

"Could you help me so I can go back to college this spring semester? I feel that the Holy Spirit is speaking to me and that I need to study and be able to warn others about what is going to happen if we don't turn our lives over to the Lord."

The urge to reach over and turn off the alarm clock was almost overwhelming. This surely had to be a dream. I should be waking up soon. Looking Steve straight in the face I said, "Tell me exactly what you said again, slowly."

"All I am saying is that I feel the Holy Spirit is working in my life and that I should go back to school. I want to be able to tell others about the Lord. In order to do it I will need your financial help. I can't afford to go on my own."

"Where do you want to go to college?" I asked.

"I think I want to go to the Adventist College in Tennessee," he replied. "I have a friend from the Academy that is studying theology there. He says it is a very spiritual school and he likes it a lot. He even asked me if I would like to room in the dorm with him."

The feeling of disbelief kept running through me. This had to be some sort of a gimmick. No one could make such a radical change from one day to the next. We sat up talking and praying for hours that night. We had a lengthy discussion on the various influences that had brought him to this point. High on the list of events were the stories about how God had taken care of our family over the years. I had no idea that he had paid any attention to most of these stories but apparently some of them had made a lasting impression on his young life.

The morning in Hawaii when I lifted him with one hand and

apparently saved him from the approaching traffic made an immense impression. Our second move to Germany was also convincing. The story about his mother and me both deciding to pay tithe when we were six thousand miles apart helped to strengthen his belief that God was leading in the affairs of our family. Apparently he was very sincere and determined to allow his life to be changed. I was definitely witnessing the process of sublimation in action.

We decided that the two of us would go to Tennessee in the next couple of weeks to see the college and make arrangements for him to register. Sleep came slowly that night. We all attended church together the following morning. The choir and the organ seemed more majestic than I had heard them in years. The sermon was apparently written just for our family. God had produced a miracle before our very eyes and I was thankful beyond expression.

The following evening Steve arrived home with his hair cropped, sporting a neatly pressed shirt and slacks. The transformation was unbelievable. The metamorphosis from a "punk rocker" to a good looking "college preppie" was as staggering as anything I had ever witnessed. His mother ran and threw her arms around him and then scrambled for the Polaroid for a dozen or more pictures. I knew how the father in the parable of the Prodigal Son felt when he slaughtered the fatted calf and threw a huge party for his lost son who had returned. All the years of praying and worrying and now my son was home.

The trip to Tennessee was planned for mid-December following Kevin's appearance in court. Steve moved back into the house and was the happiest I can remember. All he could talk about was going back to school and how wonderful the Lord had been to him. I would hear him going through house singing, which was not at all like the Steve I had known. Everything was positive. Even the government was no longer all evil and Kevin was receiving his just reward.

Kevin had his day in court and to the amazement of everybody concerned, he convinced the judge that he was not a criminal and shouldn't be sent to jail but needed drug rehabilitation. He was sentenced to finish his term in a rehabilitation center in southern Arizona.

Comfortable that Kevin was secure in his placement Steve and

159

I took off for Atlanta. We spent that night in the city and did some sightseeing in the area the following day. Then it was off to Tennessee to see the college.

Southern College was a happy experience. Steve liked the campus as well as the people he met. With his previous grade point average there was no question that he would be accepted for the following semester. I felt like a kid again myself. We had so much fun in everything that we did. After leaving Tennessee we returned to Atlanta and caught the train for New Orleans.

The train trip was a blast. Steve spent a lot of his time going through the cars waiting on people. He would run and get snacks or drinks for folks. He helped some of the elderly folks store their luggage in the overhead bins and find pillows and blankets. The rest of the time was spent visiting and just plain enjoying the scenery as we cruised through Georgia, Alabama and Mississippi. Everybody enjoyed Steve and remarked to me about my wonderful son. It was difficult to know exactly how to act. It was all so new, so completely different.

In New Orleans we stayed in a hotel on the banks of the Mississippi were we could sit and watch the large boats and barges going up and down the river. In the evening we went to old town New Orleans and listened to a group of black folks playing authentic Dixieland music. We walked and talked and laughed until I had to call a halt to the whole thing before I dropped in my tracks. It had been the best dad-and-son event ever.

The following morning started abruptly with a phone call from Sherrie telling us that Kevin had escaped from the rehabilitation center and was now considered a fugitive. No one had a clue were he might be. He had no money and only the clothes on his back. This put a damper on the day but we decided to go ahead with our plans to meet army friends from our time in Germany and have a sightseeing tour of the city.

We all met shortly after breakfast and spent the day seeing the sights including riding the trolley and experiencing the reality of the old mansions on St. Charles Street. The boat trip down the Mississippi to the zoo as well as Bourbon Street by daylight were also highlights. It was a great day and so good to be with friends who hadn't seen Steve since he was two years old.

Regardless of all the fun we were having a cloud with the name Kevin written on it hovered over our activities. Knowing that Kevin was on the run once again was devastating. I tried to put on a good front for Steve, just I am sure he did for me. No one was fooling anybody. We were both worried.

The flight home was anxious with expectation of what might be waiting at the other end. Nothing had changed by the time we arrived home. Once again there was nothing to do but wait for a call from the police or Kevin.

Neither came until the day before Christmas as the family was leaving for Flagstaff for our annual Christmas holiday with snow, skiing, and family fun. The officer that phoned simply said, "We have your son in custody once again. Rest easy."

The drive to Flagstaff was subdued as was Christmas and skiing. It was probably at that point that I gave in to the idea that we were not going to have Kevin as an active member of the family for a long time, if ever. This was a difficult concept but one that had to be faced. I threw myself into the realization that we had three other children at home who at that moment all seemed to be doing well. They needed our attention.

Steve came to me and expressed his heartbreak over the fact that he had the opportunity of going to school and knowing the Lord while "brother" seemed to be so lost and far away. We decided to make him the recipient of our prayers constantly.

Preparations for Steve's departure for college were mingled with court appearances for Kevin and pleas for "a good lawyer to get me out of this mess. I can't live in this environment with these people." One lawyer had promised to get him off for a retainer of only ten thousand dollars. Kevin gave his solemn word that if I would help him get out this time he would straighten up and fly right and never get into trouble again. The statement was so convincing that I almost gave in to his appeal. My final decision was, inasmuch as he had gotten himself into this situation it would have to be up to him to get himself out of it this time. That was the hardest decision I ever made. It was a good decision. One I would have to preserve.

With every piece of luggage that could be mustered, Steve along with his mother and me boarded a flight for Atlanta and a new start as a college freshman. The drive to the college in the rental car with Steve at the wheel and old Dad relaxed in the back seat presented a new dimension to the already radical change that had taken place in our lives.

We arrived at the college early in the morning and immediately began the process of matriculation. The fact that Steve had not spent much time in high school made the entire process completely foreign to him. While he took his entrance exams, we were out buying bedding and towels for his dorm room. This was a part of college life he had never considered.

He finished all of his entrance examinations with flying colors and everything looked good on paper. However, I sensed that his emotional maturity was far behind the other freshman there that day. He tried to be friendly yet it was apparent that his efforts were forced and his social skills were severely lacking. We talked about the fact that he had not had the experience that many of the others might have had.

His answer to any counsel was, "Oh, Dad, loosen up. You worry too much about the small stuff. Relax and enjoy the ride. Remember that I have probably learned more about life in my time out on the street than they ever learned in the classroom. I'm sure I can teach them a thing or two." Out came the old familiar phrase: "Anyhow if they don't like me the way I am, that's their problem." Then he coined a new phrase. "This is a Christian school so they have to love me the way I am."

This lack of understanding about life concerned me more than I had realized but I knew there was little I could do about it now. I chose to focus on his recent conversion and desire to improve his life. The rest would be in God's hands.

We stayed for the weekend and joined Steve at the college church for Sabbath services. The service was more inspirational than most and closed with communion. Steve asked us to take part with him in the foot-washing service where we washed each others' feet and knelt and prayed together in a secure family bond. The Lord's Supper that followed was filled with meaning for all of us. At the conclusion Steve shared with us his desire to be baptized as soon as possible. The spiritual high reached its peak as we stood with Steve between us and sang a hymn. The service was concluded with the three of us in a season of prayer led by Steve.

Back home again in Phoenix the reality of life hit hard. The spiritual high that we experienced with Steve stood in marked contrast to the depression we experienced when we realized that Kevin was going to prison. His previous "frequent flyer miles," when added to his newest charges of armed robbery and unlawful flight, gave him enough points to guarantee at least five years free room and board at one of our finer local penitentiaries. The dye had been cast. There was nothing more that we could do. This time he would have to face the music and pay the fiddler. It was with ambivalence that I gave in to the awareness that Kevin would be away for a long time. This was going to be a new way of life for all of us.

26

A Call to Perfection

Steve's calls from the school were warm and full of love for the Lord. Each call was more enthusiastic than the previous one. His major concern was that he was required to take too many secular classes such as English and Math and not enough in religion. He had some concern that the secular classes were a little too worldly for a Christian school. Overall he found the environment of the college to be to his liking and very spiritual.

I was a little concerned that he wasn't entering in with the other students as much as he should. He told me that he ate most of his meals alone in the cafeteria reading his Bible. The girls seemed immature to him and "more interested in their appearance than in the Lord."

I was in hopes that meeting a nice Christian girl might enhance the college experience, but none of the young ladies seemed to attain the necessary standard to attract him. The calls home became more frequent as the semester went on. I was beginning to get the feeling he was extremely lonely. I asked him about it and he told me he missed us a lot but otherwise he was too busy to think about much of anything other than his studies.

In mid-April I received a call from Steve late in the evening. He began with a whispered, "Dad." I knew from previous experience this particular greeting meant I was about to receive an important revelation that was not only earth shaking but something no one else had ever heard about.

"Dad," he started in," have you ever heard about the Latter Rain in the Bible?"

"Yes, sure I have," I said. "I studied about it in school. Apparently it refers to the outpouring of the Holy Spirit just before the Lord returns. What is it you would like to know?"

"I don't need to know nothing," came the reply. "I just wanted to know if you realize that we are in the midst of the Latter Rain and that it is almost over and the Lord is coming real soon."

"Yes," I said. "I know we are living in the last days and that at the time of the end, the Bible teaches that there will be an outpouring of the Holy Spirit that has been referred to as the Latter Rain."

"No, Dad," his voice was beginning to rise. "You don't get it. I have been going to a group of meetings off campus and they are telling us that we are actually in the Latter Rain right now and the world will be coming to an end real soon. Most of us will be lost if we don't get out of here."

"What do you mean, 'get out of here'?" I asked.

"We have to wake up and get out of ourselves and the worldly influence around us. Do you know that the Bible teaches that if we don't rebuke others for their sins we will be held responsible for their wrongs just as if we had committed the sin ourselves? We are the watchmen on the wall. We must rebuke the sinners."

He started talking faster and faster. "Do you know that there is only one interpretation of the Bible? The teachers at the college are teaching us things that are not scriptural. The college is becoming corrupt just like the schools of the prophets in the Old Testament. It's getting real bad, Dad. We all need to wake up and flee from the things of the world. Do you know that even the amount of food we eat and the clothes we wear and the cars we drive are a sin?"

"Hold on," I threw in. "You're getting a little off the wall it seems to me. Things at the school are nowhere near perfect, but you have a large group of well-educated professors that have spent years of their lives studying the scriptures and other historical writings. Why would you want to take the opinion of one person verses all the education of the professors at the school?"

"That's the point, Dad," he came back. "They have all of this worldly education and are teaching false doctrine. God is no longer a part of the school."

"How do you know all this?" I questioned.

"These meetings, Dad. The Bible teaches that even the most elect will be fooled in the last days. That is exactly what is happening to all these teachers with the big worldly degrees. They have been fooled into believing false teachings just like the Bible says is going to happen in the last days. There is only one interpretation of the Bible."

"You know, son," I said, trying to keep my voice under control, "I believe that there is only one true interpretation of the Bible. The fact remains we may not all see things the same way all of the time."

"That's the point, Dad. Everyone wants to interpret the Bible their own way when, if you read it correctly, you will know what it means. Do you get the point, Dad? It is just like in Old Testament times. The devil has invaded our schools. If we don't get out we are going to be lost. Dad, this is real serious. The Latter Rain is almost over. We need to wake up and get out! We have to be perfect before Jesus comes or we will be lost. There isn't much time."

"Son," I suggested, "why don't you go in and talk to your religion professor about this? What do you know about the guy who is giving the off campus talks anyway? Is he educated?"

"He isn't educated like from a worldly school. He has studied a lot on his own and the Holy Spirit has shown him that so much of what is being taught in our schools is of the world. Time is short. Christian schools shouldn't be teaching things like mathematics and engineering. They even have what they call the "Clown Ministry." These are all things of the world and we are not to be earthlings.

"The only thing that we should be reading is the Bible. One of my classes even asked us to do some of our studying from a worldly newspaper. And that was a religion class, or a so-called religion class." With that he said, "I have to go. I'll call you in a day or two." He clicked off.

His next call came a couple of days later. This time his voice was even more intense and mysterious.

"Dad," he began, "have you been giving any thought to what I told you about the Latter Rain?"

"Yes," I replied. "I have given it a lot of thought."

"Then you understand that I need to move quickly before it is too late don't you?" he whispered. "We are in the midst of the Latter

Rain and time is running out. According to Lev. 19:17, we must rebuke our neighbor frankly so we won't share in his guilt." Then he abruptly changed to another subject. "Dad, do you believe in the Ten Commandments?"

"Yes, of course I do," I answered, "why do you ask?"

"Because you drive a Cadillac and that is breaking the Ten Commandments."

"What does driving a Cadillac have to do with breaking the Commandments?" I asked, "I drive a Cadillac because I am a physician and need a dependable car. Cadillac fits my needs."

"Hold it!" Steve went on. "The Bible clearly states we are not to covet. Driving a Cadillac is coveting. So that is breaking a Commandment. As a matter of fact my sisters are coveting too."

"What are they doing to covet?" I inquired.

"Have you ever noticed all of the clothes they have in their closets? That is coveting in its worst form.

"Most of the people in the church are hypocrites because they are not following the Bible. I have to rebuke these people or take the responsibility for their transgressions. This is serious stuff, Dad. Marty tells us that the church and the college and its teachings are leading us astray. We have to be watchmen on the wall and warn the people about what is happening. You know there is only one interpretation of the Bible. All we have to do is read the Word and we will know what is right.

"Right now we have to stop everything we are doing and become perfect. That means we have to get out of the world and give up all of our earthly desires. The end is near. I can't afford to lose any time getting myself ready for the Lord to come."

He took a breath so I barged into the conversation.

"Steve, stop and think about what you are saying. You are making it your responsibility to save the entire world. Christ did that when He died on the cross. It isn't your duty to decide who is sinning and who is not. That is up to God.

"There is no way that we can become perfect of ourselves. Our perfection comes through Christ and salvation is a free gift that Christ has given us. As for the interpretation of the Bible, I am sure there is only one true interpretation of the Bible. But just because you see it one way doesn't mean that your way is that true interpretation."

"Yea, Dad. Marty said you would probably respond that way because everybody wants to interpret the scriptures their own way. That is why most of the world is going to be lost!"

"Who is this Marty guy anyway?" I was beginning to get angry. "What makes you think he has all of the answers?"

"He is a preacher who has learned to understand the Bible by taking it for what it says and not for what others think it says," Steve answered.

"Have you asked any of the teachers at the college about any of this?" I asked.

"No, Dad," he replied. "That's the problem. The teachers at the college are all being misled and are teaching worldly heresy just like the Bible teaches will happen in the last days. Surely you know even the very elect will be deceived at the end. That is exactly what is going on in our schools today. I just need to get out of here before it is too late. Don't you understand, Dad?"

"Steve, try and listen to me." I tried not to sound judgmental. "First of all, I'm not sure you understand just what it means to covet. A person can have nice things without coveting. Besides coveting is an attitude within one's own self. Unless they tell another person how they feel there is no way you can tell if they are coveting a thing or not.

"It isn't your responsibility to straighten out all the ills of the world. Salvation is a very personal relationship between you and your savior. Don't look to others. Keep your eyes focused on the Lord.

"Just because someone else is a hypocrite doesn't have anything to do with your relationship with Christ. Furthermore you can work your little fingers to the bone and you will never earn salvation. It's not what you do. It's who you know! Salvation is a free gift of God. There is nothing you or I can do to change that.

"Please son," I begged. "At least, if you don't feel comfortable talking to your teachers, talk to your roommate or some of your other friends and get more than one opinion. I don't want you to be deceived any more that you want to be. However, I sincerely believe there is always more than one side to every story. Remember the Bible teaches that no man knows the day nor the hour the Lord will return. Good admonition would be to plan your life as if you have an eternity to live and live your life as if it were going to end tomorrow."

Steve interrupted. "That's the problem, Dad, everyone thinks they have forever to get ready and they don't realize that we are in the time of the end. This is the Latter Rain.

"Most of the churches of today are teaching false teachings just the way the Bible says it is going to happen. It is going to be just the same way it was in the days of Noah when only eight people were saved. Our own church has become Babylon. You know what that means. We are the ones that are going to be lost. So you can see that even the very elect are being deceived at this very minute."

"Steve," I pleaded, "think this thing through and make sure you understand what you are saying. Give it over to the Lord and pray. You need to understand that the verse doesn't say that even the very elect will be deceived. It says they could be deceived if that were possible. I believe the admonition here is to study and keep a close walk with the Lord so that these things won't deceive us."

I tried to lighten the conversation by asking how thing were going with the studying and with school. I was informed that all the teachings of the college were of "mammon" and not of God.

Steve ended the call with, "Don't worry, Dad. You are in my prayers." He hung up. I sat for a long time in silence and prayer. How could everything be going so wrong once again? Now that drugs and alcohol were no longer a concern the very root of all I had tried to promote had become the culprit. The statement that for every good thing God has made, Satan has a counterfeit rang loud and clear in my mind. The question at this point was how to convey this to Steve.

I started by researching the people that were putting out these teachings. To my astonishment I found there is a very large group within the Seventh-day Adventist Church who often go under the name of The Independent Movement or Adventist Reform. They refer to themselves as going back to the basic teachings of the church. They have their own publications, camp meetings, and even a college somewhere in the south. There are apparently many branches to this loosely organized group but the teachings seemed to me to all be the same: "salvation by works." There didn't appear to be a move to pull away from the church in many of the groups. Rather to remain within the church and convince the members of the evil of the church itself. The Reform group apparently has their own structural organization.

The group in which Steve had become involved seemed to be independent of even the "Independent Movement." This particular group was teaching separation from the world and isolation to a more communal type of living. This environment had been established in a place unknown to me called Liberty, Tennessee.

My first thought was, I hope they don't ask Steve to go out there for the summer and pump him full of all their weird ideas. That fear was quickly realized with the next phone call a few days later.

"Dad," he began, "I am going to have to leave school!"

"You are going to have to do what?" I screamed into the phone.

"Don't get excited, Dad," Steve said quietly. "I have to leave the college and go to the farm to prepare for the Lord to come."

"When are you going to go?" I asked.

"Tomorrow," came his reply.

"But, Steve." I could hardly speak. "You have less then a month left to finish the semester. Then you can go."

"You still don't get it do you, Dad? This is the time of the end and we are in the Latter Rain. There may not be a month left before the Lord comes. I need to put away all the things of the world and get back to the basic teachings of the Bible. They will be here to pick me up in the morning. I will give you a call in a few weeks. Don't worry. God will take care of me!" Then there was a dial tone.

I wondered how, if the Lord were coming before the end of school, Steve could wait for several weeks to call home? Several weeks did pass before the first call came from the "farm." Steve's voice was in a whisper.

"Why are you whispering?" I asked.

"They are all in the next room studying the *Spirit of Prophecy* and praying. We do this about eight hours a day. The rest of the time we work in the garden and Marty's wife cooks fresh vegetables for our meals. We aren't allowed to do gluttony and we sleep for only a couple of hours a night. Most of the night is spent on our knees in prayer."

"Is Marty where I can speak to him?" I asked.

"Sure, I think so but you can only talk for a minute."

Marty came to the phone. He was very polite as he told me that Steve was a very fortunate young man to have found the truth before it was too late. Marty asked me if I was aware that there is only one interpretation of the Bible. I told him I was, but that I didn't necessarily believe that just because he said it was true made it etched in stone. He let me know how sorry he was that I did not have the intelligence to see what Steve had accomplished. At least that's the way it sounded to me. He thanked me for speaking with him then told me Steve would call again in a few weeks when he was better settled. Then I heard the old familiar dial tone.

The two months that followed seemed more like two years but finally the phone call came. It was Steve. He nonchalantly asked if I would mind reimbursing the folks at the farm for the bus ticket they had bought him for his trip home. No reason was given and I didn't ask. I simply said, "Sure, why not?"

Steve arrived by air the following afternoon without apology for the luxurious plane trip. The word "coveting" never came up either. The boy that stepped off of the plane was a complete stranger. Steve, who was already much too thin when he went away to college had lost an additional seventeen pounds during his stay on the farm. His head was shaved and although it was a hundred and twelve degrees in Phoenix that day he was wearing a flannel shirt with long selves buttoned at the wrist and the neck. He had on suspenders holding up his baggy jeans and high laced hiking boots. The final touch was the five or six long hairs hanging from his chin that were supposed to represent a beard.

I ran to him and hugged him. Then we drove home in my Cadillac. He had no luggage. He explained to me that he had given everything to the needy because he knew he could replace it if he needed too. I felt that something had been lost in the translation but left that one alone.

The rebuking began almost the minute we walked through the doorway. Sherrie was just coming in from the pool wearing a very modest one-piece swimsuit. This she was informed was completely wrong and had no place in a Christian home. Without comment Sherrie retreated to the bedroom and put on a floor length robe.

No explanation was ever made as to why Steve had decided to

come home. He did let us know that he would be spending most of his day in his room studying and in prayer.

There were a number of simple suggestions that Steve was convinced would improve our Christian lives. One biggie was the amount of food we were eating. After all it is a sin to overeat (which is probably true). The type of food should be confined to raw or natural foods. Water should not be taken with our meals. Any animal products were out of the question. That included butter, milk or eggs.

TV was a no-no, as was the playing of music on tapes or the radio. Voices were to be soft, in prayer-like tones. If any of these things were inadvertently overlooked we were kindly but firmly rebuked. The question of how to survive this new challenge in our home was a serious one. After about two weeks of trying to work out a compromise, I came to the conclusion a meeting of the minds was mandatory.

Friday evening we called Steve into the kitchen. I was armed with Bibles—several translations for clarity of interpretation—and Bible commentaries. The topic of the evening: "How to be a Pharisee in this modern world without even trying." I pointed out how Christ had criticized the Pharisees over and over again for their legalistic behavior and how similar Steve's behavior was to theirs. We read multiple passages from the Bible and the commentaries. I went into great detail about how disruptive this had been to our household. Steve sat in wide-eyed wonder.

"I had no idea I was doing this to you," he apologized. "I thought I was witnessing to you and helping you in your Christian walk. I didn't mean to hurt you. If I have, please forgive me. I won't let it happen again."

We all hugged and had prayer together. We went to bed with a huge burden removed from our lives. Steve had been so reasonable and understanding I could hardly believe it. I gave thanks to God for the large number of hurdles He had taken us over during the past few years.

The following morning after church Steve met me in the lobby. "Dad!" he shouted from half way across the room. "I am so happy this morning."

"I am too, son," I said in softer tones. "I really am glad we were able to get things settled the way we did last night."

"No, Dad," he went on. "I'm happy because I'm being persecuted for my faith. The Bible tells us that in the last days the faithful will be persecuted for their beliefs even by their families. I feel so blessed that you are persecuting me."

I don't know why but for some reason the statement took me by surprise. I just stood frozen with mouth open amazement. "Say what?"

27

Watchman at the Gate

C amp-meeting was scheduled for the following week. Steve asked to join the family for the entire ten days. I was ecstatic with the idea as I was only going to be able to attend the weekend meetings and then return to work. Sherrie and the girls were less enthusiastic as they planned to stay for the entire session.

Steve arrived in full camp-meeting attire. He was wearing the customary long sleeved flannel shirt buttoned at both the wrist and the neck. The baggy blue jeans were hanging loosely from a pair of red suspenders. Combat boots completed the ensemble, which had been chosen to survive the entire ten days without change. There was no need of luggage as that would show signs of coveting. I asked about the need for a toothbrush because of his obsessive use of garlic, but was assured that if the need for dental hygiene should arise, a swish of water in his mouth would suffice.

Steve presented himself as the watchman at the gate of the youth chapel. He positioned himself with Bible in hand, open and ready to rebuke or chastise any unsuspecting youth who might inadvertently wander toward the chambers of deception. During his time at the camp he never entered the chapel himself having been forewarned of the heresy that was being preached inside.

Several of the pastors attempted to enter into dialogues of positive reinforcement with Steve. They were promptly showered with an unintelligible barrage of theological minutia. Unanimously they were informed of their serious deception and radical misinterpretation of scripture. Any attempts to befriend Steve were met with suspicion of conspiracy.

The total camp-meeting experience was a spiritual disaster. Steve left with a reputation of being a weirdo if not completely insane. He himself felt good about the whole episode knowing that he had done God's will by rebuking sinners. Steve saw the group as Babylon due for immediate destruction with hellfire and brimstone. The ordeal was a sad commentary on Steve's lack of social skills. His zero tolerance for the beliefs of others coupled with a complete misunderstanding of what the scriptures really teach completed the picture.

Things didn't improve much at home over the next few months. The cute little girlfriend, Cindy, emerged in a pretty outfit with a skirt just slightly above the knees and a sleeveless blouse on the first day after the family returned from camp-meeting. She didn't make the same mistake the second day when she arrived in a floor length skirt, long sleeves and a high buttoned collar.

Steve and Cindy spent long hours together. Most of their time was spent sitting in separate chairs, reading the Bible in silence. Any auditory voice was in a whisper. Steve informed me the admonition of the Bible was that "women should be seen and not heard. Women were placed on this earth to serve and obey their man." I had read about the strictness of the Amish people and their dating practices. Steve and Cindy made those people look ostentatious.

Early in December Steve came to me in tears. He was wearing a pair of Levis and a short sleeved shirt, with no suspenders.

"Dad," he whimpered, "I have been such a fool. I need your forgiveness. I know that I have been a real jerk and have made all of your lives miserable. I don't know how I ever let those guys in Tennessee convince me of all the garbage that they did. I have been studying the *Spirit of Prophecy* and see that even though our schools may not be perfect we do need to have an education. There really is a place in our lives for other things than the Bible. My buddy Brad showed me there are a lot of subjects that speak of God and His creation that don't come directly from the Bible." Then he looked at me very seriously and asked, "Would you give me one more chance and let me go to Pacific Union College and finish the education that I started? This time I am sure I have come far enough so I can finish without getting off the track."

Who is this man? I asked myself. He's not the same kid that was living in the house the other day.

"What has brought about this great change in attitude?" I asked. "Just a few days ago you were totally against any form of organized religion or schools associated with the church."

"Brad thinks that I am fanatical and have gone off the deep end spiritually. He thinks that I am much like a Pharisee. He went to P.U.C. and says that it isn't like the other church schools and is very spiritual. The campus is up in the mountains and has woods all around so there isn't much room for the world to come in."

"What do you want to study?" I asked.

"Probably theology," he replied. "Or I might even go into biology and head toward something that is related to the medical field."

He kept rambling on and on. I was confused. My brain wouldn't let any of the thoughts in. I wanted to believe him and yet experience told me not to. I just stood there in dumb disbelief. Finally I came back to reality when he asked again, "Well, Dad, what do you think? Will you do it?"

"I guess so," I uttered with no emotion, "but this time there will have to be some major changes. You will have to get with the program and stop being such a freak. And you will have to do all of the paperwork and there will be no trip to look at the campus. You will have to take it sight unseen." Then I added, "You are going to have to work and pay for part of your school bill too." There was neither kindness nor enthusiasm in my voice. There was no way that a person could have such a radical change in such a short time and I wasn't about to fall victim to his antics another time.

"It all sounds good to me," he blurted. Then he gave me a big hug and said, "I love you, Dad," and off he went. Stunned would have been an understatement for how I felt. All I could do was stand there and pray, "Please let him succeed this time, please."

The next few weeks of preparation for college once again were a blast. Steve was truly a new man. There was laughter and fooling around intermingled with serious Bible study and positive discussions. The transition was unbelievable. With all the arrangements completed we were ready to head for Northern California for another go around with college.

The flight was phenomenal. Steve boarded the plane dressed in a shirt and tie, sport coat, slacks and dress shoes. He gave the appearance of a junior executive. The flight attendants hovered around us during the entire flight. They laughed and joked with him non-stop. He was even able to con them out of an extra dinner which he devoured with no thought of gluttony.

The flight was over before we knew it and we were loading our luggage into the rental car and heading into the city. We checked into a hotel at Fisherman's Wharf. We cruised the wharf watching the preparation of shell fish for immediate consumption and the icing of larger fish for storage. The smell added to the intrigue.

We hopped a cable car for a ride to the top of Nob Hill and dinner at the Tonga Room in the Fairmont Hotel. We ate Oriental and listened to the musicians on a raft in the pool in the center of the dining room. Then we had a brief walk down California Street to China Town. We browsed the shops and little markets and watched the street performers along the way. We finally arrived back at the hotel at midnight. I dropped into bed and pulled the covers over my head and told Steve to sit up as long as he wanted, but I was off to dreamland.

Steve put a towel over the light on the table in order not to disturb me, and switched on the TV. What an absolutely perfect day, I thought to myself as I drifted off. I'm not sure just exactly how long I slept or what it was that awakened me. I did wake up to find Steve slumped over the table clutching a bottle of Jim Beam in his hand. He was drunker than drunk.

"Steve," I shouted, "what in the world are you doing?"

"Just partaking in a little alcoholic beverage to get me in the mood for greater and better things to come," he said with a laugh.

I tried not to lose my temper but made it plain that I felt he was out of order.

"Oh, Dad," he slurred, "don't take it so seriously. I just need a little something to loosen me up before I fall into the routine of college life."

"But, Steve, this is so unlike you lately. Why are you doing it?"

"This isn't going to be a pattern, Dad. All I want is a little cheer to get me up the mountain. I thought you were asleep and didn't expect you to know about it in the first place. So why don't you go back to sleep like a good father and I will go to bed in a few minutes." He let out one of his war whoops that I thought would land us out on the street.

"Steve," I shouted, "you are going to get us thrown out of this place. Keep it down."

"OK, Dad," he said as he took another stiff swig of booze. "I'm on my way to bed. See you in the morning." The light went out and all was silent.

Like so many similar nights I didn't sleep much that night either. I tried to believe that it wasn't all that important but in my mind I felt it was serious. The following morning Steve acted as if nothing unusual had happened. As we headed off for the college I wondered if he had in fact even remembered anything about our conversation the night before.

The college was met with little show of emotion as was the dorm and his living arrangements. He was informed that because of his late registration he would not be assigned a permanent roommate. He might be moved around several times before he would be settled. This didn't matter one way or the other to Steve. He told the dean that he had a sleeping bag and a razor and his Bible and these were all that he needed to be comfortable. The dean raised his eyebrows but didn't challenge the idea.

I was bewildered and confused as I drove down the mountain in the direction of the airport. All of the hopes I had felt just a few hours before seemed to be in question. Was Steve really sincere about finishing his education? What was his religious experience now? Was he drinking and using drugs again? Was I being "suckered" again? Or was I just a lousy father who couldn't put any faith in his son? A father who was blowing everything out of proportion.

I beat and tormented myself all the way home and finally decided not to tell Sherrie about Mr. Jim Beam at the hotel. My cover was blown immediately by the expression on my face when she asked me how things had gone. I confided in her that I did have concerns but felt rather positive about things in general. We discussed the influence that other Christian students could have on him and even the possibility of meeting a nice young lady that could draw his interest in the right direction.

Apparently registration went smoothly and Steve was able to get into most of the classes he wanted. His phone calls home were filled with positive comments about his classes and teachers. It seemed that he had found a good balance and things were going well. He had been able to enroll in a number of religion classes and was content to take a few of the more worldly requirements such as English and math. Several remodeled utility rooms had been made into dorm rooms for overflow students. Steve had been lucky enough to get one. He seemed to enjoy living alone. I was a disappointed that he had been deprived of the social aspects of having a roommate.

The phone calls made it seem as if he had finally found his station in life and college was his bag. When I asked him about the food he informed me that he got most of his food from the market and took it out in to the woods to eat where he could study and pray. When I asked him about the social functions such as the Saturday night programs, he informed me he had much too much studying to take time off just to play around. There was no mention of girls or any special friends.

In mid-March we received a phone call asking if we could come to the college on the following Sunday for Parents' Day. He told us there would be an afternoon program for both parents and friends. The evening banquet would be just for father and son. A tour of the campus and the dorms was also on the agenda. This would be a good time to meet some of his teachers and his friends.

"Steve," I said, "why in the world did you wait so long to tell us about this?"

"I guess I kept forgetting about it," he answered. "But I really do want you to come if you can."

"I will have to do a lot of juggling to get my weekend call covered and my surgery schedule rearranged on Friday. We will give it our best shot and we will be there if we can."

I was able to find coverage and the schedule was redone. Airline tickets were purchased and off we went on two days notice. We arrived on campus early Sunday morning and found Steve waiting for us outside the dorm. It was great to see him and he seemed equally excited about seeing us. We were shown through the dorm and had a brief glance at his room which reminded me of how I might expect a cell in a convent to look. There was a small window and a small cot with a sleeping bag and a number of neatly folded clothes in the corner. I commented that it looked cozy. We headed for greater and better things.

Steve told us that he really didn't want to get all dressed up for the afternoon parents' thing. He didn't want to sit and listen to a bunch of dull talks with a bunch of people he didn't know. He asked if the three of us could just drive into town and have lunch together. The idea appealed to me so we headed down the hill. During lunch Steve informed me that he had failed to get tickets for the Father-Son banquet. Then added that he really didn't want to go to a stuffy banquet in the first place and would rather just spend the time with us.

We spent most of the day in town and returned to the campus in the late afternoon. We took a walking tour of the place for an hour or so. Returning to the dorm we sat in the lobby for a while and made small talk until it become apparent that Steve was running out of anything to talk about. It appeared it would be well for us to think about getting back to the airport for a possible earlier flight home.

As we left Steve seemed genuinely pleased that we had come. We on the other hand were perplexed. There had been no introductions to friends or teachers. We hadn't attended any of the events of the day. Conspicuously, most of the other students spoke to Steve as they passed, but never once did I hear anyone call him by name. Just as interesting was the fact that he never introduced us to anyone by name. The idea struck us hard that he was living a life of complete isolation from the rest of the school. The thought of the loneliness that he must be experiencing gave me a horrible feeling in the pit of my stomach. Everything that we had hoped for seemed to have gone out the window once again.

I debated whether or not to call him from the airport, but chose to wait until it seemed more natural before asking all the questions that were building up in side of me. At the first opportunity I called and asked, "Steve, are you really happy up there at the college?"

"Yeah, Pop," he replied. "Why do you ask?"

"Well when we were at the school you didn't introduce us to any of your friends. I guess I just wondered if you were having a hard time meeting kids and making friends."

"Na, Dad. I really haven't wanted to make friends with most of them in the first place. All the guys can think about is girls and the girls can only think about clothes and money. They all do all sorts of worldly things like going to movies and watching TV. Most of the Saturday night programs that the school puts on aren't fit for a Christian to attend either. And besides, Dad, they all think that because I want to be a Christian, I am the weird one. So I just kinda keep to myself."

"Oh, Steve," I said softly, "I wish we could have talked about it the other night. Maybe we could have helped."

"Na, Pop. They just seem to think that I am the one who is weird. If they were real Christians they would accept me the way I am. I really don't need them anyhow .Don't worry about it, pop. I'm not, so why should you?"

"But don't you feel lonely all alone up there?" I asked.

"Not really," he came back, "I really have had so much more experience in life than most of the kids up here they just can't understand what is going on in the first place. So why should I bother?"

After we hung up my heart was broken with the grief of such a sad life and so little that I could do about it. I prayed, "God, give me the strength to help my son in this hour of need. I feel so helpless and have so little knowledge about how to help him. Please, Lord, give me the ability to help him turn his life around." I sat alone for hours in sorrow for the young boy so hopelessly alone, with every advantage at his fingertips, but without the perception of how to grasp it.

The semester was finished successfully with slightly less than average grades. His return home was accompanied by a letter that suggested that unless he were willing to make some major adjustments in his attitude, it would be best for him to seek another college to complete his education.

When I read the letter I immediately got on the phone to the dean of students. The major concerns the dean expressed were, Steve's playing of loud rock music in the dorm at midnight, the war whoops he let out in the halls at anytime of day or night, the wearing of a Nazi uniform on campus, and Steve's failure to heed any of the suggestions that were offered by the hall monitors or the deans.

When I mentioned all of these things to Steve he simply remarked, "Get real, Dad. I was just goofing off and they don't know how to take a joke. It wasn't a real Nazi uniform in the first place. Really, Dad, it is all just a bunch of nonsense and they don't know what they are talking about. I really wouldn't want to go back there again anyhow."

"Listen, Steve. If you ever want to get along in this world you are going to have to learn to live by the rules. You can't barge through life with total disregard for others and expect them to accept you the way you are just because they have to. You have to learn to have respect for other people's feelings too. They really don't have to bend to you all the time."

With that Steve stood up with his arms waving and started shouting, "There isn't a Christian among them. They are all a bunch of hypocrites. I don't need that garbage and if they can't accept me the way I am, forget it!" With that he was out of there.

28

Framework of Destiny

In retrospect the five years that followed seemed to have been an experiment in futility interspersed with occasional interludes of relevance.

Shortly after finishing the Academy, Teri married a young man she had met at work. They had similar backgrounds having attended Adventist academies. They also shared a similar rebellious spirit that led them into questionable activities. Their first baby was born a year and a half after they were married. It didn't take the new father long to realize that babies were not for him so he left for greener pastures. Teri and the new baby returned home to live with us until things could be worked out.

During the same time frame Sherrie and I had agreed to accept an inmate from the state prison into our home. We were to serve as sponsors as he moved into the real world. We had never intended that he and our daughter and granddaughter would all be living in the house at the same time. But, as fate would have it, that's the way it happened. The two struck up a strong friendship from the start and in a short time chose to set up housekeeping together in an apartment across town.

Cindi graduated from the Academy and went away to Walla Walla, ironically to pursue the field of criminal justice. Her desire to achieve her Mrs. degree didn't materialize so after the first year she decided to return home. She plunged into voice lessons with great enthusiasm and became a sought-after soloist in our area.

Kevin was released from prison and came home for a few

months until he was able to reestablish his residence at a slightly more prestigious state penitentiary near Phoenix. His only offense was the illegal use of stolen credit cards and the breaking of parole by crossing the state line. After being returned from California he was able to settle into his new location to finish the sentence that had been previously set in motion.

Steve's life hit new spiritual highs and new depressing lows. He moved in and out of the house several times and was usually asked to leave due to his inability to conform. My father asked Steve to come and live with him for companionship. He asked him to leave a short time later in order to lengthen his life. It was a terribly frustrating time for everybody. There just didn't seem to be any way to get through to Steve and make him see that it was up to him to try and get along in society.

On a more positive note Cindi was baptized and I joined her in re-baptism. It was a beautiful experience for both of us and a decision I have never regretted. Following my new decision I set out to launch a program to aid members of the church that might be having problems with substance abuse.

At first the idea was met with opposition because of the false idea that it wouldn't be needed in a group of total abstainers. However, our local pastor was extremely optimistic about the idea and made it possible for me to set up an anonymous group within the church. The group was endorsed by the conference while remaining independent of the church in any way.

Brochures were printed and left on the pews without any indication of where they had come from. We established a private phone line that anyone with a problem could call, with the reassurance they would remain anonymous. The meetings were set up using the twelve steps of Alcoholics Anonymous coupled with Christian principles and prayer. The book, Steps to Christ, was used in conjunction with the twelve steps of A.A. The first meeting was attended by five individuals including myself. The group grew rapidly until there were often thirty to thirty-five attending.

Several months after establishing the meetings I received a phone call from a gentleman who identified himself as a Seventh-day Adventist named Pat who had been on drugs for many years. He told me that he had been in treatment centers over and over again and had the feeling he was coming to the "end of the road." His only request was that we allow him to bring his wife with him although she was not an addict. I explained to him that the meetings had been set up for those of us with addiction problems and thought many of the members might feel uncomfortable with an outsider in their midst.

He pleaded with me in a frantically sincere voice. "Please let Sally come with me at least for the first time. I don't think I can do it by myself."

Pat and Sally arrived at the door the following Tuesday evening promptly at seven. The figure before me appeared like a well-worn druggie with long blond hair to his shoulders and a full beard. Tattoos covered both arms. He appeared sedated but stable. His wife was a small, attractive, well dressed lady who appeared to be extremely pregnant. They were welcomed into the house and took their seat on the sofa in the middle of the group. No mention was made that his wife was not a member of the club.

When the time came for Pat to give his testimony everyone sat in stark expectation. He began, "Hi, my name is Pat and I am a drug addict and an alcoholic and I love the Lord and my wife is going to have our first baby in a few weeks and I don't want to be this kind of father to our child." He stopped talking for a long pause then whispered, "I have failed so many times that I just have to make it this time."

There was silence in the room and then it seemed as if everyone began to talk simultaneously. Without exception everyone was there to help him make it this time. After the meeting he confided to me that he was on high doses of Methadone, and had been taking all sorts of other drugs for many years. Many times he had taken an entire month's prescription of Percocet in one sitting. He added that it hardly fazed him. Then he shocked me with his next statement.

"You said tonight in the meeting that if we would ask God to take this thing from us, that He would."

"Yes I believe that," I agreed. "And I believe that you can start going off of your drugs right away but you need to do it slowly in order to allow your system to adjust."

He was very definite as he continued, "I don't have time to go slow with the baby coming and all. I have to be drug-free before it is born so that means I have to quit now. I am going to go off all drugs tonight and give it all to God!"

My faith hit a questionable low just then. I knew that God not only could, but that He would if He were asked. I also knew that people on large amounts of drugs could convulse and die if taken off the drugs too rapidly. He stood staring at me.

"Are we going to practice what we preach or aren't we?" he asked.

I have always believed that there is a great difference between faith and presumption. At that particular instant I wasn't sure with which we were dealing. We talked for a long time that evening and finally concluded that we had to exercise our faith and do it.

I told Pat that he would have to call me every few hours and if there were any signs of convulsions we would have to rush him to the hospital. He began that evening and the next day was the first day of the rest of his drug-free life. Pat was on fire for the Lord—a truly changed man. He brought more new members to the meetings over the next years than anyone else. To this day I consider him to be one of my most loyal friends.

Pat came to help me with the trees in my yard one afternoon and while there, met Steve. There was an immediate bond between them. Steve loved the idea that Pat was on fire for the Lord and had used drugs and alcohol with careless passion. The tattoos and long hair added to the intrigue I'm sure, as well as the fact that Pat ran with the biker crowd and had slipped to rock bottom and bounced back. He had a wife and daughter and preached the love of God. All of which made him the hero of the year. It was apparent from the start that Steve was going to emulate Pat in every way. With Pat as a role model I had hopes that Steve had found the help he needed to take him to the top.

Pat invited Steve to his house and the two of them spent long hours in intense discussions about the Bible and God. They found another common ground, working on the Harley in the garage. Steve admired Pat and though Pat was ten years Steve's senior they considered each other peers. Meeting Pat changed Steve's life. There appeared to be a focus developing and he even began to talk about goals.

Interestingly Steve never attended our meetings but often attended the biker meetings at Pat's house. I asked him about coming to our meetings and he informed me the people at our meetings didn't know much about life the way the guys at Pat's house did. I didn't belabor the point.

Recently I talked with Pat on the phone and told him about the book I was writing about Steve. In the course of the conversation I mentioned that it was my hope that someone out there would benefit from the book and that Steve's life would not have been in vain. Without hesitation Pat exclaimed, "There's no way that Steve's life could have been in vain!"

Then he told me how Steve had become a vital part of their family. To this day his daughter speaks fondly of Steve and tells how much she misses him. Then his voice became somber.

"Steve used to pour out his insides to me. I guess he must have told me everything there was to know about his life. Some of the time I heard things about his younger life that I wish I had never heard. He would go on for hours crying about how horrible his younger life had been."

"Was a lot of it to do with his time in Tennessee?" I asked.

"Yeah, that probably was a turning point but that wasn't all there was to it. Steve was never able to accept the idea of salvation by faith. He could talk about it in great detail and knew all the Bible had to say about it, but just couldn't get the concept that the sacrifice Christ made for us on the cross was sufficient to save him. He felt his sins were so sinister that he had to work to become perfect before God would even consider saving him. Death would be a welcome relief for a person so completely ridden in guilt."

After hanging up I wondered what there could have been in Steve's life to elicit such a comment. I quickly dismissed the thought of asking. I knew that it was none of my business and that if Steve had wanted me to know he would have told me. All that would be accomplished would be to churn things up and possibly make a lot of unhappiness without changing a thing. I decided to leave well enough alone and dismissed it from my mind. At least I tried to dismiss it from my mind. The thought still remains, were there significant things that I should have known about, or even worse, knew about but wasn't clever enough to pick up on? If I had been aware or taken the time to think it through could I have changed the course of events that transpired in Steve's life? Or could it have been simple figments of imagination in a drug-soaked mind that had so completely impregnated his soul? All of these questions have taunted me for years with no possible escape from speculation. I will never know the answers.

Pat and Sallie's lives wove a spiritual web through Steve's life for many years offering a positive influence to a troubled soul. Though Steve showed a degree of increasing maturity as a result of that relationship, the dichotomy in his behavioral pattern was becoming more pronounced. There were times when he would arrive in such a manic phase that I was convinced he was going to fly. The stages of despondency were usually accompanied by drugs and alcohol.

The actual chain of events over the next few years has become somewhat obscured, with only a few events that have stood out in my memory. What remains prominent are Steve's wide mood swings that occurred during that span of time. My reactions to his antics were poor at best. I suffered many an anxious moment over my inability to react with any creativity.

One of my pet peeves was having Steve fly down the aisle in church and land in the pew next to me with a thud. First of all it startled me and secondly it made me angry because of the immaturity exhibited by a young man in his mid-twenties. I usually "screamed" at him in a whisper, "Steve! Cool it! You are acting like a fool!"

He would usually reply with something like, "I love you, Dad. Good to see you too!" Then he would give a little chuckle because he knew he had gotten to me. He repeated this type of action at my father's funeral in mid-June of 1991. The preacher was preaching a short sermon. All the kids were there except Steve. I wondered where he might be and at the same time felt a certain sense of relief not being sure exactly how he might react.

The thought was barely out of my mind when Steve landed in the pew behind me and flung his arms around me from behind.

"Are you sad, Dad?" he asked in a voice that could be heard for three rows in every direction. "After all he was almost ninety four and had a good life. Isn't it great that he didn't have to lie in bed for months and suffer?"

"Later, Steve," I whispered. "This really isn't the time."

"When would there be a better time? After all, this is his funeral," he persisted.

"Later, Steve, we'll talk about it later!" I was quiet but firm. Nothing more was said from the row behind me.

I have often wondered what the reaction would have been if when he landed in the pew next to me I would have put my arm around him and said, "Good to see you in church again this morning, son," or, "Glad you could join us for the funeral." Maybe something simple like, "Sure have missed you a lot this week." Under-reacting really wasn't my style.

Church seemed to be that place for him to demonstrate his lack of concern for a dress code. One week he would arrive outfitted complete with suit and tie and shiny black shoes. The following week he might appear in a vest without a shirt under it and a pair of dirty Levis and sandals. The way he was dressed usually spoke loudly of how the week had gone. If I made any mention about his appearance or behavior I would get the response, "God loves me the way I am so why can't you?"

"I love you the way you are too, but it really doesn't hurt to put your best foot forward for the sake of others," I would argue.

"So what you are saying is that you want me to be a hypocrite just to make everyone else feel good. Is that what you are telling me? You want me to bear false witness just so all the rest of the world can feel good? Why can't you just leave me alone and let me be myself?"

That is a very good question, I thought to myself. Why can't I?

That thought began to plague me the more I let myself think about it. Why couldn't I let Steve alone and just let him be himself? He was a twenty-three-year-old man and I was treating him as if he were a ten-year-old child. It became painfully apparent that I needed to do some serious changing in my own attitude. First of all I would have to put away my own pride and not concern myself with whether he was embarrassing me in front of others or not. Even more important, why was he embarrassing me in the first place? Was I ashamed of him, or was it that I was ashamed of the way I had brought him up?

It was beginning to boil down to the fact that one of us was going to have to change. It was obvious that there wasn't much I could to change him, so it looked as if I would have to be the one to do the changing. I prayed hard and long about the situation and made the commitment that I was going to overlook all of the things that bothered me and start treating him like an adult.

My first opportunity to put my new resolution into practice came in about three weeks on a beautiful Sabbath afternoon as we sat in our living room at the lake. It was one of those carefree times when a few neighbors and our daughter Cindi and her boyfriend had dropped in just to visit. The French doors were open and a cool breeze filled the room.

Then, out of nowhere, Steve exploded into the room. He always seemed to arrive like a genie out of a bottle. One minute the room was empty and then it was filled with Steve. On this particular afternoon he was suddenly standing in the middle of everyone with a piercing, "Hello, what y'all dooun?"

He stood there in a dirty pair of short cut-offs, no shirt or shoes with his hair blown around as if he had just been shot out of a cannon. His eyes were glassy and on his breath the stench of old beer filled the room. From where I was sitting I could see his newest acquisition, a tattoo of a lizard on the back of his left shoulder. After commenting on all of the above except the hair I asked, "Steve, what are you doing here?"

"Just missed y'all so thought I would drop by and say how'dee. I guess by your remarks, you can tell that I have had a little alcoholic beverage to get me up the hill, but I wasn't gonna let a little thing like that stop me from dropping in, now would I? Is it OK if I come in for a few minutes?" By this time the room had emptied and our friends had excused themselves and escaped.

"Of course you can," I answered trying to recall my most recent resolutions. "Sit down and have some supper with us and tell us about all you have been doing."

He started by telling us about his new job. He said he wanted to get away by himself for the weekend so thought he would come to the mountains and say hi to us and then do a little camping. Steve had always been a tremendous camper and seemed to feel comfortable walking deep into the woods alone and setting up camp.

"The guest room is open and you are welcome to use it for as long as you can stay." Then I added in the interest of everyone present, "Grab a hot shower while you are here if you care to!" Then I gave him a half-hearted hug and said, "Nice to have you here, son!"

I wanted to kick myself over my first reaction and was determined to do my best to make up for it during the rest of his stay.

Steve hit the shower and did a little cleaning up. He put a shirt over the ugly lizard tattoo that I had only mentioned briefly in passing. By the time he got out of his twenty minute shower my guilt level for overreacting had hit an appropriate level. I felt like a real heel as Steve came back into the room.

"Steve," I said, "I'm sorry that I jumped all over you about the way you looked when you came into the house. You surprised the living daylights out of me with your impressive entrance. I didn't know that you had been camping. Anyway I am sorry that I jumped all over you in front of everyone and all."

"Don't worry about it, Dad," he replied. "I love you and it is good to see you again. After dinner I think I will throw my sleeping bag in the guest room if you don't mind and catch a little TV before I catch a few zz's."

I knew that the TV thing meant he would be sitting up most of the night watching the tube. There was also the possibility of a few beers finding their way into the house. This was going to be the true test and I was going to give it all I had or know the reason why.

We sat and made small talk while Sherrie finished getting dinner on the table. I was surprised at how pleasant a conversation could be as long as care was taken to circumvent certain subjects. Cindi and her boyfriend stopped in to let us know they wouldn't be staying for dinner so it was just the three of us. Steve made some comment about his sister not wanting to "partake of food with her barbarian brother." We laughed about it and let it go.

The evening was upbeat and the conversation smooth. Most of the talk revolved around the mountains and how beautiful and wholesome the woods were in comparison to the dirty city. Steve asked about the hospital up there and if I thought he might find work in it someday. I thought there would be a good possibility and went so far as to tell him that I would be happy to inquire if he would like me to. He thought that would be a good idea and the fact that he had worked in hospitals for some time would certainly be a plus.

Then he went on to say, "You know, Dad, I have been thinking seriously about going back to school and becoming a surgical scrub tech. I have had a lot of time to watch what they do, and I think it would be easy and I could do it. The course at Gateway College is only a year or a year and a half. Maybe I could even come back and live at home and that way it wouldn't be so expensive."

The part about the school intrigued me. The part about living at home petrified me.

"Well you know how I feel about having an education, and the way I feel about working in the operating room. They are both high on my list of good things to do," I told him. "I think you would be real good as a scrub tech. and I don't think it would be any problem at all for you to get into a school with your grades."

We laughed about us working together in the same operating room and how much fun it could be. We knew all of the same people so it would be just like old home week. The conversation drifted to the more mundane when I mentioned that I had let my driver's license expire and had to go in and take the test. My next statement should never have been made but I did say it and, very innocently I might add.

"The cashier asked me if I belonged to a tribe and I told her , 'No, I will have to pay for my license.'"

"What did you mean by that?" Steve asked abruptly.

"Native Americans don't have to pay a license fee when they get their driver's license in Arizona," I told him.

"Why should they?" he screamed back at me. "After all the white man took all of their land away from them and made them go out and live on worthless land that nobody else wanted. Don't complain to me about your having to pay a simple fee for a stupid license that you shouldn't have to have in the first place."

"Calm down, Steve." I tried to keep calm myself but it was becoming more difficult. "I know the Indians have had some real difficult times."

He interrupted me. "Don't call them Indians! They are Native Americans. As a matter of fact they are more American than you are. The white man thinks he is so superior to them because they have dark skin and have been made to live in poverty without being allowed to have an education."

"Don't forget you're a white man too," I reminded him. "Just the same as I am."

"Come on, Dad, don't try and put that kind of a guilt trip on me. All of you capitalist white guys seem to think you can take everything away from these innocent people and it's all right just because they have dark skin and you don't."

Suddenly there was a strong feeling that I was personally responsible for the Indian-American wars. Then I was informed that it was my reasonable responsibility to pay for the needs of Native Americans.

"Steve," I shouted, "calm down and listen to me!"

"Calm down nothing," he shouted back. "You are the one that needs to calm down! I don't have to put up with this kind of rubbish." With that he jumped up from the table and slammed his napkin down and ran out the front door.

Sherrie and I both sat stunned for a couple of minutes before I leaped up and ran out the door after him. I pounded on his car window as he started to back out of the parking place.

"Don't leave, Steve. Please don't leave. Come back in and stay the night. Please!" He didn't look up as he raced out of the driveway.

There was no communication from Steve for the next three weeks. I knew he was angry and wouldn't get over it for a while so I just left him alone. I did check to make sure he had gotten home safely.

When he did call, he began, "Hi, Dad. I guess I will be moving back home for a while. I got accepted into the surgical technician program at Gateway College and will be starting classes in two weeks. Do you think it will be too much trouble having me around the house again?"

There was no mention of the evening at the lake or any sign of any misunderstanding that might have occurred. I so badly wanted to say, "Hold on just a minute, you want to move into the house of someone that drove all of those innocent people out of their homeland into the wilderness?" But I didn't. Somehow I managed to keep my mouth shut, chomped my lip and welcomed him back home.

Having Steve back home proved to be a happy and fun time for the next few months. He brought home a surgical gown and gloves with cap and mask to practice operating room procedure. We spent hours together open gloving, close gloving and learning to scrub. The silverware doubled for surgical instruments to the point that even at the dinner table the passing of a knife required a slap in the palm of the hand. It became a fun learning experience and as with everything Steve had ever tried to do, he did it with exactness. The operating room appeared to be Steve's strength.

He not only excelled in the academics, but seemed to enjoy the clinical aspects as well. The two of us had finally found a common ground. There didn't appear to be any area for dispute. Often we would sit up until the early hours of the morning going over different surgical procedures with names, shapes and surgical applications of the various instruments. It was exciting to see Steve happy and doing so well. His need to rebuke others dissipated immeasurably and the curbside sermons almost vanished altogether.

One evening a family friend called. In the course of the conversation she mentioned Steve's new girlfriend. "I didn't realize he was dating," I commented.

"Whoops," she said, "I guess I let the cat out of the bag. I guess he didn't want you to know."

"Is there something I should know about this girl?"

"Not really," she answered. "It's just that she has been married a time or two and I believe she may even have some kids." She threw in quickly, "I really didn't mean to say anything so if you talk to him don't tell him who told you." Then she hung up.

I bet you didn't want to let the cat out of the bag, I thought. You couldn't wait to get me on the phone and just "happen" to mention that my son was dating a divorced woman with a couple of kids. Several days later I asked Steve if he had met any nice girls lately. He said he had.

"Anything serious?" I asked.

"Oh I don't know if you could call it serious or not," he joked, "but she is kinda cute and we have become real good friends. She works in the registrar's office at the college so we get to see each other a lot."

"When do I get to meet her?" I asked.

"I'll bring her around one of these days. I know she wants to meet you too." He went on to say that the first time he had seen her was at church and that was why he started talking to her at the school. Then he got real serious. Here it comes, I thought.

"I'm not sure you will approve of her, Dad. She's Hispanic."

"What difference would that make?" I questioned. "I have lots of Hispanic friends. You may recall that I spent three months in Mexico one summer studying language and there are a lot of Hispanic people down there," I said with just a stroke of humor. "Does she speak Spanish?"

"Mexican, I think."

"That's close enough for me. Bring her around so we can meet her." I laughed. "Don't be so secretive, we really don't bite you know. And besides she sounds like a neat lady." Then I added, "By the way what is her name?"

"Carmen."

"Well you tell Carmen that we would love to have her come over any time. I can't wait to meet her."

He brought her to the house the following Tuesday night for our regular Bible study group. The topic of the study that evening happened to be, "Jesus and the woman at the well." After the meeting Steve introduced me to Carmen. She was really very sweet and showed an intense interested in the way Jesus had treated the woman at the well, even though she had married several husbands. The fact that Carmen was at least fifteen years Steve's senior was one aspect of the relationship Steve had failed to mention.

The influence Carmen exerted on Steve was incredible. He started appearing at the house neatly groomed and wearing clean shirt and slacks. It seemed as though he was always smiling as well as being calm. I almost missed the wild war whoops that had previously erupted as he flew through the door.

He approached his studies with excitement, spending long hours developing clinical skills as well as long grueling hours perfecting the theoretical features of the operating room. There was no question in my mind that Steve had at last found his niche.

Graduation was accompanied by several awards of achievement. The most impressive was for being number one in his class academically. After the ceremony I gave him a big hug and told him how proud I was of what he had accomplished. The old Steve projected himself in living color.

"No big deal, Dad," he said. "It's all just a bunch of paper that really doesn't mean much."

"But Steve," I challenged, "you worked hard and long for this and it is worth a lot. Now you have the paper that says you are qualified to scrub in on operations and rub elbows with the surgeons. And I think you would have to admit it not only pays better than pushing a broom, but it is a whole lot more fun."

The expression on his face led me to believe what I was saying was wrong and he was right. There was no need to spoil a perfectly good evening, so I slapped him on the back and said, "Good going, son," and got lost in the crowd.

Finding a job wasn't real easy because of the need for experience. However, it was only a few weeks until Steve gave me a call with the news, "Guess what, Dad? I got a job. It's full time with on-job supervision for the first two months and then I'm on my own. I was told that I will get real money for what I do. Cool, don't you think?"

"Real cool, Steve. I think having a job and making money is real cool." To myself I thought it was particularly cool when you are the dad who has had to meet all of the expenses for the past year and a half.

One Sunday afternoon in the early summer Steve and Carmen arrived at the house for a brief visit.

"Come into the family room," Steve said. "Carmen and I need to talk with you."

Sherrie and I followed them in and sat down. All four of us sat and gawked at one another for several minutes before Steve finally broke the silence.

"Well what do you think of her?" he asked, pointing to Carmen. "Pretty nice, wouldn't you say?"

"What do you mean what do we think?" I asked feeling a little embarrassed. "You know we think she is a special lady."

"No that's not what I mean," he repeated. "What would you think about having her for your daughter-in-law?"

I choked as I gulped out a weak, "What a surprise. What a surprise, that is really a great surprise." I realized I was sounding like a fool, but that was all that would come out. "What a surprise. You guys really know how to surprise folks."

Steve started in with something about getting married in a few weeks and how he would adopt the two boys if their respective fathers would agree. He and Carmen would start sharing the same quarters immediately and all they needed to make everything perfect would be our blessing.

"Hold on, Steve," I finally was able to get the words out. "Give me a minute to catch my breath. This has come as such a shock that I really am speechless for once in my life. I have to admit that the thought of you two getting married had never entered my mind."

When I was finally able to stop acting like a goon and put my thoughts together, Sherrie and I both went over to Carmen and gave her a big hug and welcomed her into our family. We laughed and joked about her knowing what she was getting into and she assured us she was well aware.

We spent the rest of the afternoon hearing about all their plans for going to Las Vegas to get married. Steve told us that the nine-year-old boy had learned to love him as a father. He also mentioned in passing that he felt the eighteen-year-old would come around in time. Carmen confirmed that the boys were extremely happy with the idea of having a man in the house again.

Now we could close the book and everyone would live happily ever after. There didn't seem to be any way to voice my concerns without throwing cold water on the entire event. I decided I would only give my opinion if I were asked. Fortunately I was never asked.

Steve moved in with Carmen and the two boys the next day. The reports that filtered back to us were that all was happiness.

For Thanksgiving that year Cindi invited the entire family to her house for dinner. It was her first attempt at cooking a turkey and met with a degree of apprehension. She did a great job with the table setting using her roommate's china and crystal. Getting the food on the table in unison is an acquired skill which Cindi achieved with unerring accuracy.

Steve and Carmen arrived with her youngest son promptly before dinner. The maturity with which Steve conducted himself came as a complete surprise. The manners he exhibited must have come from a fairytale and were executed with precision. Carmen was introduced as his soon-to-be wife and the boy as his new son. The conversation at the table was lighthearted and filled with love in the true spirit of Thanksgiving. Carmen blended well with the family and Steve demonstrated his ability as a father with helpful hints to the boy on how to maneuver the salad fork and the napkin.

After dinner the men retired to the front lawn for a short round of Frisbee while the ladies helped Cindi repair the damage in the kitchen.

Steve and Carmen excused themselves early to meet another engagement, leaving ample time for the rest of the family to speculate about their future.

Most of the happenings of the next year and a half are related as hearsay. Steve stopped by on only rare occasions and Carmen and the boys never came by on their own. We heard that Steve had introduced several beneficial practices into the home such as prayer before eating, family worship and Bible study. It was our understanding that the boys were happy with Steve as much as he was with them. The wedding failed to materialize.

Pat continued to be a good friend to Steve and helped him in his long hours of restoring the old Harley. The motorcycle became a real passion for Steve and, as usual, he threw his entire self into the work of producing a new bike.

In the workplace it was reported that Steve was performing in an outstanding manner. He received several raises in a short time as well as personal requests from the surgeons to scrub their cases.

Rumor had it that possibly Steve was a trifle rigid with the boys for their lack of consecration to the Lord. Forced to attend church on a regular basis, the older boy chose to exert his own authority in the home. The friction continued to mushroom. Having a teenager was taking its toll on Steve. To alleviate the stress, he resorted back to the bottle. Quickly the turmoil produced by his drinking began to erode his relationship with Carmen.

It wasn't long before I arrived home one evening to find Steve standing in our family room drunker than a skunk. He was holding his overnight bag in one hand and a beer in the other. The language that was coming from his mouth would make even a drunken sailor blush.

"You wouldn't believe what that boy has accused me of," he slurred. "He stood and called me all sorts of foul names and accused me of being a hypocrite for preaching about God and living with his mother in sin. He is the one that is a hypocrite for talking to me that way! After all that I have done for those kids. I can't believe it. He has just gotten too smart for his britches."

Then he added as he tried to get me into focus, "I'm out of there. I don't have to put up with their kind of trash. If I want to have a little drink once and a while, I can't see that it is any of their business. Besides they aren't my kids in the first place."

I could see that he was extremely upset, but nothing he was saying was making much sense. His state of inebriation was too great to attempt any type of logic. I suggested that a good night's sleep would be the best thing and put him to bed to sleep it off.

The following weekend I went with Steve to Carmen's house to help him move his things. Carmen was very sweet as she described Steve's inability to come to terms with the older boy. She was sad for the younger boy who had developed a genuine affection for Steve and would miss him significantly. As she hugged me goodbye she told me she always wanted to remain friends with us. I only saw her one time after that and that was in passing at church.

Letting Steve move back home didn't fit the situation with Cindi living at home preparing for her wedding. My aunt Adeline, who had stayed on at my father's home after his death, had an extra bedroom. It was agreed that Steve could stay there. After only a few days she begged Steve to make other arrangements and find his own place to live.

Steve was on his own once again. He moved from apartment to apartment. Pat and Sally invited him to stay in their guest room. He apparently lived there with them long enough to allow some of his wounds to heal.

Somewhere along the line Steve moved in with his new girlfriend but found the situation uncomfortable when her estranged husband came home for days at a time. Life was difficult by the time he finally did settle into his own apartment.

Steve started spending more time at home which gave us the opportunity to sit up for our long discussions once again. We discussed everything from Bible truths to politics. We had great discussions, unfortunately much of the time we continued to end in screaming matches. We finally decided that this was normal behavior for us and were able to laugh about it after the fact. The experience was touch and go. There were terrific spiritual highs and times embracing the low life.

The evening of Cindi's wedding rehearsal, Steve arrived at the church smelling of beer. I suggested that a trip to the men's room for a little gargle and some cold water to the face might prove beneficial. He disappeared but instead of going to the men's room he detoured to the closest Circle-K for reinforcements. By the time he returned he was unable to do much more that take up space in the pew. Attempts at walking his mother down the aisle were almost frightening. After the rehearsal dinner I insisted he spend the night at our house under the close scrutiny of father's watchful eye.

He performed his duties the following afternoon without a flaw.

29

The New Beginning

From where I was seated in the doctors lounge all I could visualize was a silhouette standing in the doorway. As he stepped into the room with his newly styled blond hair and immaculate new clothes he looked like a prince stepping out of a bandbox. Racing across the room I grasped him by the hand and exclaimed, "Steve you look great, I mean you really look great!"

"I feel great," he said, "greater than I have felt in my whole life! Do you happen to have a couple of minutes to talk?"

"Sure," I answered. "Let's step outside on the porch where we can be alone."

We went outside where Steve began with his usual, "Dad!" But this time instead of the whisper that would denote a marvelous revelation, his voice rang out like a bell peeling the armistice and announcing that the war had been won. "Dad," he started, "I have been wrong."

"Wrong about what?" I asked.

"Just about everything," he replied. "You know, about God and the one interpretation of the Bible. About having to be perfect within myself in order to be saved. About having to rebuke everyone so that I wouldn't be held accountable for their sins. I guess salvation by works could be considered another error.

"You know, Dad, those people down South did a real number on me. They had me so scared I would have believed anything they told me. I was convinced that the church was Babylon and the college was filled with falsehood and I was being suckered into this ghoulish deception. They proved to me they had the only true interpretation of the Bible and any deviation from their theology would lead a person directly to hell.

"It didn't take a lot of talking to convince me that we are living in the time of the Latter Rain and the Lord would be coming back in a matter of days. That's why I had to get away from the school and the evil influence of the world. They let me know that to discuss any of this with the teachers at the college would only lead me deeper into confusion. The only way out was to go with them to the farm so that even though I was in the world, I was not a part of the world."

Then his face became very serious. "Dad," he said, "I'm sorry for all that I have put you and Mother through in the past few years. Can you forgive me?"

"There really isn't anything to forgive. We love you no matter what! Of course you are forgiven."

Then he got a big grin on his face and announced, "Now get this. I sold the Harley I've been building for the past year and a half. The guy gave me six thousand bucks for it, all in cash. I paid off all of my debts with the money and bought these new threads," pointing to his new clothes. "I still have forty-five hundred dollars in my pocket. Tell me what I owe you and we will be square.

"Isn't God great!" he said, flinging his arms into the air. "God is truly great. No matter how far off the deep end a guy goes He is there to pick us up and welcome us home."

"You don't owe me a thing," I said. "It is payment in full just to see you so happy and to have made such a turnabout."

"Dad," he went on to say, "that is only the beginning. I went down to the university in Tucson and applied for a job in the operating room at the teaching hospital. They took all my information and I interviewed with the chief of surgery. The lady in charge called me today to let me know I have been accepted pending a physical examination which they will do next week. The position pays big bucks and includes benefits and the opportunity to work toward my RN degree without paying tuition. I will be able to work and go to school at the same time."

All I could do was gawk at him. "You aren't putting me on are you?" I asked.

"Na, Dad. I wouldn't joke about anything as serious as this. It's for real. The schooling and all." Then he added, "I guess they really liked me or they are certainly hard up for help."

"I have to get back into the operating room," I told him. "Go home and tell your mother. She will flip. Plan to stay for dinner and we can talk more about this when I get home."

I gave him a big hug and watched with disbelief as he bounced down the steps. This has to be too good to be true, I thought. God really is great!

Sherrie pulled out all the stops and made a fabulous meal for the three of us that evening. Cindi stopped by for a brief visit after dinner and was immediately swept into the study to hear the documentary on Steve's latest adventures. The dissertation began with his new attitudes toward spirituality and progressed into the extended version which led into great detail about the possibilities for advanced degrees after completing nursing. The entire rendering took well over half an hour and left Cindi in wide-eyed amazement.

"Bro," she said when she was finally able to speak, "it sounds as if you have the whole world in the palm of your hand!"

"I do, Sis," he replied. "God has really been good to me and I want to tell the world that I am a Christian."

"Well just keep up the good work," Cindi admonished as she got up to leave. "By the way I almost forgot to tell you, I met your old girlfriend at church a few weeks ago and she asked me to give you her phone number when I saw you."

"Carmen?" Steve asked.

"No it was little Cindy. The one with the two small kids."

"Cindy!" Steve gulped. "What was she doing in church?"

"Apparently she takes her children to Sabbath School on a regular basis and then stays for church herself."

"That has to be from my influence," Steve gloated. "I knew she would come around someday. Isn't that the greatest? Little Cindy, my little Cindy, whatcha know!"

Cindi gave Steve the number and a hug then fled. Steve and I sat up late going over and over all the arrangements that needed to be made in a short time. He would give notice at his apartment right away so as not to lose any rent. Then he would tell the hospital the first thing in the morning so as to meet the two week notice requirement in order to get severance pay. The paramount goal was to get out of town in the shortest possible time for the least possible amount of money.

"Man, Dad, I guess that will pretty well burn all of my bridges behind me so I have nothing else to do but to go. Looks like you will finally have me out of your hair once and for all." He laughed. "You are the big winner!"

"No, Steve, it looks to me as if you have the winning number this time so take the ball and run with it!"

"You know I will, Dad. This is a once-in-a-lifetime chance and I'm not gonna let it get away from me."

Steve stayed the night and we all slept well from sheer excitement of the day. The following afternoon Steve dropped by with all of his paperwork for the university. His appointment for a physical examination was scheduled for the following week. I agreed to go with him and help in the search for a place to live. Steve radiated with the joy of the moment as he stood in the doorway to leave.

"Oh, by the way did you remember to call Little Cindy?" I asked.

"I haven't forgotten," he assured me. "I plan to give her a call as soon as I get all of my paperwork together and can stop long enough to take a breath." Then he added as if I had no knowledge on the subject, "You just can't begin to imagine all the work it takes to put all of this together." With that he was gone.

"Keep me informed," I yelled as his car pulled out of the drive. I saw his head nod in the direction of not to worry.

There wasn't any word from Steve over the next three or four days and I began to feel a sense of uneasiness. You worry too much, I told myself. He probably just has so much to get done that he hasn't had time to come by. On about the fifth day when I couldn't reach him at home I decided to give him a call at work. The blood in my veins ran cold when the nursing supervisor told me that they hadn't heard from Steve in about a week.

"That really isn't at all like him," she was saying in the phone. "He is always real good about letting us know if he is sick or even if he is going to be a little late. We have all tried to call him at home and some of his co-workers have even gone to his apartment. The landlord told them he had given notice and was moving. We finally concluded that he had just left without further notice and we were left high and dry." The lady was still talking but I had tuned out. My mind was racing in all directions and kept coming to the same crossroad, Little Cindy.

I wracked my brain to remember her father's name. Finally after a day of searching I was able to find his phone number and I gave him a call. When I reached him I asked for Cindy's home phone number.

"She and the kids live here with me," he informed me.

"Is she there now and may I speak with her?" I asked.

"No," he replied, "I haven't seen her in about a week. I have the kids here with me but have no idea where she is."

I laid the phone down as a wave of hopelessness pounded over me. It was several days before the phone call came. It was Steve with a barely audible whisper.

"Dad," he whimpered. "Dad we need help. Can you bring us some money?"

"Money for what?" I asked.

"They are trying to throw us out of our hotel room. They want us to pay up or they are going to call the cops."

"What happened to the four thousand plus bucks you had the other day?" I screamed. "Where is all that money?"

"I don't know, Dad. All I know is all the money is gone and the manager is going to have us in jail if he has his way. Can you help us or not!?"

"What do you owe," I probed.

"About five hundred bucks," was the feeble answer.

"Five hundred bucks!" I yelled. "Where are you staying, the Waldorf Astoria?"

"Come on, Dad, later with the lecture I'm not in the mood to be preached to!"

"Well I do think I should have the right to know where my money is going!" I tossed back at him.

With that there was a click and the phone went dead. He was gone! The next call came about four hours later. The "gentleman" on the other end of the line sounded like what I think a Chicago gangster would sound. The filth that came out of his mouth was unprintable.

The essence of the conversation was that if I didn't pay the money that "I" owed him he was going to call the cops. If the cops were to come to the hotel and see what had been going on in that room for the last week or so, my kids would be thrown into the slammer and would never again see the light of day! There was no question about it, this guy meant business.

"What makes you think that I am responsible for this bill?" I asked, trying to remain calm.

"Do you want your kids to go to the electric chair?" He swore.

"No not really," I answered.

"Then pay up and everything will be fine!" he said with a very convincing inflection. I agreed to pay the bill.

Since then I have wondered if that was one of the biggest mistakes I could have made in my life. Steve was bailed out once again, financially destitute and broken in spirit. The one redeeming factor was that during the week in the hotel he had had enough sense to call the university and postpone his physical examination until the following week. At least his new job would still be secure. But, the day before we were to go to Tucson Steve called with a pleading request.

"Dad," he whispered, "I really need your help."

"What now?"

"Could you give me a clean catch urine specimen for my physical tomorrow?"

"No Steve," I snapped. "First of all it wouldn't be honest and secondly there is no way you could get away with it without getting caught."

"But, Dad," he pleaded again. "If I turn up with a 'dirty' urine I might just as well kiss my future goodbye."

The silence that followed was deafening. In my mind I knew that smuggling a urine sample in for a routine physical probably wouldn't be all that difficult. More important, I knew we were about to cross the line of honesty. The line of a future or no future. The line of life or death. I prayed, "God don't make me make this decision. How can I do the right thing and be so wrong?"

My mind was spinning through all of the possible solutions, none of which seemed to produce an answer. The choice loomed before me, lose my own soul or lose my son. I didn't have the courage of my convictions so I told Steve, "I will give it some thought. Call me back in a couple of hours."

Steve called in an hour and said, "I'm sorry I put you in such a position, Dad. I was wrong. You shouldn't have to take all the flack for me. I know you really would want to help me but that you know right from wrong and I really admire you for that. I will go down tomorrow and just pray that my system will have cleared by then. Maybe they will forget to take a specimen. Anyway, Dad, pray for me and thanks for everything."

The next day was black Thursday. The urine sample came back "dirty." Steve was advised that he could reapply in one year for possible reconsideration. The job was gone. The money was gone. The education was gone. All of Steve's self esteem was gone.

The hospital agreed to give his old job back with a cut in pay and loss of seniority. This meant that he wouldn't be able to pay for an apartment. He asked to move home. We agreed on a temporary basis.

30

Decision to Move

The summer of 1994 came and went, fading into an uneventful fall. Cindi and her new husband were busy setting up their new home while Teri and her husband reconciled their differences and were expecting their second baby. Kevin was secure in his penitentiary in the valley, being protected from all outside influences. Steve, in spite of his severe setback, was gainfully employed as a surgical tech. and doing well emotionally.

The time seemed appropriate to think about retiring and moving to our Condominium at the lake. Our major concerns were Sherrie's parents who were in their eighties and my aunt Adeline who had stayed on in my dad's condominium after his death and was now in her nineties. We were Adeline's only "children," so it stood to reason she would come to the mountains and live with us when we moved.

Sherrie's parents posed another problem. They were dogmatic about not giving up their independence and there was no way they would consider moving into an assisted living situation. They were also incapable of living alone. Rosie managed to park her car in the dining room of their home by driving through the back wall of the garage. My father-in-law chose to ignore stop signs and the arrows on one-way streets. The three a.m. phone call from my mother-in -law to the police claiming there was a strange man in the house necessitated my getting out of bed and driving across town to identify my father-in-law. The night Rosie was found walking down the middle of a four-lane thoroughfare in her nightgown was the deciding blow. We had to find a home for them.

Finding a home for my in-laws and getting them to move into it is a book in itself. The impossible was accomplished shortly before Thanksgiving when they finally agreed to move into an assisted care facility. They shared a room and took their meals in a common dinning room. One of us visited them every day and took them for walks and an occasional ride in the car. Rosie chose not to go in the car so it was usually just Earl and myself.

Their minds deteriorated rapidly. They lived in the past and often had difficulty identifying family members. The situation was sad. There was very little tenable communication between us. All of our kids were good about visiting their grandparents. Steve showed a particular interest and stopped in to see them regularly. They never recognized him or acknowledged any relationship.

Adeline on the other hand was sharp as a tack and excited about moving with us to the lake. We found a live-in housekeeper to stay with her in her condominium until the move. With the house on the market Steve's clutter was sometimes a bit cumbersome for the realtor, but tolerable. Shortly before Christmas he found himself financially secure enough to move into his own apartment. We now had all of our "ducks in a row" for the move. I gave my notice to the hospital for the first of June 1995, completing twenty years of service.

Christmas Eve was spent at our home with Cindi and her husband's family. Adeline was also there and so was Steve. We ate a delicious dinner before retiring to the living room for package opening around the ten foot Christmas tree. There was a fire in the fireplace and the entire evening glowed with festiveness. I played the piano while Cindi led the group in Christmas carols. Then we opened our gifts one at a time. We had a good time and everyone oo'ed and ah'ed appropriately as each one opened another package.

Steve was nicely dressed that evening. He arrived with gifts for the entire group. It seemed as if the spark had come back into his life. He laughed with everyone and helped Adeline open her gifts as he explained how he had picked them out and wrapped them himself. One of the fondest pictures I have is of Steve on the white couch with Rex our Labrador resting his head on Steve's knee.

Sherrie produced a birthday cake with lighted candles for Steve to blow out. For once in his life he seemed pleased to have us sing

"Happy Birthday." He blew out his candles in quick order and made a wish. That Christmas Eve was Steve's twenty-eighth birthday. It was also his last birthday.

Standing in the living room I took in the beauty of the lighted tree with its glistening ornaments. The crackle of the fire and the laughter within the group suggested a family filled with love. The thought hit me that this would be the last time we would all be together like this in this room. Little did I understand the prophetic truth of my thought. I quickly dismissed that thought and went on to cherish the memories we were making at that moment.

Christmas day was spent at the nursing home with Sherrie's folks. We all had dinner together and opened some gifts but the festiveness of the previous evening was lost with the realization that the beautiful people I had once enjoyed were there only in body. The once brilliant hostess sat almost motionless staring into the face of a man she no longer recognized as her husband. She made some mention of seeing her father that morning and following him around the field on the farm. She thought he would probably come over that evening but wasn't sure. Her voice trailed off and her chin dropped onto her chest as she appeared to doze. Sherrie held her mother in her arms for a few moments, tears rolling down her checks. It didn't seem fair a body could be so well and fail to house a mind.

31

A Night to Remember

T he long evenings of January were warm in Phoenix that winter. Steve and I were visiting together commiserating about the happenings of life. We sat by the swimming pool with only the light of the moon and stars reflecting in the water. Steve had regained the self-respect he had thrown away the previous spring. Although still financially destitute he had received a raise at work and was working on fixing up his apartment.

The past was over and there was no reason to keep reiterating the damage that had been done. His maturity had begun to surge. That particular evening he seemed to want to ventilate about some of the important events that had influenced his growing up. There appeared to be a special need to pour out his heart as he began with a rather startling disclosure.

"You know, Dad, I have always been bummed by the fact that my birth mother didn't want me. And even more bummed that the folks that were originally going to adopt me decided they didn't want me either. So you were stuck with me whether you liked it or not."

"Steve," I interrupted. "That's not the way it happened at all. I really believe your mother, as young as she was, had your best interest in mind. She could have kept you and may have been able to give you a good home and all, but she was wise enough to realize there was a good possibility that she couldn't. There is no doubt in my mind that the only thought she had was for the well being of her baby. Also you have to realize she may not have had a lot to say in making the decision to give you up. She must have had parents and they may have made it very difficult for her to keep her baby."

"You know I had never really thought about the fact that she may not have had the last say in making the choice," Steve said. "My only thought for all these years has been, all she wanted to do was to dump me so I wouldn't interfere in her life. Thanks, Dad. You know that really makes me feel a lot better about my old lady."

"Why not get in the habit of referring to her as you birth mother?" I asked. "Seems to me that is a little more respectful."

"I will have to give that some thought too," he replied. "I'm sure you're right. But just remember a lifetime of feelings can't be changed in one evening."

He went on to talk about his love for music. "I have always loved to play the guitar. When I was a kid I would walk around the room as if I were on a big stage. I became the rock star of all times. I not only wanted to play like the one I was idolizing, I wanted to be exactly like that person. The old saying of drugs, sex and rock-and-roll was my goal in life. All of the time I knew you didn't approve but I really didn't care because you were an old man and couldn't be expected to understand in the first place. You know, Dad, there were times I really felt sorry for you because you couldn't understand about sex, drugs and rock-and-roll. You grew up not knowing how to have a good time and that's sad. You never did go to a real party!"

I wanted to say that I had been to a lot of parties in my time, but the words popcorn, ice cream and marshmallows didn't flow well in that particular setting.

He quickly jumped to the next and more important subject. "I have always felt that God was the great dictator in the sky. His only job was to make us toe the line and if we didn't we would get zapped. You are my earthly father and held the same position here on Earth. Government officials also held the same authority and all they wanted to do was to make sure we were all miserable. That included anyone who was in charge of anything."

My instinct told me we were getting onto some serious turf and I wanted to make sure we didn't get on a runaway craze and blast the entire discourse out of the water. I approached the situation with kid gloves and sincere sympathy.

"Steve," I began, "you have had some bad hurts in your life haven't you?"

In the dim light I couldn't read the expression on his face but his voice reflected a sense of surprise. "People have tried to hurt me," he whispered, "but I never let them. I have always felt that if they didn't like me the way I am that's tough."

I thought I had heard that sentiment expressed before, but for once in my life I let it pass without saying a word. It did serve as a springboard for my next question.

"Would you like to tell me again about what happened that spring in Tennessee?"

"What do you mean, what happened? You know what happened. I messed up my life that's what happened." His voice sounded a little edgy before he caught himself.

"Sure, Dad, I would really like to talk about it. You know I told you I have always felt that God was sitting up there on His posh throne just waiting to catch me on some minor offense and ban me from the kingdom. I knew I couldn't live up to all the expectations that He had for me so I was lost. I wanted to be a good Christian and thought that everyone should believe the same as I did. It really upset me when others didn't see things my way.

"When I was in Tennessee and went off campus to attend those religious meetings, the people there seemed to see things more like I did. So I took the whole thing in hook, line and sinker. But when they told me the Lord was coming in a matter of weeks it scared the living daylights out of me. I knew I was lost and doomed to be tormented in Hell for ever and ever.

"Dad, you will never know how scared I was. I have had to lie to you in the past and have even run from the cops, but have you ever thought about how it would be to have to run from an all-knowing and all-seeing God?

"The preaching began with talks about the Latter Rain in the very last days of history. They convinced me that we were living in that time. Then they led me to believe there was only one interpretation of the Bible. It never occurred to me that their interpretation might not always be the right one. One of the text they emphasized was 'Be ye also perfect.' To be perfect, they told us, meant to live a life in strict

213

obedience to the letter of the law. There was only one strike and you were out.

"The college was, in their minds, nothing more than the devil's workshop preaching Satanic evils. Another text that was paramount was the one, 'We are in the world but not of the world.'" This essentially meant that anything that was produced by man was evil and had to be given up. Emphasis was placed on the fact that "worldly" subjects were being taught at the college that would do nothing more that prepare us for a "worldly" job in a sinful world.

"Supposedly this was the same thing that had happened in Old Testament times in the Schools of the Prophets. God had condemned the school then and He was condemning the college now. Students were being required to read secular articles such as the daily newspapers that were doing nothing more than a good brainwash job.

"They believed the church had become Babylon and was no longer led by God but strictly under the direction of man. This is where the text about 'even the very elect will be deceived' was presented. There were no ifs or ands about it. We were all being deceived and had to get out of Babylon before if was too late.

"The list of do not's was inexhaustible. They started with the way we dressed, the way we ate and the places we went. No form of entertainment was acceptable. That included dancing, card playing, roller skating, movies ,TV, bike riding and checkers. You name it. Even walking through the city streets could be a sin if you were not extremely careful where you looked and who you talked to. Any type of convenience was considered sinful. And any kind of luxury was coveting.

"The text 'pray without ceasing' didn't mean to have an attitude of prayer it meant to be in actual prayer all of the time. The final presentation told us about the farm that had been established where we could serve the Lord without any uncertainties. The altar call was for those who were willing to accept the responsibility of giving up self and turning their lives over to the Lord before it was too late. I knew I had to do it! It was my only salvation. I jumped to my feet and was welcomed at the altar by the director who put his arms around me as we fell to our knees in prayer. It was a prayer of complete surrender of my life to God with no looking back. I knew I must get out of the world!

"To my astonishment I was the only one in the entire congregation that answered that call. I was assured that others would follow but few had the courage of their own conviction the way I did. My heart ached for all the ones who had heard the word but would not yield their hearts to the way of right. Not only did my heart ache for these lost souls but I felt a terrible responsibility for letting it happen to them. The knowledge that they were damned to Hellfire and brimstone because of me just about tore me apart. The director tried to alleviate my fears by telling me that with our prayers and by our witness their hearts would be softened and they would slowly be turned from the ways of man and turn to the way of right. He added that as 'watchmen on the wall' it was our responsibility to rebuke sinners for their wrongdoings.

"I couldn't sleep much that night as I waited to be taken to the farm the following morning. I knew you would be madder than all get out. However, the Bible does teach that our families will turn against us and persecute us when we surrender our lives to Christ. I felt extremely sad that you and Mother had been suckered into the ways of the world and would be eternally lost. I can't remember ever being so scared or feeling so alone. So few weeks left and so much to do."

At that point I wanted to put my arms around him and tell him how sorry I felt about everything, knowing full well that anything I might say right then would seem shallow and unimportant. I simply asked, "What happened when you got to the farm and what did you do all day?"

"When we got to the place," Steve said, "the director's wife took me to the room where most of the guys slept. Then the director gave me a rundown of the day's activities. There was a garden that had to be maintained to provide food for the table. This would be the responsibility of the men. The women would be in charge of preparing the food.

"Extreme caution was to be taken to abstain from gluttony, one of the major weaknesses. The diet would be strictly vegetarian including abstinence from meat, chicken, fish, or any dairy products Water was available at all times but was never to be served with meals.

"The men's dress would be in accordance with Christian

principles, which dictated overalls with a long-sleeved shirt buttoned at the collar. The hair should be shaved.

"Early on I was told there were possible misinterpretations of the Bible. To be on the safe side I should always adhere to the principles set forth in the *Spirit of Prophecy* books. I really never found any discrepancies between the two but it did bother me a little that the *Spirit of Prophecy* seemed to be held in higher esteem than the Bible.

"We would all sit in a circle for hours in silence reading the Great Controversy. The book we had was the original publication because there have been so many changes made by man that later editions couldn't be trusted.

"After our evening meal, which consisted mainly of a small bowl of fruit, we would have worship and go to our rooms for prayers. Our prayers lasted for most of the night. We were informed that to pray without ceasing meant that sleep was secondary and that the majority of the night must be spent on our knees in prayer. Some of the time I just couldn't stay awake and would fall asleep. When someone would wake me up, I felt so guilty there was no way I could go back to sleep. I was tired and hungry all of the time. That made me feel guilty because if you were keeping all of the health principles a person shouldn't get tired or hungry. I needed to strive harder for perfection.

"Sabbath was a day of meditation with no thought or talking about anything that involved the world. From sundown Friday night until sundown Saturday night there was to be absolutely no work. The day was spent in study with an occasional break to go to the bathroom and eat a small portion of food that had been prepared the day before. We didn't do any singing and spent most of the day on our knees.

"Swimming was an approved sport as long as it was only men with men and women with women. Swimming nude was sanctioned. So the men would go to a nearby pond and swim. This served a dual purpose. We got our bath while having some recreation. That type of recreation wasn't considered a sin because we weren't wasting God's time.

"Most of our conversations were in whispers. Laughing out loud or making jokes is strictly forbidden in the Bible, you know." He gave a brief snicker. "At least that's the way they taught us."

"How many were there in your group?" I asked.

"Ten or twelve," he replied, "but I would rather not talk about the others if you don't mind. It was a sorta private group if you know what I mean."

"How could you be so private and take the Gospel to the rest of the world?" I asked.

"We did pray for the other people of the world. Frankly I guess we felt that time was so short there wasn't a lot of hope for others anyway. When we went into town we made it a point to avoid unnecessary contact with anyone. We did hand out *Spirit of Prophecy* books but took care not to get into controversy with any of the worldly people. My own feeling was that I couldn't do anything until I became perfect myself. Then if there was still time left I would try and save others."

It was getting late. The moon had disappeared behind the trees leaving only the light of the stars reflecting in the swimming pool. It was evident that Steve was eager to talk on into the night so I turned up my jacket collar in anticipation of the late night chill and settled in for the duration.

"Do you remember the night I came home and told you I wanted to start keeping the Sabbath and would probably loose my job as a result of it?" he asked.

"How could I ever forget that night? It was one of the greatest nights of my life."

"Well, Dad," he went on, "I knew then that if I were to survive I had to get away from the lifestyle I was leading. Going away to a Christian college seemed like the only way to escape the temptations of the world. When you told me you would send me to Southern Missionary College I knew God had answered my prayers. In my heart I knew that if I stayed here in the city my habits would kill me.

"When I got to the college I was on a Christian high like you wouldn't believe. The thought of being with a group of 'saints' made me warm all over. I pictured small Bible study groups and long sessions of prayer late into the evening with my fellow students. It would be so easy to be holy because everyone else would be holy too. I knew the conversations at the dinner table would be about God and how we could save souls for the kingdom. There would be no sinful thoughts because there would be no external stimulus to generate them. The

217

fact that I was going to a Christian college made me feel as if I had already attained heaven.

"The delusion faded quickly. It didn't take long to recognize that many of the people at the school were no different than the 'worldly' people I had been associated with right here in Phoenix. The first thing the lady in the registrar's office told me was that she was sure I would be happy as soon as I found myself a girlfriend. Dad! You know I didn't go there to find myself a woman! All I was interested in was finding the Lord.

"The very first weekend I was invited to the home of one of the faculty members. They told me they had a bunch of the kids over every Saturday night for ice cream and to watch a movie. The very thing I was trying to get away from.

"I guess I was so naive that I thought everyone was on the same spiritual high I was experiencing. You know, Dad, the reason I chose Southern was because I wanted to be a preacher. There is no way to tell you how disappointed I was when they told me I would have to take a bunch of general classes that didn't even interest me or pertain to God and that I would only have one small Bible course. I was crushed to say the least and even went to my counselor and tried to squeeze in a couple more religion classes. They told me I needed to have the general courses in order to graduate. I let them know that I really didn't care if I graduated or not. All I wanted was to learn how to be a preacher and serve the Lord by winning souls. That was considered a good attitude with the wrong approach.

"All the rationalizing in the world wouldn't sway that administration. The answer still came up 'no way man.' You can imagine my excitement when my roommate told me about a guy who was preaching off campus. I was told this guy was a real preacher and not afraid to tell it the way it is.

"I was glued to my seat the following night as he told the story of how the church had strayed so far from the original movement. He explained that in many areas it is impossible to tell Seventh-day Adventist from any other church. Our church had gone the same way the Roman Catholic church had in deviating from the original apostolic church. He told us that he represented the Adventist

Church in its purest and most basic form. Their movement taught the truth that most other churches had forgotten.

"The next day I skipped my classes in order to read up on all the things I had heard the night before. With no one to drive me to the church the next night I walked over two miles just to hear the meeting. It was even better than the first one. The preacher showed us many of the examples where man had misinterpreted scripture. He talked a lot about cheap grace where all you have to do to be saved is believe on the Lord Jesus. He showed without a doubt that without rigid adherence to the Ten Commandments there is no salvation regardless of one's relationship with the Lord.

"After the meeting I stuck around to meet the preacher. He thanked me for staying and shared with me how happy he was that I was fortunate enough to get in on this end time message."

"What about all the other teachings you were being taught?" I asked. "Didn't it seem strange to you that one person would have all the answers and all the others be wrong?"

"No, Dad," he exclaimed. "Because he had everything that I was looking for. A set of rules that all you had to do was check them off and stay on the straight and narrow. Also there was very little to think about because the Bible was interpreted exactly as it reads. There was no room for error and I was completely protected from the temptations of the world. This was still the church I had been brought up in but it had been narrowed to the few remnant who were teaching the pure gospel. The remainder of the church had become Babylon. When I heard that the Lord was really coming in the next few weeks there was nothing to lose by leaving and everything to lose by staying.

"Dad, you sent me to a missionary college in good faith to learn about the Lord and literally cast me to the wolves! I was so focused on getting away from the enemy in the outside world that I couldn't see the enemy within. The thought of the devil taking something spiritual and twisting it around for his own benefit didn't enter my mind. Although when you think about it where else is there that he would have a more captive audience than in church?

"Anyway, Dad, the rest of the story is history," Steve said with a yawn. "I guess we have spent enough time whipping a dead horse and better spend more time thinking about how to whip the future."

219

"You're right, son, and all I have to say about the whole thing is I thank God daily that you got through the entire mess with only minor abrasions."

"Yeah, I really could have been messed up pretty bad for the rest of my life. It gives me the shivers when I realize how I was sucked into that whirlpool of fanatical deception. You know I didn't have a clue what a fanatic was until you called me one and I looked it up in the dictionary," he said with a laugh. "I guess I was just too busy being perfect to concern myself with fanatical."

32

Forfeited Honor

The next two months went by smoothly. Our house was on the market without so much as a nibble which we had anticipated as a possibility from the start. Moving day was still scheduled for the first of June nevertheless. Adeline was excited about the move and had her things in readiness to head for the hills. I had already found part-time work that had the suggestion of becoming full time in spite of my intentions to cut back. Steve was thinking in terms of applying for a position near our new home which pleased me. Everything was ready for the big move.

In mid-March I came home from the hospital early and found Steve standing in the kitchen talking on the phone. He gave me a nod and went on with his conversation.

"What is Steve doing here in the middle of the afternoon?" I asked Sherrie.

"Don't tell him that I told you," she began. "I think he just lost his job. He is on the phone right now talking with his supervisor to see if he can straighten things out."

"Why would they fire him?" I asked. "I thought things were going so well."

"I thought they were too," she replied, "but apparently there have been some problems with him not showing up for work or at least not coming in on time. He asked me not to tell you about it so don't let on that you know anything."

When Steve walked into the room he looked as if he had been shot through the heart. He was pale and he stood there with a blank gaze in his eyes for a long moment before he said anything.

"They canned me," he groaned. "They canned me without so much as giving me a second chance. Why wouldn't they forgive me and give me a second chance? Why would they just fire me on the spot like that and not have a forgiving spirit? Haven't any of them ever made a mistake before? I just don't get it!" His arms were beginning to whirl about his head and I was detecting a spirit that had dominated the old Steve.

"What did you do to get them so upset?" I asked trying to sound sympathetic.

"Nothing," he fired back. "Nothing at all. I just didn't hear my alarm clock this morning so when I did wake up I called and told them what had happened and they told me not to bother coming back. I just got off the phone with the nursing supervisor. She told me this had happened one time too many times for me to keep my job."

"Have you missed work or called in late before?" I asked.

"She says I have and I guess I may have once or twice but that's no reason to fire a guy. Don't they have any forgiveness in their hearts at all?"

"Steve," I asserted, "they have an operating room to run and they can't do it if people don't show up for work. Why were you so tired that you couldn't wake up in the first place?"

"Now you are accusing me of partying," he wailed. "Why do you always think it's me? You know they could be wrong too! I just think they need to give a guy another chance. The Bible says that a person should be forgiven seventy times seven times. I just don't get it. I do a good job for them and this is the thanks I get. As far as I am concerned I don't need their stupid job. There are a lot of other places to work in this world where they know how to treat a guy right!" With that he was out the door.

My first question was, "Do you think he is using drugs again?"

"Sounds like a good possibility to me," Sherrie responded. "Just pray that we are wrong."

There weren't a lot of other places to work. As it turned out, Steve was on a collision course with disaster and there didn't seem to be any hope of blocking it. One after another the hospitals in the area closed their doors on his requests for employment. Even temporary employment wouldn't fly. There was nowhere to turn.

He could no longer afford his apartment so was forced to move. This time he chose not to ask to come home. He found a room and bath in a small complex near the hospital and moved in with one suitcase and a sleeping bag. An old overstuffed chair dominated the room and his clothes were "hung" in the corner on the floor. There was no bed or table, just that one pathetic old chair and his army green sleeping bag embellished with a feather pillow that had more feathers on the outside than in.

When I walked into the room unannounced I found Steve sitting on the floor smoking a cigarette. The pawnshop ticket in his hand represented his beautiful, expensive electric guitar. Holding up the ticket he lamented. "That was my best friend but I had to let her go even though we have been through a lot together. She is just too expensive for me right now."

"Steve, why didn't you come to me if things were getting so tight? I could always float you a loan until you get on your feet again."

"Not this time, Dad," he muttered looking completely dejected. "You have always bailed me out in one way or another in the past. This time I've got to make it on my own no matter what."

"Do you have anything to eat?" I asked.

"Not a hot lot," he admitted, "but I was well trained in not overeating while I was down South. So I guess there is no reason that I can't survive for a while."

"Come with me and we will go get some food," I begged.

"Thanks but no thanks," he answered. "I got myself into this mess and I will have to find my own way out! Now if you don't mind, Dad, I have a few things I need to sort out. I will let you know how things are going in a few days. There is a chance I can get on over here at a little fast food joint. Two of the people that live here are working there now and are willing to share some of their hours with me. So don't worry about me. I really am going to be OK."

He made a gesture toward the door then said, "I love you, Dad. Thanks."

Walking out the door I spotted what appeared to be a couple of empty beer cans on the kitchen floor. "Take it easy on the sauce," I cautioned.

"Don't sweat it, Dad," he replied. "A little alcoholic beverage is good for the soul and might be the answer to all my chaos about now." With that he stood up and closed the door behind me.

A few nights later I arrived home late to find Steve's car in the driveway. A wave of excitement ran through me as I thought, maybe he has decided to come home for a while and get a grip on his life. My hopes were smashed when Sherrie told me the police department had called and asked to have me pick up Steve at the station.

"What do you mean pick him up at the station?" I hollered. "His car is sitting in the driveway."

"I didn't know that," she said. "All I know is an officer called and said they had Steve down there and that he appeared to be very drunk. You need to go pick him up. Here's the phone number. Call them yourself!" Sherrie was crying and upset. But I still wanted to know why Steve's car was in the driveway. Questioning Sherrie didn't prove to be profitable so I resorted to making the phone call to the police department as requested.

"Yes Steve is here," the officer confirmed. "Yes, he is very drunk, and yes, you need to come and get him and take him home as soon as possible."

At the police station the story was revealed that Steve was heading south when an officer spotted him and attempted to catch up with him. Steve turned into our street and was parked in our driveway before the cop was able to get there. Since Steve was not in his car when the officer arrived he couldn't be sited for a DUI so the officer took him in on disorderly conduct.

Steve was seething as he came out of police station. "They are telling you a bunch of lies," he slurred. "I was going north so they couldn't have followed me. I could tell for sure which way I was going. All they want to do is make trouble so don't believe them."

I was convinced that Steve didn't even know what town he was in let alone what direction he was traveling. Dragging him into the house wasn't an easy maneuver but the challenge was met and Steve was thrown unceremoniously into a heap on the bed to sleep it off. It was difficult to discern whether I was angry, hurt, or just plain relieved that Steve was safe in his own little bed again.

Looking down on his miserable drunken form on the bed I could hardly imagine this was the same young man I sat with by the pool just a few weeks earlier. The emotion of the evening swallowed me as I slid to the floor and sobbed openly. My sobs were barely audible over the snoring of my unconscious son.

"God, where are you hiding this time?" I cried out loud. "Where are You?" I laid on the floor beside the bed for several hours, my mind pounding with questions. Was this ever going to stop? Is life just one valley after another? What had I done wrong and how could I make it right? Same old questions—same old answer.

33

Realities of Life

Time was getting short and the monumental job of moving loomed ahead of us. Steve was acting like an spoiled child and refusing to work unless he could go back to work in the operating room.

"Steve," I pointed out, "if you don't have enough money to buy food to eat, I think you might do well to take just about any job that pays money. Anything would be better than nothing."

"I'm trained to scrub in the OR," he said. "I'm not getting another job until I can go back to that!"

I argued until I was blue in the face but there was nothing I could do to change his mind. It was their fault that he wasn't working and that was that! So he guessed they would have to suffer.

"OK then would you come to the house and help us get things packed for the move?" I asked. "I'll pay you and I can certainly use the help."

"How can I find another job if I'm working all the time for you?" he asked with a smart grin.

"Just be there in the morning and stop being such a jerk!" I shouted as my self-control flew merrily out the window. "Just get yourself over to the house and get busy and help your mother tomorrow with some packing!" I stomped out of his disgusting little room and jumped into my car and flew down the street.

He could make me so angry and at the same time I wanted so badly to help him. The thought of going back and shaking him until his teeth rattled made me feel better even though I knew he was too big for me to do it. I still have a hard time understanding how I could love someone so much and want to beat him to a pulp at the same time. It seemed to me that same feeling had been with me all of his life. One of us needed to grow up. That one was probably going to have to be me.

Steve didn't show up the following day and when I did finally got in touch with him the next week he told me he had a job. He was finally willing to work for minimal wage in lieu of starving to death. He asked me to go with him to trade his Firebird in on a more economical small truck. I agreed and we went down the following day and traded his car in on a very used, very utilitarian truck. It was pathetic to see his beautiful car go. Under the circumstances I didn't volunteer to stop the transaction.

There were a number of important decisions that needed to be made before the move. Number one was what to do with my in-laws. We chose to leave everything "as is" for the time being and make different arrangements after we were settled. Adeline would be going with us and was happy with the idea. Steve was thinking about moving to the mountains and finding a job in the hospital up there. I secretly prayed he wouldn't want to live with us. My emotional constitution was too frail to withstand the added stress.

The week before moving day I was visiting with Adeline at her condominium. We had a nice visit and she expressed excitement about moving to the lake. She described to me how she loved to sit in her room up there and watch all of the different kinds of birds on the water. Then she went on to tell me how wonderful we had been to take her in and help her in her old age.

"Just remember," she said, pointing her finger straight at me, "if anything ever happens to me don't do anything heroic to try and save me! I'm an old lady and have already lived a lot longer than I should have!" She was emphatic about her point. I knew she meant business.

"Don't you worry," I replied. "If anything should ever happen to you I will be happy to let you die."

She laughed and said, "I bet you would too."

I realized what I had said and grabbed her in a huge hug and laughingly said, "You know that isn't what I meant. I just meant I wouldn't do anything heroic."

"I know what you meant and I love you!" She gave me a big squeeze. I kissed her on the cheek and told her I would see her tomorrow and said goodnight.

Walking to my car I thought what a wonderful blessing Adeline had been to me. All my life she had been my favorite relative. We had always had so much fun together when I was a child. The fact that she never had children made her seem more like a second mother to me and she always got a kick out of me introducing her as my mother. Yes sir, I thought. I certainly have been blessed.

The phone call from St. Joseph Hospital the following morning was to inform me that my aunt, Mrs. Adeline Mack, had been brought into the emergency room a few minutes earlier and was being prepped for surgery. She apparently had fallen during the night and sustained a blow to the head and also fractured her hip. Her caregiver had found her on the floor when she went to get her up this morning. The neurosurgeons were planning to take her to surgery for an immediate craniotomy. If that procedure was successful the orthopedic surgeon would repair her hip at a later time. I was informed she was unconscious and intubated on a respirator at present and probably had a large blood clot on the brain.

"We need you to come in and sign the consent form as soon as possible," the lady on the phone explained. "The doctor has an OR reserved and feels that time is of the essence."

"Don't do anything until I get there!" I shouted into the phone.

"But the doctor says—"

"I don't care what the doctor says," I interrupted. I quietly explained that I would be there in about twenty minutes and for her to tell the doctors not to so much as breathe on my aunt until I walked through that door!

Even with Adeline's admonition of just a few hours earlier the decision was difficult. I told the doctors to pull the tube and let nature take its course. They all agreed that at ninety-two that was the best choice. Cindi came in and we all sat and watched as her breathing become more shallow. Our pastor arrived later in the afternoon and led us in a season of prayer. Adeline never regained consciousness. Her breathing ceased at about two a.m. the following morning.

The move to the lake went smoothly although it was overcast with a cloud of sadness. Adeline had been a wonderful part of our family for many years. The new house seemed desolate without her. The downstairs bedroom was furnished as a guest room but always remained "Adeline's room" in our hearts.

Moving was not a new experience to us but moving from a large house into a small condominium was. The garage was floor-to-ceiling furniture. We pushed and tugged until most of our belongings found a spot.

I began filling in at the hospital and within a few weeks found that I was working more there than I had before I retired. Sherrie spent much of her time back in the city taking care of business and her parents. My father-in-law's diabetes continued to worsen. His feet had so deteriorated he could no longer walk. His mind was so poor he could hardly communicate.

Late in June I received a call from Sherrie letting me know that her father had lapsed into a coma and would probably not live through the night. She sat at his bed side until he breathed his last breath. She brought her mother in to view the body. There was no acknowledgment that this man had any relationship to her at all. She wasn't even aware that he wasn't alive. Just a silent cold stare before she asked to return to her room

We had a small memorial service a few days later and Cindi sang in remembrance of her grand father. Steve appeared to be incommunicado. Repeated attempts to contact him at home or by calling the neighbors phone failed. He had been seen coming and going but for some reason didn't get the message that his grandfather was gone.

Following the memorial service friends gave a dinner for the guests at our home. Toward the end of the dinner there was a phone call from Steve.

"Hey, Dad," he began. "What's new in your life? Sounds like you have a bunch of people at the house."

"Yes," I said, "we are having a dinner after your grandfather's memorial service. He passed away three days ago. We have been trying to get in touch with you but no one could find you. I'm sorry you couldn't have been here. It was a nice service and the dinner mother's friends fixed is out of sight."

"I didn't know grandpa was even sick," Steve said with an element of surprise. "What happened to him?"

"You now he had severe diabetes and heart problems and only one kidney. Plus he was in his eighties. All in all I guess he just got old and wore out."

"But I thought grandma would die first," Steve contested.

"That's the problem with life," I threw in. "You never know how long you are going to have it."

"Can I come over and eat now?" Steve asked.

"Sure," I replied, "only you will need to hurry if you want to meet any of the guests. Most of them are about to leave soon I would imagine."

"I will have to take a shower and put on some clothes before I come. Oh, by the way I did have just a little alcoholic beverage a little while ago. And I guess I will have to have you come and pick me up."

"Why can't you drive your own truck over?" I asked.

"That's another story, Dad. I'll talk to you about that later."

"Why don't you just stay the way you are and don't bother cleaning up. I will grab a few plates of food and bring them by on my way to make rounds. I can bring enough to feed most of the apartment complex."

"Sounds good enough for me," he said. "I was just going next door to have a beer with my friends so you can find me there."

Guilt engulfed me when I hung up. There was no doubt in my mind that I was taking food to him to keep him from coming to the house and embarrassing everyone by his appearance and alcohol enhanced breath.

When I arrived at the apartment Steve was standing outside waiting for me. "Sorry about grandpa," he began. "But you know he was an old man and really wasn't much good to nobody anymore nohow."

Thank you Steve, I thought to myself. You really have such a way with words. I stood looking at him in his short shorts, bare feet and without a shirt. His hair was long and unkept. The bouquet of old beer on his breath was sufficient to give testimony to the amount that had been consumed earlier in the evening.

"You look good," I said in an outright lie. "What has been going on in your young life?"

"I'm working part time at a fast food joint down the street. Three of us hold the same job so when one of us is working the other two can just hang out. It works great."

"What do you do with all the money you make?" I asked in a minimally sarcastic tone.

"Don't worry, Dad. We make enough to pay the rent and put food on the table."

Yea and buy beer and cigarettes I bet. I didn't say that out loud but came close.

"The thing I called to tell you was that I had my truck stolen the other day. Yesterday it was found on the other side of town smashed into a tree. There is no clue who could have taken it." His next question sent chills up my spine. "How much do you think I can make off of the accident?"

"Do you mean how much will insurance pay?" I asked.

"Yea, Dad, I need to know how much they will pay and how soon I can get the money. I guess it is probably totaled so I should get the whole bit, don't you think?"

"Have you reported this to the insurance company?"

"I called them yesterday," he answered. "They wanted to know where it was stolen from and if I had any idea who might have taken it."

"What did you tell them?" I asked.

"I told them I didn't know. All I knew was that it was gone."

"When you first knew it was missing did you call the police?" I asked.

"No," he whispered.

"Why not?"

"I don't know. I guess I just didn't think it mattered that much."

"Was there an accident report filed?" I asked.

"I guess not," he conceded. "I guess nobody saw anything. They just found the truck smashed into a tree and wrecked." Then he added, "The insurance company asked a bunch of questions like where were you at the time and when did you drive the truck last. They wanted to know if I had ever had a DUI."

"What did you tell them?" I asked.

"I told them that was none of their business."

"Have you ever had a DUI?"

"Yeah, Dad I guess I have. They say I was driving drunk a few weeks ago. I don't think I really was but what's the difference anyway? You can't fight City Hall!"

"Did they actually give you a DUI? Or did they just say you were driving drunk?" (Dumb question on my part.)

"They gave me the real thing. I have to appear in court in two months unless I can come up with some sort of a hot shot lawyer that knows how to get around the law. You know there is no way I can ever hire a lawyer unless I can come up with some big bucks in a hurry."

The story about the truck being stolen was beginning to take on the appearance of a deception. It took everything I had to keep from accusing him of telling me a bold face lie. I followed my better judgment and didn't approach the subject of insurance fraud. In my mind I knew something wasn't right but couldn't make myself get into it right then. Instead, I told Steve I had to get going and gave him a hug.

"I love you, Dad," he said with a laugh.

"I hope everything will be all right," I shouted back to him over my shoulder. "I hope everything will really be all right."

"Yeah, Dad," he laughed. "Everything is going to be just fine. I'll call you when I find out something about the truck."

I walked to the end of the walk and for some reason stopped and turned to look at him. He was still standing there holding the plate of food in his hand. That picture remains indelibly imprinted in my mind. His wild blond hair, bare feet and cutoff shorts. He just looked at me with no expression on his face then turned and walked into his apartment. That was the last time I saw Steve.

I left for the mountains the following morning to await the arrival of my father-in-law's body for burial. I was already at the cemetery when the hearse arrived. The gravediggers were working frantically to get the grave dug before the casket arrived. It was raining with occasional lightning and thunder. My only thought was to get out of there before all of us got zapped by lightning.

The mortician had the gravediggers help carry the coffin to the side of the grave. He took me completely by surprise when he asked,

"Being you are not having a service today would you care to say a few words before we bury your father?"

"No," I answered, "everything that could be said has already been said." Then I just stood there and looked ignorant. I have always wondered why I didn't at least say a short prayer or just say something. But no, I just stood there and said, "everything has already been said," and left it at that.

Sherrie stayed in the city to finish cleaning the house before the escrow closed. There was a lot to be done in our new home which helped rid my mind of the recent tragedies that had plagued our home.

The beauty of the lake in the summertime painted a picture of tranquility. The sunsets were exquisite splashing the sky with brilliant reds and yellows which were picked up by the clouds in the sky and the ripples in the water. The water birds were restless and gibbered wildly as they scurried from place to place preparing for the night. Finally God was in His heaven and all was right with the world.

By mid-July the usual Phoenix inferno had set in. Sherrie was at the house making final preparations to close the sale when Steve called asking to come over for the day while his apartment was being fumigated. He arrived in the early morning with three of his friends. According to Sherrie it was one of the nicest days she had ever spent with Steve.

Most of the day was spent in the pool floating on rafts and making small talk. Steve was in an all-time high spirit. There was no evidence of alcohol or drugs. The conversation was directed toward all the good things that had happened in life. About God and His wonderful mercies. For lunch they had pizza brought in, followed by a nap by the pool.

For Sherrie it was a good break from the responsibilities of caring for her mother and packing the house. They agreed early in the day, no type of work would be attempted. The time was set aside strictly for pleasure and the renewing of a mother-son relationship. The day was a complete success on all counts. For Sherrie the memories of that wonderful day will be forever engraved in her heart. It was the last time she saw Steve.

34

The Day Time Stopped

There are certain events in life when a person remembers the exact circumstances of the moment. For example the day president Kennedy was shot. The day the Challenger exploded or the more recent event when the space shuttle Columbia disintegrated. I remember I was playing in my sandbox when my grandfather came out and told me Pearl Harbor had been bombed by the Japanese. I had no idea who the Japanese were, or for that matter what Pearl Harbor was. I did know that everyone was upset. For some reason that moment has stuck in my mind for all these years as if it were yesterday.

There is another day in my life that stands out in the same way. The morning of August 7, 1995.

I was working in the front yard when Sherrie called me to the phone. "Beth wants to talk to you on the phone," she called.

"Tell her I will call her back," I hollered back.

"She says it's important and she needs to talk to you right away!" she repeated.

"OK tell her I'll be right there." I put down the hose and headed for the house. There isn't anything that I can imagine Beth wanting that couldn't wait for a few minutes, I muttered to myself. Beth had been a secretary in our office for nearly seventeen years and if Beth couldn't handle it, nobody could!

I ran up the stairs to get the phone in the bedroom. "Hi Beth," I razzed. "What's going on in your young life that would make me put my shovel and hoe away? You know I had to run up two flights of stairs just to speak with one of the world's greatest living secretaries?"

I started to add there have been greater but they aren't living when she interrupted.

"Keith," she said, sounding very serious. "I think I may have some terrible news."

"What's happened?" I asked as I began to realize the seriousness of the call.

"I just got a call from the homicide division at the police department," she started. My heart started to pound. What had Steve done now? Could he had killed somebody accidentally when he was drunk or stoned? Or could there have been some horrible accident? Time stood still until she finally continued talking again.

"The investigator said he's not sure who it is but thinks it could be your son."

"Who what is?" I gasped. "What has happened?"

"I'm not sure I know what has happened," Beth was almost crying. "This guy called from the police department and said they had found a body in an apartment over by Lincoln Hospital and they think it may be your son.

"Oh Keith," she sobbed, "I hope they're wrong. He gave me his number and asked me to have you call him as soon as possible."

I scribbled down the number. "I'll call you back as soon as I know something," I told her and hung up. Then a strange sensation rushed over me. I felt a sense of relief that Steve had not harmed someone.

The horrible devastation that he could be dead instantly struck hard. The word dead made me feel sick to my stomach and I knew I was going to vomit. I put down the phone and blindly ran down the stairs purposefully avoiding going through the kitchen where Sherrie was working. Stopping only briefly to vomit in the bushes I directed myself toward Carol's house at the end of the block. I needed to call the investigator before I said anything to Sherrie. In my heart I knew this whole thing had to be one big mistake.

Carol wasn't in the house but I could see him standing down by the lake. When I stepped onto the back porch he saw me and immediately recognized something was wrong. All I said as he stepped into the house was, "Steve's dead."

He grabbed me and put his arm around me as I sobbed violently with my head on his shoulder. Moments later Sherrie burst into the house screaming. "I knew something like this would happen if we left him home alone and moved away!"

"Something like what?" I asked.

"Steve has killed himself, haven't you heard? He's dead. I knew we shouldn't have moved away."

I held her in my arms in a futile attempt to comfort her. Her body felt limp as if she were about to faint.

"We aren't even sure that the body they have found is Steve's in the first place. I came down here to call the police before I said anything to you." That was the first time the question of how did she know about this hit me?

"How did you hear about it?" I asked.

"Cindi called me."

"How did she know about it?" I asked.

"She was at work in the emergency room when the investigator came in and asked to use the phone. She showed him to the phone and when he laid his papers on the counter she saw Steve's name written across the top of the page.

"That's my brother's name," she told the investigator. "What's it doing on your report?" He told her, "We just found his body in an apartment across the street and think it is a case of suicide."

"I guess Cindi fell apart and ran and called me."

I began to feel more in control. "We need to talk with the police before we jump to any conclusions. After all, Beth told me they weren't sure they even had the right person."

I called the number on the paper and got the switchboard. "He's out investigating a suicide. If you want to give me your number I will have him give you a call as soon as he calls in."

"I think he may be investigating my son's death so I really need to talk to him in a hurry," I told the lady on the switchboard.

"That's probably what he's doing," she said in a matter-of-fact tone. "I'll have him give you a call as soon as he calls in."

"Do you think it is a suicide?" I asked.

"Sounds like it to me," she replied. "I'll have him give you a call."

The hours of waiting were unimaginably painful. Not knowing

the answer to the question, "Is he dead?" was to me more painful than death itself. My thoughts turned to Christ on the cross. I wondered if God looked down upon His Son with any expectation of uncertainty.

Everything seemed to be vanity. Even God's plan of salvation seemed to have lost its meaning. How could anything hurt so badly without killing a person? I knew this had to be an absurd dream. There was no way something like this could be happening.

When the phone did finally ring it took every ounce of strength I had to pick up the receiver. The gentleman on the other end of the line began to speak. Immediately I knew my worst fears were about to be realized.

He began by saying, "I'm sorry. Your son's neighbors have given us a positive identification. Your son is dead. He probably died sometime during the early morning." Then he went on to say, "This has to be terribly painful for you. I have kids myself and can understand in part what you must be going through. We have all the identification we need on your son, so I would suggest that you not view the body unless you have a personal need to do so."

He continued by explaining that because this was a case of an unexplained death the body would become the property of the coroner. The process of determining the cause of death would take about a week. After that the body would be released to the family. He suggested cremation as a means of internment due to the length of time from the death until burial. The remains would be available for a service by the end of next week.

Thanking him for his consideration I hung up. His phone call has had more impact on my life than any phone call I have ever received yet to this day I don't even know his name.

At the mortuary the following day, in an attempt to alleviate some of my pain, the funeral director told me about the death of his own son who had been killed at the age of twenty-nine. He told me how comforting it has been when many have seen his son at family functions. His son has made it known he is living in a place far superior to this earth. The fact my Steve was living in heaven should be a comfort rather than a sorrow. He quoted several passages from his "bible."

I didn't use any tact as I corrected him by explaining that in scripture the Bible does not teach that a person goes directly to heaven when he dies. Rather, it clearly teaches the dead remain in a state of unconsciousness which Christ often referred to as sleep. This state continues until the day Christ returns and the graves are opened and the redeemed are raised to spend eternity with the Lord.

Catching myself I stopped short of producing a handful of scriptural proof text to confirm him wrong before diving into the subject of the Book of Mormon. I felt embarrassed as I realized I was sounding exactly like Steve with my zero tolerance attitude. The remainder of the arrangements were made without additional discussion of the subject.

Another dear friend called to tell me how she had felt such comfort in knowing that Steve was darting through the clouds clowning with the angels about all the silly stuff he had done on earth. When I explained that I believed he was asleep in the grave as the Bible teaches and not clowning with anyone right now her only comment was, "That's a pretty way out way of thinking. I've never heard of anything like that. Everybody knows you go to heaven when you die." Not the way my Bible teaches it, I thought to myself. I knew she was trying to console me and I greatly appreciated it. There was no reason to preach her a sermon on my beliefs about the state of the dead.

Ten days can be a lifetime when you are waiting to bury your son. A particularly long time when you are plagued with a multitude of pertinent questions. Questions such as, did Steve deliberately commit suicide? Did he accidentally take an overdose or maybe have been given bad dope? Could he have been murdered? What about the night last week when he called asking for money? Could that have been a plea for help that I completely overlooked? In that phone call Steve told me there was a warrant for his arrest. The money he needed to clear the warrant was about two hundred dollars.

"What is the warrant all about?" I had asked.

"Do you remember when my truck was stolen? Well the insurance company is saying that the vehicle wasn't really stolen. They accused me of wrecking my truck and then running from the scene. Then they accused me of insurance fraud by trying to collect the money for my truck. Dad, they are just making all of this up so they won't have to pay for my car." His voice had began to trail off.

"If I send you the money will that clear you of all the tickets being held against you?"

"Yeah, Dad. I promise this will be the last time you will ever have to bail me out!"

Once again they were prophetic words that have haunted me ever since. Then he'd said, "Please, Dad, just this one more time. I don't want to go to jail."

"I'll send you the money but you will have to promise me two things. First that you will use the money to pay the court and second that you will get a hold on your boot straps and fly right."

"Yeah, Dad, I promise. Thanks a lot." Then he had added in what sounded like a very sincere statement. "I love you, Dad."

The check was endorsed by Steve for cash only. In my heart I believe the money was used to buy the drugs that killed him. No evidence of a warrant has ever appeared.

Sherrie left for the city to help Cindi and Steve's neighbors get his things together and clean the apartment. I should have gone but couldn't. I had to stay and struggle with my own self-pity and sort things out alone. The battle was on and it appeared that depression would be the winner. Every known emotion I had ever experience surfaced.

At first I felt like a newborn infant. All I did was cry and kick my feet and wonder why no one could understand what I wanted. Friends brought food to the house and gave me words of comfort and compassion. Still no one seemed to understand what I was trying to tell them.

The wide mood swings took me to a more adolescent emotion. That of rebellion and anger. In my mind no one knew anything. Everyone was against me. Friends told me they understood but I knew they didn't have a clue. God had abandoned me and no longer cared. The confusion of feeling so alone and yet not wanting to be with anyone was completely foreign to me. My friend Carol was my only comfort. He sat listening for hours at a time not saying a word. He seemed to accept my stupefaction without reproach. There is comfort when a friend just sits and listens. An attribute I hadn't fully understood previously.

Toward the end of the week I achieved a more adult emotion and began to realize the needs of my wife and three remaining children. Then I felt the shame of my own self-pity. Calling Sherrie helped, especially when she told me that according to the neighbors Steve had spent most of his last day reading his Bible.

Then came the most difficult emotions of all. Bitterness and blame. I blamed Steve's natural mother for giving him up in the first place. The grandparents for not accepting him in his younger years. What about the law enforcement agencies that didn't have the intestinal fortitude to stand up for right and take the drugs away from him? They had caught the kids in the act and just shook their heads and said, "Sorry!"

Then there was the Adventist Reform group in Tennessee that convinced Steve to drop out of college and sent him on a downward road of destruction in search of perfection. When perfection was unobtainable drugs eased the pain. There has to be blame there! The paradox began.

And the years of my own battle with alcohol. The addiction that had to effect the life of one as young as Steve. The burden of having been such a role model weighed heavy on my heart.

The rock music with stars that glorified sex, alcohol and drugs. They should also have to carry the weight of some of the blame. And what about the young girlfriend that helped him squander all of his money and self-dignity on drugs? Shouldn't she have to bear some of the blame?

We often think we understand our own emotions until it becomes necessary to deal with them personally one by one. Everything in life has to have a reason. Justification for a situation like this requires blame. Just blame someone. Anyone or anything will do. Then everything will be better!

The heart-wrenching truth came with the realization there really wasn't any one thing or any one person to carry all of the blame.

35

One Bright Light

The day of the funeral arrived. To my surprise not only family members arrived but many friends had been willing to drive the hundred and fifty miles from Phoenix to support us on that terrible day.

Teri flew in from Montana and drove up from the valley with her sister. She was having an especially hard time accepting Steve's death because she had failed to stop and visit him on her trip to Arizona the month before. We all had our times of regret that stemmed from the words "if only I..."

There is a beautiful poem by Edward R. Sill in which he writes the words:

"The ill timed truths we might have kept
Who knows how sharp they pierced and stung.

"The word we had not sense to say
Who knows how grandly it had rung."

The closer we were forced toward the cemetery the more removed from the situation I became. As we left the car and walked up the little hill toward the canopy that housed the chairs for the family everything slipped into slow motion. Hoards of people seemed to be walking slowly and silently toward me. Most of them were without faces yet I was aware many of them had tears. Although some of the folks were speaking I couldn't make myself hear the sounds. It was like a dream where you want to run but can't make your legs move.

Finally seated beneath the canopy I caught a glimpse of a squad car parked behind a nearby tree. I knew Kevin and his escorts had arrived. He found his way to the family group while accepting hugs and kisses from friends. Having him there brought me back into focus. Looking at him I came to the understanding I still had a son. It was a wonderful feeling but short-lived as I noticed the guards who would tear him away from me again at the conclusion of the service.

My eyes focused on the sun's bright glow through the canvas overhead. Multiple rays of light radiated from the central bright spot to form a large star. Losing myself in the brightness of the light my mind went back to the happy times Steve and I had enjoyed together in the years gone by. The happy moments that only a father could share with his son.

I could picture a small blond-headed boy against the backdrop of the Italian Alps, his body perfectly poised over his well controlled skis. The smile on his face testified to the fact he knew he had done a good job.

The morning in Hawaii when God had delivered us from the approaching traffic and transported us safely to the curb without a scratch. I remember thinking at the time how fortunate I was to have my son alive and well with a lifetime of happiness ahead of us. I was sure God had a work for both of us to do.

I remembered the little boy who laughed and giggled and produced a most obnoxious laugh at inappropriate times. The kid whose greatest crime was spraying a fire extinguisher into an empty school bus. The one whose report card always glistened with A's.

He was a great kid. So full of life and vitality.

That day in Heidelberg when we sat on the river bank with Steve on my lap watching and waving as the barges passed back and forth. He had been so tickled at the underwear hanging on the line at the back of the boat.

The violins played, the tenors sang and the church bells rang in the piazza St. Marco in Venice as Steve ran through the throngs of pigeons. He was so young and carefree. Completely unaware of the beauty around him or the snares that would entangle him.

Many were the times I would see him strutting around the patio appearing as a rock star while playing disgustingly audacious music on his guitar.

The evening we sat together under the stars just a few short months ago. He was a young man so full of life and hope. The maturity he exhibited that evening assured me there was nothing ahead for him in life but success. His entire world was filled with God and reassurance. How could it all be gone now?

The bright light reflecting through the canopy seemed to personify the son I loved so dearly. He had been the light of my life. I wondered if God in His great wisdom and mercy was seeing him in that same beautiful light that removed all of the rough spots leaving only a perfectly faceted stone.

The service was over and the strains of "Amazing Grace" were fading into oblivion. I was standing alone with family and friends in an unreal world. The worst possible scenario of my life had just taken place. It was over.

As I stared at that little wooden box I was aware that it was no more than a few handfuls of ashes. However, it was the only tangible evidence that remained of a living vital person. I had to speak to it. Somehow I had to let Steve know how much I really loved him. The knowledge that we can't go back pierced through me like a sharp knife.

Talking to the little box I made one final appeal. "Steve, you know I just told you I have always loved you. But I don't think you really have any idea how much. If only we could go back to the night by the pool. Everything was so perfect then. So completely perfect!

"Why did you hit on drugs again?" I was sobbing, imprisoned in my own guilt. "It had to be me. I tried so hard to be a good dad. It has to be my fault otherwise why would this happen? Please forgive me."

Someone took me by the arm and ushered me toward the car. We stumbled down the hillside into the darkness of my own self-pity.

"It was so perfect, Lord. Why did You let him slip away? Why, dear Lord, why?"

36

Alone With God

It was cool and misty as I climbed the slight incline of the cemetery garden early the next morning. I was alone with only the thoughts of yesterday to consume me. The absence of people and the missing canopy and chairs gave a feeling of tranquility to the scene. I noticed the gravestones of others that I had completely overlooked the day before. I became acutely aware of the suffering of others represented in this place.

A light rain seemed to mingle with the tears on my face. Standing above the graves I stared at the four small mounds of dirt that represented my mother, my father, my aunt Adeline, and now my son Steve. To the left was the fresh grave of Earl my father-in-law and the unopened grave of my mother-in-law whose mind had died while her body lived on.

As I gazed at the sight before me the flood of emotion that had been held in for so long began to pour out from within. The dam broke and I fell to my knees sobbing uncontrollably.

There was a bright flash of lightning followed by a loud clap of thunder. The pad of dust that lay under my knees represented a large part of my family. Beneath me lay a lifetime of memories and experiences. I could feel the pounding of the heavy rain on my back. I was drenched through and through as I laid on my face thrusting my fingers repeatedly into the newly forming mud. I could understand the lives of the elderly, but why Steve? How had a life so filled with opportunity crumbled and been snuffed out to end in such a senseless way? Where were my prayers going? If God is so caring why wouldn't He give me some answers?

Lying there on the ground blaming God for all the misfortune in my life, the rain stopped as suddenly as it had begun. As if God had extended His hand and placed it on my back, the warmth of the sun radiated its comforting calm over me. It felt as if the promises of God were being poured out directly upon me from heaven. My son had suffered a useless death. How much more had the Son of God died a death that should never have had to happen? Satan had sentenced both of our sons to die.

Then some beautiful promises of hope filled my mind. God's promise that He so loved the world that He gave His only son to die for me and for my son. That if we would believe we would not have to perish but would be given everlasting life. He went on to say that it wasn't His purpose to condemn the world but rather to save the world and all of its inhabitants.

My thoughts skipped back to the Old Testament where God told Samuel that man looks on the outward appearance but God looks on the heart. What a beautiful statement, I thought. God does the judging and He alone knows the workings of our hearts. Equally as important is the fact that Jesus Christ who died for the sins of each of us will stand before the Father as our advocate to plead our cases.

I felt the promise of John 14, where Christ said, "Let not your hearts be troubled. You believe in God. Believe also in Me." Then He told the disciples that in His Father's house there are many mansions. Christ is going to prepare a place for us and will come back again for all those who love Him.

Romans 6:23 says the wages of sin is death but the gift of God is eternal life. The part Steve was never able to understand is that the Law demands death for sin, while the gift of eternal life is the result of God's grace.

The most beautiful promise of all comes in Revelations where we are given the assurance that after Christ returns, Satan and all his angels will be destroyed. Sin will be eradicated and there will be no more death. There will be a new heaven and a new earth for all who love the Lord to inherit for all eternity. The great controversy between God and Satan, between Life and Death will be finished. God will have won. There will be no more tears.

Walking down the hillside I felt the potential of a new beginning. Although the life of Christ should never have had to be taken, His sacrifice gives us the assurance of salvation.

My hope is that the useless loss of Steve's life might in some way serve as a redemptive source to save others whether young or old from the pitfalls that plagued his soul.

As parents we have all made some horrible mistakes. Satan would have us dwell on the heinous circumstances of our lives. God's law requires perfection. Christ provides perfection with His righteousness. The ransom for our mistakes has been paid.

So if the devil tries to make you feel guilty because of your past, take a moment to remind him of his future.

Epilogue

God has greatly blessed our family since that day when Steve left us.

Kevin has moved into the free world. The life of honesty without drugs, alcohol or tobacco has proven to be a satisfactory alternative to his previous lifestyle. Three years ago he took a lovely and intelligent lady to be his wife. Together they are finishing college with honors and plan to continue in the master's program.

Teri suffered a painful divorce. She has since remarried a fantastic Christian gentleman. Together they have a new daughter who is a wonderful addendum to her other two girls. They live on fifteen acres of rolling hills in a beautiful custom log house in Montana. The stable contains horses for the parents as well as one for each of the older girls. Prayer is their common bond and love the holding tie.

Cindi is happily married to the same man she promised her life to at their wedding eight years ago. He is a good husband, father and provider. Our two little granddaughters are not only beautiful but they are talented. Cindi has continued to pursue her career as a singer. She performs regularly in the churches of the metropolitan area and is presently working on cutting her first CD. Together she and her husband are bringing their children up in the love of the Lord.

Sherrie's mother mercifully died this past year in a nursing home after more than ten years of severe Alzheimer's disease. She was eighty-seven.

Since my retirement last year Sherrie and I have moved into our motor home and are currently serving as volunteers with an evangelistic team traveling around the U.S. and Canada. Home is where we park it!

My recurring dream is of the Coming of the Lord. It's a brilliant display with a thousand times ten thousands of angels. Trumpets sound as lightning flashes. The angelic chorus swells to symphonic grandeur as myriads of angels raise their voices in adoration to God. Then I look up and see the most beautiful sight of all. Jesus Christ in the clouds of glory coming as the "King of Kings" to take His people home.

As Christ descends toward the earth one by one each of my three children seek me out. Then there are our parents who departed so long ago. My grandchildren are all there shining brighter than the brightest star. Sherrie is there as well as our closest friends.

Then from somewhere deep within the multitudes of people I hear a familiar voice.

"Hey, Dad."

I turn and ask, "Is that you, Steve?"

"Yeah, Dad, it's me."

The end

In Loving Memory

1966-1995

Steve   Kevin
Cindi   Teri

Teri, Dad, Steve, and Kevin in Palm Springs.

Steve, Teri, Cindi, and Kevin.

Kevin and Steve in the summer of 1982.

Steve on Aspen Trip.

Steve and Rex in 1994.

Steve on Christmas 1994.

Steve in 1995.

Dad and Steve at Southern College.

Steve and Sherrie on their last visit.

Teri, Sherrie, Cindi, Kevin and Keith at the funeral in 1995.

Cindi, Keith, Sherrie, and Teri with her daughter Bobbi.

I'll tell you about a truth so pure,
It comes from Heaven above,
It is a message of eternal love.
What people know so little of.
It comes from some time ago,
Now it is here on the earth below.

'Cause you see I've been to the mountain top,
I've even been to the bottom of the sea,
But I never quite learned just how to be free.

Ya, I've been so high,
I even touched the sky,
But I still find the tears to cry.

—Steve Mack 1982